Ex Libris
Arthur E. and
Nora A. McGuinness

for Art McGuinness

connoisseur of fleeting

moments . . .

all best wishes

Roger Cardinal

September 88

Figures of Reality

A PERSPECTIVE ON THE POETIC IMAGINATION

ROGER CARDINAL

CROOM HELM LONDON
BARNES & NOBLE BOOKS
TOTOWA, NEW JERSEY

© 1981 Roger Cardinal
Croom Helm Ltd, 2-10 St John's Road, London SW11

British Library Cataloguing in Publication Data

Cardinal, Roger
    Figures of reality.
    1. Poetics
    2. Imagination
    3. Creation (Literary, artistic, etc.)
    I. Title
    808.1   PN1041   80-49928
    ISBN 0-85664-085-9

First published in the USA 1981 by
BARNES & NOBLE BOOKS
81 ADAMS DRIVE
TOTOWA, New Jersey, 07512

ISBN 0-389-20064-6

Typeset by Jayell Typesetting · London

Printed and bound in Great Britain by
Redwood Burn Limited
Trowbridge & Esher

CONTENTS

ILLUSTRATIONS

PREFACE

Those who write about poetry are faced with the problem of establishing an appropriate relationship between the secondary discourse of
criticism and a primary discourse characterised by its complex differentness from ordinary speech, its dramatic strangeness and unpredict-
ability. One solution has been to adopt the manner of dispassionate
objectivity in the belief that the critical discourse can best function if
it is as cool and unwavering as the poetic original is febrile and shifting.
Certain contemporary writers in the field of poetics and literary criticism, and especially those drawn to semiotic and linguistics-based
approaches to things literary, have begun to promote an ideology within which the critical discourse is seen as necessarily technical and aloof.
  Now I would not say that the language of poetry should never be
subjected to technical analysis. It is obviously useful to be able to
notice and refer to such features as phonic patterns, verse forms,
rhythms and tones, semantic densities and tensions, the mechanisms
of metonymy or metaphor. Yet I suspect that the idea that the critic
should remain totally unruffled and objective as he goes about his tasks,
is a myth which has value only up to a point. I believe that critical
detachment is a desirable posture only if one is pursuing certain limited
ends, such as the enumeration of linguistic and stylistic data. When
faced with descriptions of poetry which are at such obvious pains to
remain formal and non-speculative, I have more and more found myself
possessed by the feeling that this is not enough, that an honest account
of a reading experience should not restrict itself to the signs on the
page, but should equally take note of all the intellectual and affective
responses which those signs arouse. I can see why the idea of critical
distance can seem compelling, and yet I continue to find myself uneasy
with a regulation that says I should keep silent about the moments I
most prize in my actual reading of poems, when a text touches vulnerable parts of my sensibility, creating flurries of association or a passing
dizziness which cannot be accounted for in rational terms. To censor
this dimension of response seems to me, simply, to be to adopt an incomplete view of the situation, a way of keeping poetry as it were in

the deep freeze, rather than letting it flourish on the window-sill in the sunlight.

This book attempts to show how the poetic imagination moves towards its meanings, in the light of the avowed ambitions of poets and of the poems they write. My thinking has been guided by the supposition that poets go about their task with reference to certain guiding fantasies or controlling models of the poetic function. Of course, it would be an exaggeration to suppose that every poem is the deliberate illustration of an *ars poetica* (though works do exist which have been carefully constructed in accordance with a strict theoretical blueprint). What I am suggesting is that when poets come to write, they do so under the influence of certain implicit presuppositions about the nature of the process in which they are engaged. Whether consciously or unconsciously, the poet has a lively sense of what the poetic is, and what status the words he is putting together have in relation to the world beyond the text. I believe that there is, so to speak, a phantom poetics which hovers in the writer's mind as he works, a powerful though often indistinct paradigm. Probably this phantom is also extremely volatile, in that it may change its appearance while the poet is still working, tempting him by a succession of alternative seductions like some protean vision before Saint Anthony. What I have sought to do here is to isolate some of the typical manifestations of this phantom and to set them out, for clarity's sake, in the form of a series of simplified models.

I begin at one extreme by examining the model of the poem as a locus of unreality. If one theory of language has it that words are inherently abstractive, then a poet may choose to situate his work in a perspective whereby poeticity is envisaged in terms of an assertion of verbal autonomy. It seems to me that poets of all sorts of persuasions have at one time or another been responsive to the idea that words acquire a special glamour if they are absolved from all responsibility to the real world and are instead encouraged to play together in a nonreferential way, so that the ensuing poem ends up floating as a self-reflexive artefact with no ties to life. In the first part of this book I explore some corollaries of this view, advancing the notion that it is typical of the poetic temperament that it should respond pleasurably to those encounters with the unreal which take place within the bounds of perceptual experience, and that the writing and reading of poems may be understood as an extension of this primary delight, a conscious toying with artifice. In this perspective, poetry can be appreciated as a capricious yet engrossing activity which thrives on the refutation of normality. The fact of its attractive strangeness gives rise to the further hypothesis that poetry often engages the reader precisely because he cannot at first grasp its meaning: our tolerance of obscurity in poetic texts is, then, a function of our willingness to be fascinated by the unreal.

However, my argument switches direction soon after this point when, in the second part of the book, I propose an important adjustment of focus. Far from the poetic flirtation with counter-realities being an escapist indulgence, I argue that on the contrary it may have the effect of obliging the reader to refer back to his awareness of actual reality. That is, in order for him to make sense of the strangeness transmitted by the poetic text, it becomes necessary for the reader to set aside his intellect and instead to consult the associative suggestions supplied by his low-level sensibility. It is here that I sketch a theory of creative reading whereby the recipient of the poetic message — provided he genuinely lends himself to the situation and seeks to facilitate the transitivity of figurative speech — is able to give meaning to the ancient Orphic myth of poetry as magic revelation. The poem is now seen as the locus of impulses that radiate beyond the page, the figures of poetic speech sensitising the reader to corresponding figures within reality at large.

The third part of my project is a review of certain aspects of the poetic perception of the natural world. The model here is of the poem as the locus of an epiphany, the record of a tremor of poetic insight induced by an elective place, a favourite object or a privileged element. Often such tremors turn out to be ephemeral, only just noticeable; there is even a category of the poetic which resides in the 'not quite' of an unfulfilled promise of epiphany. Yet when a poet does fulfil the ambition of eliciting presence through poetic utterance, he confirms the central intuition, shared by many poets, that the natural world outside the poem functions as a compendium of fertile correspondences, a runic script whose revealing signs may be deciphered through procedures of scanning and analogical combination. And these are in turn to be seen as strictly equivalent to the procedures used to make sense of textual figures.

In the last part of the book, I stress the importance of analogical thinking as an instrument in man's general quest for an intimate adjustment to his environment. Because the confrontation with verbal metaphor prompts us to marshal our non-rational associative faculties. poems may be said to sponsor fluency within our mental and sensory circuits, making us more alert to the ways in which the perceived world around us is shaped and reshaped. All of which leads me to advance what is essentially a Romantic, even a utopian model of the poem as a medium of enhanced perception, a lens which can transfigure the reader's vision of the real. At this point I am at pains to resist the seductions of another mode of unreality, the notion of a mystical transcendence of sense impressions. Instead I view poetic transfiguration as a reconciliation of the Real and the Ideal, poetic truth being inseparable from the encounter of mental reality and material reality here and now. These lines of André Breton evoke the power of the utopian image to enact the gesture of contact, to cross distance and hover into focus as a perceptual certainty:

> Quel est donc ce pays lointain
> Qui semble tirer toute sa lumière de ta vie
> Il tremble bien réel à la pointe de tes cils

>   (Breton, 1966a, 179)

(What then is this distant realm/Which seems to draw all its light from your life/It trembles a true reality at the fringe of your eyelashes)

I make no secret of the fact that these are arguments rooted in a sympathy for the ideas and expectations of a number of favourite poets. I am especially aware of what they owe to the poetics of both German Romanticism and French Surrealism, the names of Novalis and Breton being frequently enough invoked in the following pages for this indebtedness to be foregrounded. In a sense, what I have tried to construct here is an intellectual case for treating the lyrical propositions of such poets as entirely serious and worthwhile. They are not offering escapist fantasy or daft inconsequentiality as aesthetic ideals, but are instead the adherents of poetic principles which are as modern as they are meaningful and which the contemporary critic may quite properly accommodate within his secondary discourse.

My perspective on the poetic imagination is illustrated by quotations from a range of poets writing in French, English and German. What I have instinctively felt is that, idiosyncrasies and aberrations aside, there is a common chord which resonates through the poetry of the past two centuries or so. The Romantic yearning for certainties lying beyond the visible, the Symbolist aesthetics of absence, the Surrealist campaign to establish the primacy of the imaginative act, the Expressionist piercing of aesthetic surfaces to disclose emotions which impinge on our innermost being, the endeavours of the Imagists and the later Phenomenalist poets of America to pinpoint insights within a revealing nexus of perceptions — these seem to be so many variations on a basically simple set of recurrent themes concerning the essence of the poetic and its status within general experience. Octavio Paz describes the poetry of the West during the nineteenth century as an 'analogical system', a plural yet unified field within which 'each work is a unique reality and at the same time a translation of the others — its metaphor' (Paz, 1974, 67; tr. Rachel Phillips). This intuition of analogical relatedness, of a continuity amid multiplicity, has prompted me to quote freely from a wide variety of sources (including even non-European ones), in the expectation that I might thereby arrive at a representative statement about what poets feel they are doing. I hope that the result is not too caricatural a stylisation, and that my preference for citing the writers with whom I feel most affinity has not weakened the aspiration to mediate a general consensus.

In order to highlight my theme of situating poetry in direct relation to the world, I decided that I must give most scope to the primary texts, rather than repeatedly discuss things in terms of what other theorists and commentators have had to say on the subject. Much of my thinking about poetry has been influenced by my reading of a number of admirable critics (in particular in the orbit of phenomenology), but I have elected to express this debt through the Bibliography rather than overload my text with critical acknowledgements or disagreements. This is another way of saying that I have dropped the ballast of scholarly cross-reference in order to give more buoyancy to the poetic argument proper.

I am conscious that at times my impatience to pursue a line of discussion has prevented me from dwelling sufficiently long over a given quotation, and that I may therefore not have done justice to the inherent virtues of the text in its singular right. What I hope my secondary discourse does not diminish is the sense of the poem as a vital experience to be embraced, and not a dead letter to be dissected. Wallace Stevens once wrote that

> The poet speaks the poem as it is,
> Not as it was.

> (Stevens, 1955, 473)

This notion of immediacy emboldens me to adopt the precept that the most urgent thing to attend to is not the poem as other people have seen it, nor indeed the poem as its author may be supposed to have seen it (interesting though these may be) — but the poem as it comes off the page at me, the poem as I encounter it *now*. I feel that it is vital for the reader of poetry to resist any suggestion that he is one who arrives too late upon the scene. True, the exegetes may have passed this way before, but since the essence of the poetic experience is located in that unique sense of participation which links consciousness to sign, the reading of a poem is something which each reader initiates afresh for himself: he alone can make the decision so to situate his sensibility in relation to the text that it begins to embody a presence meaningful for him. It is in this spirit that I have written this book, seeking to transcend critical aloofness and abstraction, and above all to communicate an appeal to the reader of poetry not to neglect his own imaginative resources, without which his reception of the words on the page will remain conceptual and incomplete. Nothing less than full imaginative participation will suffice to elicit the full meaning of a poem, or indeed the full meaning of any experience in life. As William Carlos Williams has observed, 'it is the imagination on which reality rides' (Williams, 1970, 139), and without its enlivening collaboration we cannot expect really to get hold of anything.

ACKNOWLEDGEMENTS

The author and the publisher wish to thank the following for their kind permission to reproduce material:

Verlags AG 'Die Arche' for an extract from 'Gadji beri bimba' in Hugo Ball, *Gesammelte Gedichte*, © Die Arche 1963;

Georges Borchardt Inc. for an extract from 'Clepsydra' in John Ashbery, *Rivers and Mountains* (© 1962, 1963, 1964, 1966 by John Ashbery);

Carlisle Museum and Art Gallery for *Wittenham Clumps* by Paul Nash;

Columbia University Press and Jonathan Cape Ltd. for 'I Climb the Road to Cold Mountain' from *Cold Mountain* by Han-shan;

José Corti for 'L'Averse' from *Liberté Grande* by Julien Gracq;

Courtauld Institute Galleries, London, for *Woman at a Window* by Edgar Degas;

Association pour la diffusion des Arts graphiques et plastiques for *L'Objet invisible* by Alberto Giacometti;

Faber and Faber Ltd for extracts from George Barker's *Collected Poems 1930-1955* and Louis MacNeice's *Collected Poems 1925-1948*;

Faber and Faber Ltd and Alfred A. Knopf Inc. for extracts from *The Collected Poems of Wallace Stevens*;

Éditions Flammarion for an extract from Tristan Tzara's *Œuvres complètes* and the poems 'Route' and 'Nomade' from Pierre Reverdy's *Plupart du temps*;

Éditions Gallimard for extracts from Guillaume Apollinaire's *Œuvres poétiques* (© 1959), and *Les Champs magnétiques* (© 1967) by André Breton & Philippe Soupault; 'Fréquence' and 'Congé au vent' from René Char's *Fureur et mystère* (© 1962); 'Vos bouches mentent' from *Domaine public* (© 1953) by Robert Desnos; 'N'être plus avec toi' from *L'Embrasure* (© 1969) by Jacques Dupin; extracts from Paul Éluard's *Œuvres complètes* (© 1968); 'Que distraitement le promeneur' from *Tout Instant* (© 1957) by Jean Follain; extracts from Stéphane Mallarmé's *Œuvres complètes* (1961) and Gérard de Nerval's *Œuvres* (1974); an extract from 'Palindrome' by Georges Perec in *La Littérature potentielle* (© 1973); extracts from Saint-John Perse's *Œuvres complètes* (© 1972); and an extract by Charles Tomlinson from *Renga* (© 1971);

Éditions Robert Laffont for an extract from 'Sais-tu' by Benjamin Péret;

Liveright Publishing Corporation for an extract from *The Complete Poems of Hart Crane*, © Liveright Publishing Corporation 1933;

Otto Müller Verlag, Salzburg, for 'Untergang' from Georg Trakl, *Dichtungen und Briefe*, © O. Müller Verlag 1969;

the Trustees of the National Gallery, London, for *Apollo and Daphne* by Antonio and Piero del Pollaiuolo;

New Directions Publishing Corporation for 'The Southern Room over the River' and 'A Thousand Mountains' from Kenneth Rexroth's *One Hundred Poems from the Chinese* (© 1971 by Kenneth Rexroth) and *Collected Shorter Poems* (© 1966 by Kenneth Rexroth);

New Directions Publishing Corporation and Laurence Pollinger Ltd for extracts from Configurations (© 1971) by Octavio Paz;

Oxford University Press, New York, for an extract from *Preludes* by Conrad Aiken;

Penguin Books for extracts from Bashō's *The Narrow Road to the Deep North*, and Li Shang-yin's 'Phoenix tail . . .' from *Poems of the Late T'ang*;

Suhrkamp Verlag for extracts from Rainer Maria Rilke's *Sämtliche Werke*;

Wesleyan University Press for 'In a Train' from Robert Bly's *Silence in the Snowy Fields*.

The author wishes also to express his gratitude to Sigrid Taylor and Dora Musi for their generous assistance with the typescript, and to Pamela A. Duesbury for her painstaking concern for the index.

Note on Translations and References

Translations into English are by the author, except where another translator is credited.

The sources of quoted material are given in the text in the laconic Harvard style (author's surname, date of publication, page number). All items mentioned are set out in a complete form in the Bibliography.

Part One

GETTING AWAY FROM REALITY

1   THE ATTRACTION OF THE UNREAL

Poetry advances where ordinary reality falters. As soon as the strict adequacy of our habitual view of the world is called into question, imagination springs into action to offer alternative ways of seeing. We rarely allow that this is a frequent occurrence, for routine mentality tends to frown upon flights of fancy. We may all muse for a minute with glazed eye, turn our head to locate something glimpsed through the window of the train, sense an obscure attraction in a picture in a magazine which someone else is reading on the bus; yet few of us are likely to place any confidence in such fleeting experiences as being possible sources of discovery or deep pleasure. The suspicions that the common man harbours with regard to poetry may well be linked to an obscure yet probably quite justified hunch that poetry is an unsettling force that thrives on disruption and the shaking of security, a force which may even seek to topple the fixities of received opinion, the collective picture of the world 'as we know it'. Poetry seems to draw its strength from all that is at variance with normality, all that is disquieting, alien, unreal.

One evening in Paris some years ago, I was walking towards Les Halles after a day spent reading at the National Library. My way took me past the sombre walls of the French National Bank. As I looked up at the roof of the building some forty feet above, I suddenly saw a woman jumping from the top, her dress billowing out around her. A moment later, and I had realised my mistake. What I had taken for a woman leaping to her death in flowing robes was nothing more than a large flag fixed to the front of the building, which had happened to swirl out in a gust of wind just as I passed below. In real terms, the leaping woman had not the slightest claim to existence: she was an optical illusion, a momentary hallucination not really different in kind from the many trivial visual misunderstandings we experience in ordinary life. All the same, a strong sense of the exceptional remained with me. My emotional reaction to the illusion had been dramatic enough to leave a strong trace, so that it became a habit thenceforth to glance cautiously up whenever I passed that building.

The affective aura of such experiences tends to counteract our sage concern for a purely empirical approach to experience, an approach implicit in the collective picture of the world to which we normally feel obliged to adhere. Certainly it would be silly to suggest that my leaping woman had any objective reality. Yet it would be no less silly to try to diminish her impact, her plausibility to my consciousness, even if this were limited to a brief moment in time. As far as my imagination was concerned, she had been a reality, and, as Octavio Paz once put it,

> La irrealidad de lo mirado
> Da realidad a la mirada

> (Paz, 1971a, 188)

(The unreality of the seen/Makes real the seeing. Tr. C. Tomlinson and G. Aroul.)

The woman's sudden irruption into my picture of the world – and her no less brusque disappearance – effected an intriguing breach in the stable continuity of physical facts, presenting me with a sample of unreality whose value lay in its capacity, however short-lived, to challenge the assumption I might otherwise have made that the French National Bank was incapable of surprising me.

In *Anima Poetae* Coleridge has a note about 'a pretty optical fact'. He was returning from a walk one day when he saw a noble kite soaring high in the sky. He gazed at it for a long while, whereupon he turned round and was surprised to see two like birds floating close together in the air at a similar height. It then occurred to him that he had never previously noticed two kites hovering in unison like this: no sooner had he registered the thought than the vision disappeared. What he had taken for two birds was in fact two pairs of leaves, strongly resembling wings, on a fruit tree a few feet from his nose. Coleridge comments that 'the magnitude was given by the imagined distance, that distance by the former adjustment of the eye, which *remained* in consequence of the deep impression, the length of time I had been looking at the kite' (Coleridge, 1957, 139). In effect, the investment of attention into one natural phenomenon had created a temporary perceptual fixation which gave rise to something akin to an hallucination. We may note that the illusory image was dispelled immediately the poet allowed himself to query the strangeness of the vision, passing from wonderment to analysis. Illusion, it seems, does not last long once rational thought is applied to it. None the less Coleridge was obviously excited by the episode and recorded it with care. We may assume that the passing exhilaration of this brush with the unreal was not necessarily cancelled out by the objective explanation of the incident. Indeed the 'prettiness' of the 'optical fact' resided in large part in the 'mental fact' whereby the poet was able to *reflect* upon it as an instance of the conjuncture of perception and imagination.

Suzanne Lilar relates a number of analogous confusions in her book *Journal de l'Analogiste*. One of these concerns a magical transformation she witnessed one night while walking home in Antwerp along the utterly uninteresting Avenue Brialmont. Under the influence of the moonlight, the familiar setting was marvellously altered and took on the appearance of a distant and totally different place: the Belgian street turned into the Grand Canal in Venice, something dull becoming something radiantly beautiful. Indeed, Lilar insists, the metamorphosis was so extraordinary that the beauty of the illusory Grand Canal seemed to outshine by far that of the actual Grand Canal — Venice itself had never shown itself to her other than as something predictably beautiful. Whereas the Avenue Brialmont had *surprised* her, throwing off its placid bourgeois garb to assume the noble, sumptuous garments of the exotic. 'I kept on tirelessly comparing this vision with the one I had had on other days, confronting the one with the other, exploring the space which separated them . . .' (Lilar, 1954, 14). Her ability to draw renewed pleasure from the transformation had nothing to do with a sense of being muddled or disoriented: on the contrary, that pleasure was associated with a perfect awareness of the falsity of the vision.

In his book *L'Image fascinante et le surréel*, Maurice-Jean Lefebve seeks to analyse the fascination of such visions and images, encountered in material life or else in books and pictures. He offers the consideration that our awareness and enjoyment of the 'fascinating image' are governed by our full consciousness of the *unreality* of that image. That is to say, the object of our attention intrigues us precisely because, at the same time as we witness it, we also hesitate to ascribe any reality to it. Its propensity to assert itself as being 'as large as life' is never realised: 'On the contrary it is in our full consciousness of the unreality of this object that we are led to identify the source of this fascination' (Lefebve, 1965, 24). Lefebve suggests that what we feel in such circumstances is a special form of poetic pleasure. One of Lefebve's examples has to do with sitting in a train about to leave a station, and is an experience that most people have had at one time or another. One looks idly out of the window at the train at the next platform. Perhaps one vaguely hopes that one's own train will pull out first. Then one realises it is moving, and one experiences a full sense of movement. Full, that is, except for any of those sensations of jerking or swaying which, presumably, one normally registers in an unconscious way. A moment or two later, the brain has received some sort of message of alarm from the senses other than sight, and one realises that one's own train cannot in fact be moving – it is of course the train on the *other* platform which is pulling out. Lefebve analyses three stages in the experience, a movement from actuality through illusion and back to actuality. And he locates the *pleasure* which is undoubtedly aroused by the experience at the moment of transition from the second to the third stage. In this moment, the sensation of movement persists even though one is in the process of recognising that one has made a mistake. The moment is therefore one in which illusion and reality may be said to co-exist. As Lefebve puts it, it is like 'travelling inside a metaphor' (Lefebve, 1965, 85): for a moment, one's mind runs along both a literal and a figurative track, reality exactly parallel with unreality.

Such pleasures are frequently evoked in the travel sketches of Sacheverell Sitwell, who seems particularly receptive to unreal appearances in natural spectacles. In a piece about the Great Skellig, a massive desolate rock off the Irish coast, he describes the view that the besieged inhabitants of that place have as they look across to the fertile slopes of the mainland, which they can only hope to reach during comparatively rare periods of calm sea.

> The wild mountains were of unreal green, changing with every hour of the day, and of so wide a prospect that the mind could never tire of traversing their aromatic slopes where every step bruised the mosses and the lichen. When the sun came [. . .] the mainland looked appreciably nearer and lay suspended like a vision in the clearness. This would happen upon very many days when approach to it was impossible by boat. It had, therefore, not only the appearance of a vision, but, as well, its unreality and intangibility. (Sitwell, 1942, 65-6)

Sitwell's appreciation of the scene is very much a flight of fancy: for one thing, it seems improbable that the tough folk of the Skellig would be the sort of people to have such thoughts as he attributes to them. All the same, the example bears out the point that for a poet there can be genuine delight in witnessing a semblance of unreality, an unreality whose poignancy derives from the perception of quite real physical phenomena – actual hills and vegetation lit by the sun – which are desirable yet out of reach.

It might seem that the examples investigated thus far are not of a piece. The first was of a woman who seemed real, yet proved to be unreal. Coleridge's kites looked plausible, then became illusory. The movement of the train seemed real, yet was in fact unreal. But the Avenue Brialmont was real enough, even if it looked like the Grand Canal. And the mainland seen from the Great Skellig was definitely there, despite its unreal appearance. I think, though, that these are all complementary examples, in that each support Lefebve's general contention, which I will summarise thus: the source of the fascination of an illusory image lies in our *consciousness of its deflection from reality* — whether or not it derives from an involuntary or a cultivated aberration of perception. What I want to underline is that there *is* a response on the part of the person involved in such experiences, and that this response, which in many cases is so strong as to stick in the mind vividly for a long time, is dependent on that person's willingness to find something attractive in things which depart from the expected norm. Poets are people who are prepared to respond in this way: they have no hesitation in attributing value to experiences of the unreal, and indeed they cultivate a veritable taste for such experiences, actual and imaginary.

One of the most extreme statements of an attachment to the unreal is the half-lyrical, half-programmatic text *Introduction au discours sur le peu de réalité* by André Breton. With a Surrealist's typical faith in the capacity of imagination to adumbrate solutions to the problems of existence, Breton launches in this text on a critique of the conditions which tend to hamper the spontaneous flowering of poetic feeling and especially of 'that foreground reality which prevents us from getting anywhere' (Breton, 1970b, 28), i.e. from getting to a different sort of life than the one now on offer. Moved by a consequent 'desire for the unreal' and a 'love of the improbable', Breton puts his head between his hands and sinks into a reverie in which his thought becomes a sleeping woman to whom he makes love while the world outside is ravaged by an earthquake from which the lovers can never be rescued . . . As her lover, he watches over her, while outside everything else collapses: 'The end of the world, of the external world, is expected at any minute.' There could be no better end to his life, he muses, than to make love to this woman — his thought — while the physical world falls apart all around them (Breton, 1970b, 15-16).

In this fantasy Breton is exploring a temptation to which other poets have been no less drawn, that of ascribing to mental fantasy a character far superior to that of perceived reality proper. For as Breton writes elsewhere, the world of brute sensation is a thick fog which hides from us the things which the poet feels to be precious (Breton, 1955, 188).

Breton liked to quote the example of a young soldier he had met in a military hospital during the First World War, a man who had been withdrawn from the front line after an incident in which he had stood up on the parapet in the middle of battle, to wave his arms at the shells whistling overhead. His explanation of his conduct was that he had seen through the 'plot', and now knew the war to be nothing more than a show put on for his benefit, with sham bullets, bogus bombs and simulated wounds (Breton, 1952, 29-30). This man's conviction of the validity of his picture of the world was such as to impress upon Breton the fact that our reality *can* be shaped according to the way we choose to perceive it. Thus the message of his 'Introduction to the discourse on the depletion of reality' is that poetic imagination is perfectly justified in asserting its own rights, and in erecting an unreality in place of the given reality. Maybe it is only our articulation of the world which sustains it in its present form? 'What is, what might come to be, how insufficient that seems to poetry! Nature, she denies all your reigns; things, what do your properties count to her? She will know no rest until she had laid her negativistic hand upon the whole universe' (Breton, 1970b, 20).

There are occasions when the modern poet, in certain cases, will take his cue from the psychotic and reject the evidence of his senses in favour of a version of things which emanates entirely from himself. There is a particular thrill in the idea that all else can be eclipsed by the singular will of the creative imagination. Someone who can, so to speak, let the air out of reality and let it collapse into his pocket, immediately acquires full power to assert his private, unreal world in its place. The poet Joë Bousquet, whose actual direct experience of life was brutally curtailed after a shell wound in the war left him bedridden for life, managed to project onto the white screen of his immediate reality — his bedroom, from which he scarcely ever emerged, was a bare, whitewashed room with the shutter invariably drawn to — a whole pageant of fabulous adventures, imaginary encounters, poetic images. Almost effortlessly, he was able to confound fact and call forth an unreality so stunningly *present* that it took on the consistency of actual perceptual reality. Thus when Bousquet writes of an ideal love, his imagination is so intense that the creature of fantasy partakes of tangible reality.

Nue, elle devient réelle, inoubliable comme le jour. Elle ne rit plus, étendue sur ton lit elle est l'eau dormante de son rire. A sa prière, tu as éteint toutes les lampes, et le visage penché sur ses genoux, tu as distingué les dessins du tapis, puis ses cuisses, il y avait dans les ténèbres une nuit moins épaisse que dans tes yeux. Elle était si présente que tu n'avais pas besoin de la lumière pour la voir. (Bousquet, 1946, 92)

(Naked, she becomes real, as unforgettable as the daylight. She has stopped laughing, and outstretched on your bed, she is the sleeping water of her laughter. At her request, you have put out all the lamps, and with your head leaning on her knees, you have made out the patterns of the carpet, then the outline of her thighs: there was in the shadows a night less dense than in your eyes. She was so much a presence that you had no need of light to see her.)

Where an unreality can achieve such consistency, achieving the paradoxical effect of material presence while remaining manifestly immaterial, there seems no doubt that the poet enjoys a pleasure ranging beyond the one he might feel in lying beside an actual mistress. Here it could be said that for Bousquet the sensual impulse has become rarefied into a purely poetic impulse: the erotic thrill depends precisely upon the awareness that the naked girl is only as real as a dream may be said to be 'real'.[1]

That optical illusions and other sensory aberrations can be a source of fascination and poetic excitement is a proposition that many poets would want to endorse. Louis Aragon speaks for them when he writes in praise of what to the normal run of mortals must constitute a prospect of total insecurity, the collapse of certainty about the status of his perceptions. 'I no longer wish to hold myself back from the mistakes made by my fingers, by my eyes. I now know that they are not merely gross traps, but curious paths towards a goal which nothing other than they can reveal to me' (Aragon, 1926, 13). Without as yet being able to identify the precise nature of the revelation to which he feels he is being led, Aragon maintains his confidence in the capacity of the poetic sensibility to derive valid profit from the encounter with patent unrealities.

There are many poets whose fascination with the unreal has encouraged them to experiment in actual induced illusions of sensation. One could cite a whole string of poets from the nineteenth century on who have explored the poetic possibilities of hallucination as provoked by the taking of such drugs as opium, hashish and mescalin. Texts like De Quincey's *The Confessions of an English Opium Eater*, Baudelaire's *Les Paradis artificiels*, Cocteau's *Opium* and Michaux's *L'Infini turbulent* testify to the persistence, among poets of a certain disposition, of

the hypothesis that hallucination of the senses — the deliberate induce-
ment of an experience of something which is known to be unreal and
yet which has all the appearance of reality — constitutes an important
analogue for literary creation at large. It is with this in mind that I turn
to perhaps the most extreme case of a poet drawn to hallucination, that
of Arthur Rimbaud.

I do not wish to enter here into a detailed account of the background to Rimbaud's experiments with drugs (a list of which would
include not only hashish but also wine and absinthe, along with the
factor of lack of food, which may have enhanced the effect of the drugs
proper). Suffice it to say that Rimbaud's individual revolt against
literary orthodoxy, proclaimed in such texts as the 'Lettre du voyant'
and 'Alchimie du verbe', took the form of a studied campaign to exorcise normality by way of a cultivation of deviant sensory experience. In
order to create a new poetry, Rimbaud felt it necessary first to establish a new sensibility, one that would arise only after the violent suppression of the old. In effect he was hoping to displace existing reality
by the construction of a monstrous unreality. Dislocating his normal
awareness of the world by means of 'a long, immense and calculated
derangement of all the senses' (Rimbaud, 1960, 346), Rimbaud sought
to become a *voyant*, a seer poet capable of imposing upon the whole
world the tyranny of his personal vision. As he tells us in 'Alchimie du
verbe', the peak of aberration was reached when he found himself able
freely to substitute one thing for another, as though able to call up such
miracles at will. In my own example cited above, I was an involuntary
participant in the transformation of a flag into a leaping woman: for
Rimbaud, anything could be changed into anything else by the mere
application of his sovereign imagination.

> I schooled myself in the habit of straightforward hallucination: I
> could quite frankly see a mosque in place of a factory, a school of
> drummers composed of angels, carriages racing across the highways
> of the sky, a drawing-room in the depths of a lake; monsters, myster-
> ies. In the end I found something sacred in this mental disorder.
> (Rimbaud, 1960, 230)

This is the time to air an objection that might be raised as to the
relevance of such an example to the theme of unreality in poetry. In *Le
Plaisir poétique*, Jean Hytier maintains that an illusion is not of itself a
factor of poetic pleasure. If it is the case that a genuine hallucination is
experienced as an undisputed *reality*, it cannot *at the same time* be the

bearer of that 'bitter after-taste' which Hytier sees as characteristic of poetic pleasure, and which derives from the reader's awareness of the *non-reality* of an image at the moment of tasting its attractiveness (see Hytier, 1923, 26-31). On this argument, it would be open to Breton to admire the disturbed soldier for the tenacity of his version of things, but not to attribute to that version any specifically *poetic* virtue. A person hallucinating submits to the experience, not knowing that reality has been eclipsed. It may be surmised that for the genuine psychotic, the hallucination is perceived as an integral part of experience at large, not as an isolated aberration which can be bracketed off.[2] Whereas poetic pleasure, Hytier maintains, lies essentially in the perception of a subtle *difference* between the image and reality proper.

If we leave aside the extreme (and by definition unverifiable) testimony of those who are fully convinced of the reality of their delusions, we will, I believe, find that the conditions for poetic pleasure outlined in Hytier's analysis are in fact met in the examples advanced so far. I have already suggested that the emotional aura attaching to Suzanne Lilar's vision of the Grand Canal in a Belgian town was a function of her realisation that *in fact* the canal she saw was a fiction. If the transition is exactly pinpointed, I think I can reconcile Lefebve's analysis of the poetic charge of illusional experience with Hytier's assertion that it is improper to call genuine hallucination an experience of 'unreality'. I would suggest this reading of the sequence of events. First, Lilar turns a corner and finds herself standing before an expanse of water in the moonlight which she recognises as the Grand Canal. She has a hallucination, that is: the Canal is, if only for a moment, an undisputed reality. Then she realises she is in fact looking at the macadam surface of a street in Antwerp. Her grasp on true reality has returned. Hytier's way of looking at the situation would be to say that there has been a transition between one order of reality and another. Lefebve would say that unreality has intruded upon reality for a moment. But wherein lies the poetic pleasure which Lilar undoubtedly derives from the incident? 'I kept on tirelessly comparing this vision with the one I had had on other days.' Lilar does perceive a subtle difference between image and reality, in Hytier's terms — though *not at once*. The poetry derives not so much from the immediate experience as from its reenactment in memory. For where the hallucination proper is involuntary, the retrospective exploration of it is willed. Indeed pleasure derives from the subject's being able to toy with the transformation, switching back and forth between them, 'exploring the space which separated them'. The same analysis applies to my experience of the flag/woman. My pleasure lies in being able to re-run the mental film at will on my memory screen: in my mind, even at a distance of several years from the actual event, I can still savour the transition itself as the locus of pleasure.

Rimbaud of course saw himself acting deliberately when he engaged in his experiments. He would scarcely have spoken of the 'sacred' in connection with his mental disorder if he were subject to hallucinations over which he had no control at all. However closely he may have skirted to the madman's position of losing all control, he does not appear to have actually succumbed to psychosis. The point is important: for if we accept that Rimbaud was sponsoring a 'deliberate derangement' of his senses, it follows that in the moment of hallucination he would have been aware of the unreal status of what he perceived. In this, he would have been in a position to appreciate them rather as Bousquet appreciates his imaginary visitor, as a presence all the more appealing because of its avowed unreality.

Thus far I have been content to examine examples of the poetic as it attaches to experiences of the unreal which are not confined to the pages of a book. This I have done in order to provide a firm point of reference in the field of sensory reality before entering on an exploration of the attractions of the unreal in literature. Now, there is an obvious sense in which *all* that is written is unreal in the sense of being set at a remove from the realm of sensory immediacy. Jorge Luis Borges has a poem called 'The Other Tiger' which describes how the author thinks of a tiger, pictures its stripes, its motions, its strength: sitting in Buenos Aires, he can follow that tiger along the bank of the remote Ganges. Yet, he eventually comes to realise that this creature is no more than 'a tiger made of symbols and of shadows', a construct of words and echoes from encyclopaedias. In desperation, he seeks out the 'other tiger' which is not the creature of his poetic fantasy:

Against the symbolic tiger, I have planted
the real one, it whose blood runs hotly,
and today, 1959, the third of August,
a slow shadow spreads across the prairie,
but still, the act of naming it, of guessing
what is its nature and its circumstances
creates a fiction, not a living creature,
not one of those who wander on the earth.

(Borges, 1972, 66; tr. Alistair Reid)

To point at each new tiger is to turn it into yet another fiction, so the writer must resign himself to the fact that real tigers can never be planted within the confines of a poem — to imagine, to name, these are acts which strip reality of its substance, and retain only the shadow or the form.

In effect Borges is putting the case that all literature is inherently fictional: everything placed within its bounds will be unreal, since no act of description or evocation is adequate to the task of calling forth the intricate richness of the thing itself. And yet, charming though Borges's poem is in its insistence on the impossibility of netting a tiger in a poem, I do not think it countermands the collective experience of what I imagine to be a majority of poets, namely that the written word is *not* in fact a diminished area of experience, a depletion of the real. For they would contend that language is a medium which amplifies experience, giving it a new consistency or 'meaningfulness' — perhaps not a literal physical solidity (the real Bengal tiger remains solid whether or not Borges writes a poem), but none the less a deeper significance, a special radiance. Borges's paper tigers may end up having more meaning for us, indeed, than the animal pacing the jungle, for they have impact upon our minds proportionate to the speed with which they fade into shadowiness. Like Carroll's Cheshire Cat, they delight us most because they manifest their unreality, and therefore remind us of the distance between image and fact. And this, as we have seen, is an ingredient of poetic pleasure.

Let us return to Rimbaud and his hallucinations. We can at this point — given that the discussion has now switched from actual experiences of unreality to the literary recording of unreality — direct our attention away from hallucinations *per se* and towards *the way hallucinations are formulated* in words. An actual illusion, being the subjective experience of an individual, cannot in any event be scrutinised by others: we have to rely on the report that the eye-witness gives us, just as with someone's dream we have to go by his account of it, unable as we are to project *his* dream onto *our* mental screen. In Rimbaud's case, we have an interesting situation in which the actual hallucinatory experience ('straightforward hallucination') is mediated for us through the agency of language, which we are now beginning to suspect may be uniquely suited to the establishment of unreality. Where Rimbaud is concerned, such a medium was perfect: for did he not seek above all to 'escape from reality'? (Rimbaud, 1960, 225). The momentary flicker of a deranged optic nerve which enabled him to *see* carriages dashing across the sky could be rendered permanent by being recorded in words.

Rendered permanent, and, more importantly, rendered more attractive to the degree that the image became more patently unreal. It needs little reflection to see why the procedures of induced hallucination might become redundant once the seeker of novelty and unreality comes to realise the power of language to alter reality and to sponsor unreal forms in its own right. Rather than persist in inducing 'illuminations' and then copying them down, Rimbaud may — possibly at an early stage in the composition of the *Illuminations* — have abandoned drug-induced unreality in favour of 'the hallucination of words' — his own phrase (Rimbaud, 1960, 230). This argument is put forward incisively in Breton's text 'Le Message automatique', where the surrealist poet insists on the primarily verbal nature of Rimbaud's fictions. In the final stage, Breton contends, Rimbaud was writing in an undirected, exploratory fashion, not describing an experience he had already had. The strangeness of the resultant texts, their hallucinatory shock-effect, is therefore due to the spontaneously unreal nature of his language. The poet would in these circumstances experience his illumination *a posteriori* — he would 'see' the illusion only when he read the poem (Breton, 1970b, 185-7).

If it is the case that poetic pleasure can derive from savouring the splendid plausibility of the impossible, then it is not difficult to appreciate why such pleasure may be best mediated through language alone. Words are poetically intriguing because they tell lies so easily. In the poem 'Barbare', Rimbaud cannot resist inserting into the text itself an unambiguous reminder to the reader that the things he is speaking about are lacking in all reality. He wants to make quite sure that the reader does not take the poem as a realistically conceived document about some unlikely though actually experienced series of events.

> Bien après les jours et les saisons, et les êtres et les pays,
> Le pavillon en viande saignante sur la soie des mers et des fleurs arctiques; (elles n'existent pas).

> (Rimbaud, 1960, 292)

(Long after the days and the seasons, the people and the countries,/ The flag of bleeding meat on the silk of the seas and of the arctic flowers; (they don't exist).)

It is ironic that Rimbaud's explicit avowal — 'they don't exist' — should not have prevented some literalist commentators from seeking out links between elements in the text and actual things and incidents in Rimbaud's biography (in so far as these can be ascertained with any measure of certainty in the absence of any diary or similar record). Here, for instance, the flag of bleeding meat has been interpreted by one critic as the Danish flag which Rimbaud would have seen on his arrival in Iceland en route for Java in 1876. The reference to arctic flowers might be thought to corroborate this. Rimbaud's interpolation is however quite explicit: the flowers he is talking about have *no real existence*, and we therefore would be wrong to attribute any reality to 'the flag of bleeding meat on the silk of the seas' either. Moreover, if I understand Rimbaud rightly, the whole point of such objects is that they are seen not to originate in real experience, but instead in language. They parade themselves as textual fictions whose *raison d'être* is that they have *no* 'reason to be'. This is a poetry which nourishes itself on images of the unreal: it exploits its fictive nature to the utmost by capitalising on the incredible capacity of language to designate not just the things which exist in the real world but also, and more excitingly, things that do not exist anywhere. Poetic pleasure is, here, very much dependent on our ability to enjoy swaying between accustomed reality and the unreality we encounter in reading.

I have tried to describe the way in which experiences of the unreal, occurring in ordinary waking life, can create a species of poetic agitation in us, encouraging us to reflect pleasurably on the moment of an illusion as it insinuates itself into the continuum of perceptual habit. I think it is equally the case that descriptions of the unreal which we encounter in the form of poetic texts tend to jolt consciousness through an analogous sequence: from the normality of our ordinary reading habits into the surprises of the poem, and then back to normality again. The intensity of the poetic shock will not simply be a function of poetry's being, as Borges implies, an intrinsically fictional enterprise: rather it will lie in the fact of transition itself, in our awareness of a gap between poetic language and the language we associate with prosaic transactions in the world of facts. Let us now look more closely at the ways in which writers of poems deliberately undertake the construction of unreality.

THE MAKING OF UNREALITY

Fantastic voyages are the very stuff of imaginative literature. The writer who wishes to take leave of reality for a while has only to dream up a realm that does not exist and people it with the creatures of his fantasy, following thereby an ancient tradition of the traveller's tale which dates back at least to Apuleius's *Golden Ass*. In *Au Pays de la magie*, Henri Michaux describes a purely fictional country where there exist seven varieties of magic fog, where fire lacks heat, where people store oil in paralysed blocks and it is illegal to laugh before noon. One of the provinces of this strange land is called Stomach, and those who cross it are liable to have their feet digested as they go (Michaux, 1946). In more sombre mood, Charles Baudelaire, in the prose poem 'Anywhere out of the world', passes under review the various escape routes available to his world-weary soul. He evidently needs a holiday in a place entirely different from anything he knows. At first he pictures Lisbon, transmuting it in his daydream into a desolate city above a cold sea whose inhabitants tear out each least trace of vegetation in hatred so as to maintain its character of mineral sterility. But Baudelaire is not satisfied: he goes on to think of Rotterdam with its masts rising like forests above the roof-tops. Still unfulfilled, his mind moves on to Batavia in Java, which embodies a mixture of tropical wildness and European elegance. But even now his soul is unable to find rest: 'Fuyons vers les pays qui sont les analogies de la Mort' (let us flee to the countries which are analogous to death) (Baudelaire, 1961, 304), he exclaims, and by way of Torneo, a town close to the Arctic Circle, he comes to think of the North Pole itself. At last he has found the perfect place, a setting where night and day are infinitely extended and life lacks all rhythm. Surely this would be the perfect antipodes to his present real existence, in a Paris bustling with life yet also stifling and depressing. 'Anywhere out of the world' thus describes a progression toward an unreality whose attraction lies in its reversal of all the colour and naturalness of normal existence.[3]

When we go on long journeys, or when we only dream of travel, or, again, read about other people's dreams of travel, we often do so in order to provoke sensations of unsettlement and strangeness which give rise to a form of poetic pleasure. When we come upon a place – or a description of a place – which we do not recognise and which impresses us, we feel a mingled fear at the prospect of entering upon that which is alien to our experience, coupled with the thrill of adventure. 'To succumb to fascination is to abandon oneself to that which is *other*', writes Lefebve (Lefebve, 1965, 123), and poets have frequently shown that the allurement of the strange is a rich vein of poetic invention. It is not very far to move from Baudelaire's North Pole to the remote realms evoked in the poetry of Georg Trakl, a world so alien as to make the unprepared visitor shiver and wish he had stayed at home:

UNTERGANG

Über den weissen Weiher
Sind die wilden Vögel fortgezogen.
Am Abend weht von unseren Sternen ein eisiger Wind.

Über unsere Gräber
Beugt sich die zerbrochene Stirne der Nacht.
Unter Eichen schaukeln wir auf einem silbernen Kahn.

Immer klingen die weissen Mauern der Stadt.
Unter Dornenbogen
O mein Bruder klimmen wir blinde Zeiger gen Mitternacht.

   (Trakl, 1972, 64-5)

(DOWNFALL / Over the white pond / The wild birds have flown away./ At dusk an icy wind blows from our stars. / Over our graves / The broken brow of night bends down. / Under the oaks we toss on a silver boat. / Still the town's white walls keep ringing. / Under arches of thorns / O my brother we blind hands climb towards midnight.)

The stark landscape is presented without explanation or comfort. It is a frozen place where those who exist do so in conditions of menace: their graves lie ready and they are caught in a silver boat on an empty pond. Time moves on inexorably, it seems: the speaker and the one he calls his brother are caught in a relentless progression towards some form of ultimate anguish, moving as blindly and as mechanically as the hands on a clock ticking towards midnight. This world is certainly strange, and we may find that our fascination with it is not undissociated from the knowledge we keep at the back of our minds that all this, thank goodness, is unreal.

In his book *Techniques of Strangeness in Symbolist Poetry*, James L. Kugel tells how he came to crystallise the poetics of the French

Symbolists in the formula of 'poetic strangeness', following the realisation of a similarity of presentation in a poem by Maurice Maeterlinck and a song by Bob Dylan. In either case the information given was skeletal, and served not to set out a story or a scene in detail, but rather to 'provide a direction for the reader's imagination without offering it a means of satisfaction' (Kugel, 1971, 5). By systematically withholding the full information that the reader expects to receive, Kugel argues, writers in the Symbolist mould create an ambiguous sense of strangeness, at once offputting and compelling. It would be easy enough to illustrate the point with one of Kugel's examples from writers like Maeterlinck and Nerval; instead it may be instructive to turn to an example of poetic strangeness coming from a more distant culture. This is an untitled Chinese poem by the T'ang poet, Li Shang-yin, who even within his own culture had a reputation for being 'difficult'.

> Phoenix tail on scented silk, flimsy layer on layer:
> Blue patterns on a round canopy, stitched deep into the night.
> The fan's sliced moon could not hide her shame.
> His coach drove out with the sound of thunder, no time
>   to exchange a word.
> In the silent room the gold of the wick turned dark:
> No message since has ever come, though the pomegranate is
>   red.
> The dappled horse stands tethered only on the back of
>   drooping willows,
> Where shall she wait for a kind wind to blow from the
>   South West?

>   (Graham, 1965, 149; tr. A.C. Graham)

The situation described in the poem is not very clear. Working backwards through the lines we can detect a slender anecdotal thread. There is a female person who is waiting for some sort of relief or salvation. There is a horse on which she might escape, though it is not clear whether she will attempt this solution to her predicament. She awaits in vain a message which seems unlikely to materialise, now that so much time has elapsed since certain earlier events which, it seems, determined her present state. Those events gave rise to a sense of shame, and culminated in the brusque departure of a man, who had no time to speak to her. She is left all alone, it seems, and her sole activity is sewing by night, producing silken patterns like the tail-feathers of an imaginary bird . . . Coming upon the poem as we do without knowledge of its cultural context, we will not have available the suggestion that red pomegranate wine is drunk on the wedding night, and that the girl may be working at the canopy of her bridal bed: we would therefore not necessarily guess that the poem was about a bride cruelly abandoned by her bridegroom. Rather we would respond to the poem's indirect-ness for its own sake, savouring a poetic atmosphere whose capacity to intrigue us depends above all on the incompleteness of our information. Indeed it could be argued that our pleasure in the poem is deepened by our ignorance of its anecdotal basis: we respond to the sequence not as a meaningful series of explicable events, but as a series of floating motifs — a phoenix-tail, a fan like a sliced moon, a thunderous coach, a horse by a willow — whose virtue lies in their suggestive discontinuity. We might call our experience of the poem one of unreality in the sense that we find it hard to piece things together into the coherence we are used to finding in normal presentations of meaningful situations.

It is not surprising that short poems tend to create this sense of strangeness, instilled as it is by an embargo on exhaustive explanation. Poets are by definition writers who prefer lyrical density and allusion to the long-winded clarification of prose. But the widespread tendency of poets to be lapidary in their style is one that has particular impact where the creation of unreality is concerned. What could be more simple and unstrained than the following piece by Wallace Stevens, and yet what a lot of background explanation we would need if we were ever to argue that it depicted a plausible reality!

He rode over Connecticut
In a glass coach.
Once, a fear pierced him,
In that he mistook
The shadow of his equipage
For blackbirds.

> ('Thirteen Ways of Looking at a Blackbird' in Stevens, 1955, 94)

An unidentified protagonist rides out across a territory in the United States of America. Connecticut exists. However, does 'he' really exist? That he rides in a coach with an equipage suggests that he is a person of some authority: but who rides out in a glass coach in real life? There is an element of the fairy tale here, associated with echoes of Cinderella's glass slipper and her magic pumpkin-coach, or of the transparent or more to the point: illusory clothes of a certain gullible Emperor. So far we know that this person is riding in an unreal coach across a real space. The presentation is completed not by an explanation of the discrepancy, but by a specimen experience which functions as a shorthand description of his psychological state: he experiences the kind of illusion one has when glimpsing something out of the corner of one's eye. His retinue, presumably sombrely clad and riding on horse-back (though here I am already extrapolating), are momentarily transformed into blackbirds. Now this tells us something about the mentality of the protagonist in that it carries a fairly clear suggestion of an omnipotence which cannot entirely relax, being pursued by intimations of treachery. In this spirit, one could argue that the illusion described tends in the direction of adding substance to the man: he is that much more real to us by virtue of the poet granting us this information. Yet at the same time, the poem dissolves into a caricature of reality: the focus tilts from the fairytale reality of the man travelling in a glass coach to an unreality a further degree removed. To summarise: if we take the reference to *Connecticut* to be our basic reality, then the *glass coach* tilts us towards unreality, that is towards a stylised, fairytale substitute for the real. Now the *blackbirds* come into the poem (further stressed by the reader's being conditioned specially to look out for them if he has read other poems in the set of poetic variations on the blackbird motif from which this poem is taken). Their effect is to plunge us to a further level of unreality in that they are not an actual but a *delusional* experience of the man in the coach. In other words this brief poem wraps up two layers of unreality and leaves us not merely with the sense of strangeness dependent on our being deprived of adequate information, but with a neat demonstration of the capacity of the poet to flip us out of reality by the merest turn of phrase. The poem boils down to an unreal journey punctuated by an illusion: our poetic pleasure, if we join in the spirit of the game, lies in the gentle uplift afforded by the scarcely detectable jolt that takes us from the real and places us, so to speak, in a mental no-man's-land. We arrive at a space of perfect unreality, what Stevens elsewhere calls 'Reality as a thing seen by the mind, / Not that which is, but that which is apprehended, / A mirror, a lake of reflections in a room . . .' (Stevens, 1955, 468).

Strategies of displacement and dislocation are part and parcel of the work of many poets in a tradition initiated by Rimbaud. His is one of the most varied experiments in the modes of making unreality, and the techniques he developed may be taken as exemplary for all poets intent on the literary escape-route out of the real world. The poems of *Illumi-nations* read like nothing less than a series of demonstrations of the poet's capacity to 'strangeify' the normal world to the point where recognisably real objects and situations give way to a more plausible because more intense unreality (Rimbaud, 1960, 253ff.). For example, he places things in settings where they do not belong: 'Madame *** sets up her piano in the Alps' (one has an almost comic image of a lady strumming at the keys upon a mountain peak), or 'they are playing cards at the bottom of the pond'. The normal spatial properties of things are turned in reverse: 'There is a cathedral reaching downwards and a lake stretching upwards'. Things are animated, so that flowers can look and speak, or else objects are posited whose substance is highly abnormal: castles built out of bones, or grass composed of steel and emeralds. Colours are attributed to objects in an unthinkable fashion: we read of a white sunset, red mud, scarlet pigeons. Fantastic scenes are evoked in which bridges criss-cross a fabulous city, or façades and railways people a promontory which is at the same time a palace. In the end, the reader learns to adapt to this giddy world and to savour its unreality as a genuine poetic pleasure. As with all fictional illusions, one enjoys the unreality not simply because it is inadmissible in real terms, but because one can, without actual risk, venture in one's mind along the path towards accepting the poet's version of things at its face value. The delight of reading such poetry is subject to our readiness to entertain some measure of belief in the validity of the unreal. We respond with a momentary gullibility to a Surrealist poet like Breton when he voices the poetic challenge, 'I hold that nothing is inadmissible' (Breton, 1970b, 26).

The eventual effect of a sustained subversion of the categories on which rests our notion of the normal world is to achieve a global derealisation. That is, the poet of unreality ends up by creating a universal ambience such that *anything* introduced within it is at once emptied of its natural substantiality. A Surrealist example, from a poem by Benjamin Péret, amply demonstrates what I will call the technique of total derealisation.

Ma tête de papier de verre frottant tant et plus sur une coupe de cristal
faite à ton image d'oiseau qu'un sanglier empêche de prendre son
    premier vol
est pleine de l'embrun de tes yeux semblables à deux oranges qu'on
    ne cueillera jamais
tes yeux qui sont peut-être une pierre éclatée comme un arbre
    foudroyé

   ('Sais-tu' in Bédouin, 1961, 118)

(My head of glass-paper rubbing ever so hard on a crystal cup / made in
your image which is that of a bird that a boar prevents from launching
on its first flight / is full of the fog of your eyes similar to two oranges
that will never be plucked / your eyes which are perhaps a stone split
open like a tree struck by lightning)

The extract begins with the poet speaking of his head, yet at once he
inserts a qualification which robs this head of all reality: it is made of
glass-paper. Without pausing, Péret goes on to speak of this glass-paper,
which is mysteriously at work smoothing down a crystal cup. Without
explanation, he proceeds to describe this cup in terms of its resemblance
to an unspecified *tu* (which it is convenient to identify as the poet's
beloved, though no strict necessity to do so is voiced in the poem). Yet
before this resemblance is fully articulated (and certainly before the
reader has had time to visualise what it might mean), the woman's
appearance is qualified as being bird-like. Again this is not a point to
dwell upon, for the mention of a bird sponsors a brief anecdote about
the bird caught by a boar. All this has happened by the time we reach
the main verb in line three and learn more about the poet's head. Now
the poet plunges into an obsessional evocation of the beloved, whose
eyes create the fog which swells within his head: two further sub-
qualifications ensue whereby her eyes are compared to two oranges or
to a stone split open.

The writing here is characterised by the compulsive specification of
each new item as it is introduced into the orbit of the poem. Far from
helping us to adjust to each new item, the specification operates on a
principle of startling incongruity so as to deprive it of any reality practically at the moment of its first being mentioned. Images abound,
generating further images: there is even a simile secreted inside a metaphor, as when the stone identified with the woman's eyes is likened to a
tree struck by lightning. In the end the reader feels that the process is
one of endless generation: the poem seems to need just one initial
stimulus (the mention of the head) for it to propagate an infinite series
of unrealities.

In its simplest form, this process of zany generation was perfected
by Lewis Carroll in the 'He thought he saw' verses which are interpola-
ted into the narrative of *Sylvie and Bruno*. Each verse is constructed on
the same model.

He thought he saw an Albatross
 That fluttered round the lamp:
He looked again, and found it was
 A Penny-Postage-Stamp.
'You'd best be getting home', he said:
 'The nights are very damp!'

   (Carroll, 1939, 342)

Each verse in the poem introduces a subject in its first line (here, the Albatross), only to re-define it radically in line four (here, the Stamp). In the space of a few lines, a flagrant contradiction of sense occurs as attention leaps from one thing to another. The function of the couplet at the end of each verse is to convince the reader that this new subject is indeed worthy of attention, and yet the scandal of the homely scrap of paper that can be mistaken for a massive marine bird is scarcely diminished. Such a poetic structure constitutes an automatic 'derealising machine' which absorbs realities at one end and spouts forth unrealities at the other.

By now it will have become clear that the major force in the poetic subversion of real properties and relations between things is most completely engineered by the application of techniques of verbal assertion. Just as I argued for the view that for Rimbaud the 'hallucination of words' outstripped the sensory dissociations induced by drugs, so it can be said that with Péret, as with most Surrealist poets, the release of language from its contractual obligation to reflect the conventional order of things, and in particular a style of free association encouraged by grammatical structures which facilitate metaphors and similes, leads to a poetry whose kaleidoscopic brilliance is completely at odds with the more or less uniform colouration of our normal life. If we as readers may be said to 'enter' such poems, it is by virtue of our surrendering all handholds on the world of fixed relations, with its steady gravitational pull, and submitting to an experience which equates to that of extreme sensory deprivation. One of Rimbaud's more anguished moments comes when he realises what he stands to lose in the process of derealisation:

Décidément, nous sommes hors du monde. Plus aucun son. Mon tact a disparu. Ah! mon château, ma Saxe, mon bois de saules. Les soirs, les matins, les nuits, les jours . . . Suis-je las! (Rimbaud, 1960, 222)

(We are decidedly out of the world. No more sound. My sense of touch has vanished. Ah! my castle, my Saxony, my willow wood. The evenings, the mornings, the nights, the days . . . How weary I am!)

It is as though, at the final stage of the derealisation process, there were a literal shift 'out of the world'. The eclipse of the poet's normal sensibility has led him to a point where nothing seems real: the only remnants of material existence take the form of memories of a past now out of reach, a time of regularly alternating days and nights which is in complete contrast to his present undifferentiated, almost abstract experience, one which is presumably akin to Baudelaire's imagined experience of the North Pole.

The process of retreat from empirical reality thus reaches a decisive point of withdrawal. This is the moment so often caught in Turner's water-colours, the point where a recognisable aspect of the material world, the outline of a boat for example, still lingers on, while the major part of the picture has begun to drift away from representation into sheer colour texture bereft of any representational justification. At this stage it is debatable whether a given expanse of blue-green still constitutes an allusion to the way water looks under a particular sort of light, or whether it already manifests nothing other than sheer abstract colour.

Of course in a general sense, as Jean Bazaine has pointed out, all art is 'abstract': art is not nature, but 'a contraction of the entire real' (Bazaine, 1953, 47). Art does not and cannot exactly duplicate the tangible world in whole or in part, and the most 'realistic' artist who attempts to carry something of that world into his work will find that what actually comes through is something more in the nature of an imprint or a figure or a sign. The situation is implicit in Borges's complaint that he is unable to introduce into his poem 'the other tiger', the creature of flesh and blood. But my argument goes further than this. The processes of derealisation in poetry proceed beyond the primary stage where experience is simply aesthetically stylised or formalised as a set of signs. It goes beyond the fictional mirrorings, contractions or configurations which stand for aspects of the real world. It advances to the logical extreme, the total eclipse of *all* allusion to that world. The voyage into unreality thus ends up with the complete suppression of all trace of material imprint.

The archetype of the poetry of total derealisation is that of Stéphane Mallarmé. Where Rimbaud was intent on erecting a counter-reality out of the dislocated fragments of his sensibility, an unreality which had strange colours, but at least *had* colour, Mallarmé practised the cooler

Symbolist technique of gradually filtering off from his writing all direct or indirect allusion that might link it, however remotely, to perceptual experience. His aim was to distil experience into a quintessence so pure that it would rise above the contingencies of phenomenal reality and assert itself on the untouchable plane of the Idea. Many of his poems are constructed around objects which have been so refined as to disappear completely; that is, Mallarmé creates a poetic form about the 'absence' which is the sole residue of an extinguished object. The two quatrains of the famous 'Sonnet en -yx' exemplify this passion for nothingness in almost caricatural style.

> Ses purs ongles très haut dédiant leur onyx,
> L'Angoisse, ce minuit, soutient, lampadophore,
> Maint rêve vespéral brûlé par le Phénix
> Que ne recueille pas de cinéraire amphore
>
> Sur les crédences, au salon vide: nul ptyx,
> Aboli bibelot d'inanité sonore,
> (Car le Maître est allé puiser des pleurs au Styx
> Avec ce seul objet dont le Néant s'honore).
>
> (Mallarmé, 1961, 68)

(Her pure nails lifted high to dedicate their onyx, / Anguish, the lamp-bearer, carries at this midnight hour / Many a vesperal dream burnt by the phoenix / Which are not contained in any crematory urn / Upon the sideboard in the empty room: there is no ptyx, / That extinguished bauble of sonorous inanity, / (For the Master has gone to gather sobs by the Styx / With this one object which Nothingness deigns to countenance).)

The poem refers to a room, and there are even sideboards, but this is about all the materiality that is left. It is midnight, the hour when ordinary earth time modulates into eternity. A figure appears, but she is no more than a personified abstraction, Anguish, recognisably female only by virtue of the fact that *angoisse* is a noun of feminine gender and of the oblique reference to her polished fingernails as they glint in the lamplight. Our attention is directed, however, not at this creature's hands but at what she holds in them, and this is — nothing. She bears dreams which have been burnt, that is: annihilated, and even if she *were* to have brought their ashes, the room lacks any container in which to place them. No urn? No, not even a *ptyx*. Here Mallarmé compounds his negations by introducing an imaginary object which has no material reality whatsoever. Mallarmé's *ptyx* – a word without vowel, without space to breathe – is thought to derive from a Greek word meaning a fold, which is to say: it has the form of something which enfolds, but not the substance itself. Mallarmé is said to have been delighted by the word in that it gave rise to the painful challenge of composing a sonnet with four rhymes in -yx. The *ptyx* is in fact a sublime artificial pretext, a thing appropriate to its context inasmuch as it lacks all real content and justification. As Mallarmé goes on to say, it is an empty, echoing thing of no consequence (*bibelot*). And in any event, he insists, the object is not there – it is now *nul* and *aboli*, nullified and obliterated. The only past history it can claim is the slender anecdote set in brackets: the Master (i.e. the Poet) has gone to gather tears in it by the river of oblivion. But since one cannot hope to retain that which oblivion sweeps beyond reach, the object is finally instituted as the perfect emblem of Nothingness.

Mallarmé's *ptyx* may be taken as the end-product of the development I have hoped to sketch thus far. It is an object whose poetic virtue lies in its utter lack of reality. It fascinates us in the way that a purely hypothetical entity may intrigue our minds. Perhaps this is what mathematicians feel about the square root of minus one: it has the nagging fascination of something we know to be impossible, yet which continues to titillate our speculative faculties. This notion of an attraction emanating from a thing bereft of substance or presence is movingly depicted in a sculpture by Giacometti called *The Invisible Object*. It consists of a slender female figure who stands in a seemingly protective posture, her slender fingers encircling an object which is not there. Her stylised face indicates a mixture of anxiety and perplexity, and this gives rise to a number of possible interpretations of her situation. Is the invisible object something precious which has just vanished into thin air? (The sculpture is occasionally referred to by the title *Hands Holding the Void*.) Can the figure feel anything between her hands? And if the invisible object were to suddenly become real to her, could she recognise it? Or would it remain a source of anxious perplexity to her? Giacometti's figure is a marvellous evocation of that atmosphere of wistful yearning that arises from the contemplation of poetic images of absence. The invisible object remains unseen, and yet its transparency haunts us as a seductive promise of contact and discovery. It is what we grasp when we let go of everything else.

'a seductive promise of contact'

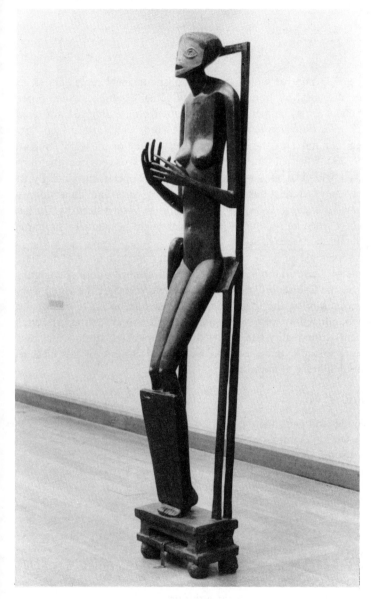

Alberto Giacometti, *The Invisible Object*
Source: Aimé Maeght Collection, Paris © by ADAGP Paris, 1980

3 TOWARDS THE LOGOLOGICAL EXTREME

The *poésie pure* of which the Symbolists dreamed represents an extreme distantiation from the world of actual experience. Such poetry lays claim to an hermetic space within which are arranged not words which refer outwards to real things, but words which are, in Jean-Pierre Burgart's phrase, 'of the colourless transparency of the wind' (Burgart, 1969, 29). When all hint of an external context is censored, the verbal artefact will float as a watertight, anchorless object, sustained by the purely internal relations of its component parts and impervious to external pressures. It begins to resemble an ideal voiced by Gustave Flaubert when he spoke of a book which might be uniquely 'supported by the interior force of style'.

An example of such 'watertight' poetry might be one of the early poems of Pierre Reverdy, the literary equivalent of Cubism in painting. Just as the Cubists broke down the configurations of the visual world and redistributed the fragments in a picture according to endogenous formal principles, so Reverdy may be said to have extracted certain elements from reality and arranged them in a new pattern which owes nothing to the external context and indeed is more or less bleached clean of all trace of immediacy.

ROUTE

Sur le seuil personne
   Ou ton ombre
Un souvenir qui resterait
La route passe
   Et les arbres parlent plus près
Qu'y a-t-il derrière
    Un mur
      des voix
Les nuages qui s'élevèrent
Au moment où je passais là
Et tout le long une barrière
     Où sont ceux qui n'entreront pas

        (Reverdy, 1969, I, 176)

(ROAD / At the threshold nobody / Or your shadow / A memory that might remain / The road goes by / And the trees speak closer to / What is there behind / A wall / voices / The clouds which rose up / At the very moment I was passing there / And all along a barrier / Where those are who shall not enter)

Ostensibly the poem is 'about' a road, though the lack of article to the title might indicate that the text of the poem proper is not so much an account of a road as a sequence of statements forming a purely mental 'route' or progression of ideas. The poem contains various words which seem to signal the presence of a number of concrete things: a threshold, a road, trees, a wall, clouds, a barrier. Yet each thing is apprehended in terms of a lack of physical immediacy. If there is a threshold, then it fails to function as a threshold should, since nobody is there to transform it from an arbitrary place to a place of significant arrival or encounter. There is a road, yet it is merely said to pass, with no indication that it leads anywhere. There are a wall and a barrier, but their role is to implement a sense of numbness by functioning as hindrances to contact. Then there are trees and clouds. The former seem to be an embodiment of presence inasmuch as they speak, and speak in an intimate manner ('les arbres parlent plus près'). And yet their actual message is censored within the space of the poem, and what lies 'behind' – namely the dual entity 'Un mur / des voix' – represents a unit in which a firm negative force (the solid wall) is juxtaposed with an indistinct positive force (voices, an incorporeal half-promise of human presence), the dominant accent thereby placed upon the unlikelihood of contact. The clouds that seem to react to the motion of the unidentified protagonist ('Les nuages qui s'élevèrent / Au moment où je passais là') may suggest the notion of a natural environment sensitive to the behaviour of man. But we have nothing more to go on, since the sentence apparently beginning with the subject 'Les nuages' fails to arrive at any main verb. This omission of the crucial word in the sentence at the one point where decisive meaning seems called for, may be seen to reflect a general strategy of nullifying activity. As for the unusual variety of conflicting tenses – present conditional, present indicative, past definite, imperfect, future – these establish such a complex web of antagonistic implications about the poem's chronology that they ultimately achieve the effect of cancelling out all sense of development, of denying *any* action at all. The reader is left with a handful of inconclusive phrases, and no more than a hint of hoped-for presence at the threshold: 'ton ombre', the merest shade of a person.

As it stands, the poem is a scatter of signs drifting without orientation. Admittedly the reader can sometimes lean heavily on such poems and force onto them a guiding context, inventing, say, a novelette about a lonely lover who waits for his beloved by a doorway, straining to hear her approach, studying the sound of trees and the motion of clouds in the hope of eliciting some indication of hope – and so on. In this way, he would let some reality into the poem. But to do so would be to damage the delicate suspension on which the poem is founded. Rather it asks to be regarded as a frozen collocation of whiffs and hints refined out of all immediacy, a set of immaculate, neutralised patterns which have no application to extra-aesthetic experience. The poem is what Maurice Blanchot has called a 'language object' (Blanchot, 1955, 39).

If it is possible to envisage that a totally self-supporting verbal microcosm can be conjured up by language in contradistinction to the physical flux of the macrocosm, it is only natural to expect some poets to hit upon the notion that language might be capable of 'supporting itself' even if it were not directed to this end by the poet's will. The Surrealist practice of automatic writing was just such an experiment. Now, many poets distant from Surrealism have been known to veer in this direction, and even such a balanced and meticulous verbal craftsman as Mallarmé can write of the pure work of poetry as implying the 'elocutionary disappearance of the poet, who cedes the initiative to words, in the shock of their mobilized inequality; they are illumined in reciprocal reflections, like a virtual train of sparks over jewellery' (Mallarmé, 1961, 366). But the Surrealist poet goes much the farthest in ceding the initiative to his medium. If he follows Breton's recommendations as laid down in the *Manifeste du surréalisme*, he will put all thought of creating literature out of mind, and distantiate himself from all aesthetic or moral considerations. Having reduced his commitment to its purest form – he simply wants to write, with no idea as to *what* he wants to write – he proceeds to record whatever passes through his head, avoiding pauses and corrections. The resultant text will, according to one theory, reveal the workings of the poet's unconscious mind, and may be a source of insights into his secret life. Alternatively, as one might also hold (and this second view is not incompatible with the first, as the Surrealists themselves were prepared to argue), the text is a pure product of language, the result of a process of self-generation which Breton and Éluard in one work were to allude to as an 'immaculate conception'. My example of such a linguistic virgin birth is drawn from a book which Breton composed with Philippe Soupault, *Les*

Champs magnétiques, held to be the first authentic Surrealist text. The following passage is one of Breton's contributions:

> Le lac qu'on traverse avec un parapluie, l'irisation inquiétante de la terre, tout cela donne envie de disparaître. Un homme marche en cassant des noisettes et se replie par moments sur lui-même comme un éventail. Il se dirige vers le salon où l'ont précédé les furets. S'il arrive pour la fermeture, il verra des grilles sous-marines livrer passage à la barque de chèvrefeuille. Demain ou après-demain, il ira trouver sa femme qui l'attend en cousant des lumières et en enfilant des larmes. Les pommes véreuses du fossé, l'écho de la mer Caspienne usent de tout leur pouvoir pour garder leur poudre d'émeraude. Il a les mains douloureuses comme des cornes d'escargot, il bat des mains devant lui. Tout l'éclaire de son raisonnement tiède comme un corps d'oiseau à l'agonie; il écoute les crispations des pierres sur la route, elles se dévorent comme des poissons. Les crachats de la verrière lui donnent des frissons étoilés. Il cherche à savoir ce qu'il est devenu, depuis sa mort.
>
> (Breton, 1971, 78-9)

(The lake one crosses with an umbrella, the disturbing iridescence of the earth, all this makes you wish you could vanish. A man walks and cracks nuts, folding back on himself from time to time like a fan. He walks towards the drawing-room, where he has been preceded by the ferrets. If he arrives at closing-time, he will see submarine gates open up to let through the honeysuckle craft. Tomorrow or the day after, he will go back to his wife, who waits for him while sewing up lights and threading tears. The mouldy apples of the ditch, the echo of the Caspian Sea exert all their power to preserve their emerald powder. His hands are as painful as a snail's horns, he claps hands in front of himself. Everything sheds light on him with its tepid reasoning like the body of a dying bird; he listens to the puckering of stones on the road, they devour each other like fish. The spitting of the casement gives him starry shivers. He wants to find out what has become of himself, since his death.)

It can at once be seen that the Surrealist voice tends to observe the rules of normal syntax: the sentence construction here is relatively simple, and almost all verbs are in an uncomplicated historic present. The natural expectation of the reader is that the sequence of statements should build up to a plausible coherence, and where events are specified in sequence, that they should add up to a story. But only one factor remains constant: the references to a man, whom we follow through a majority of the sentences. This figure sometimes acts, sometimes reacts: now he is purposeful ('il se dirige vers le salon'), now he submits to alien forces ('les crachats de la verrière lui donnent des frissons étoilés'). We learn nothing of his personality: we know him only through what he does, and this knowledge is no more than a list of unexplained movements. The man walks, cracks nuts, bends his body, claps his hands, looks and listens to things. We do hear of a wife who waits for him patiently. That her patient waiting involves sewing and tears suggests a cultural association with the story of Penelope waiting for Ulysses, though it is hard to gauge whether such associations add very much to our understanding of the text, whether or not we decide that the allusion is in some sense 'intended'. There is a reference to an actual geographical place, the Caspian Sea, but it amounts to little more than a flicker of exoticism in this context. (The only characteristic of that sea which might be thought relevant is that its size is progressively decreasing.)

All in all, we have here the slenderest anecdotal thread on which dangle a series of incongruities. One does not cross lakes with an umbrella, the earth does not ordinarily give off rainbow-coloured light, ferrets do not normally visit drawing-rooms, stones do not contract. Admittedly these events are not physically impossible, merely implausible. They are, however, by contiguity, implicated in the process of derealisation engineered in the correlation of more wildly ill-assorted words or groups of words. 'La barque de chèvrefeuille', for example, enacts a marriage of disparates sufficient to create a strong sense of the absurd: it is a Surrealist image of a standard type, whereby two nouns of alien provenance are linked by the preposition *de*, a stylistic device which imparts a spurious credibility to a semantic aberration by virtue of its syntactic correctness. In other words, the objection 'But you can't say that!' is an objection to the sense of the phrase, not an objection that would hold up in any grammatical court. Éluard it was who pinpointed the issue here in his lines

> La terre est bleue comme une orange
> Jamais une erreur les mots ne mentent pas
>
> (Éluard, 1968, I, 232)

(The earth is blue as an orange / Never a mistake words don't lie)

Of course the statement about the colour of the earth – an inadmissible mixture of the blue and orange! – is at odds with physical fact.[4] In this blunt sense, the claim that 'words don't lie' is unjustified. But in the terms which Éluard intended, these words are truthful: within the strict space of language there *is* no way in which accountability to the physical facts can be enforced. If he has a mind to do so, the poet can say what he jolly well wants and still contend that his statements have validity – albeit a validity restricted to the verbal space within which they are framed. The prospect of unlimited freedom of utterance is precisely what attracted the Surrealists to automatism: a situation in which words could 'make love', in Breton's phrase, is a situation in which the enticing surprises of unreality will be maximised. Breton's automatic text contains several pointers to what might be said to be the underlying theme of the passage: namely, that the world in which the protagonist moves is a world of unrealities, of physical impossibilities – in short a world structured entirely on a fragile network of syntactical relations. The main protagonist is a ghostly being whose experience develops only to the extent that sentences run on and give rise to further sentences. He thinks about vanishing ('tout cela donne envie de disparaître'), but is incapable of making resolutions about his future actions, so that when he tries to find out what his status is in this undependable world, the sentence articulating this search winds up with the definitive decree that he is dead, and has been dead for some while (since the beginning of the paragraph, as it were!). The man is a phantom in a world without substance: like Borges's fictive tiger, or Rimbaud's arctic flowers, he does not exist, and can therefore enjoy no purchase on physical certainties. He is no more than a flicker crossing the automatist's mind, and can be blotted out at any time. The word *mort* and the final full stop do indeed curtail his brief and tenuous career in the book.

A further advance towards inchoate unrealness in *Les Champs magnétiques* is manifested when Breton comes up with impenetrable formulas like 'Suintement cathédrale vertébré supérieur' (Breton, 1971, 46) (Seepage cathedral superior vertebrate), where the running together of nouns has no semantic and very little syntactic justification (arguably, these juxtaposed nouns could be read as being in apposition). The formulation attains a pitch of impeccable incongruity, and is a model for the whole process of literary depletion of realness and meaningfulness. It is, in short, a piece of pure nonsense.

A technique of juxtaposing separate phrases without evident consequentiality had been developed prior to Surrealism by Guillaume

Apollinaire, especially in some of the poems in the sequence 'Ondes'. In the following extract from the poem 'Arbre', glimpses of consistency occur from time to time, but only to fade away into the overall inconsequentiality.

> Tu t'es promené à Leipzig avec une femme mince déguisée en
>   homme
> Intelligence car voilà ce que c'est qu'une femme intelligente
> Et il ne faudrait pas oublier les légendes
> Dame-Abonde dans un tramway la nuit au fond d'un quartier désert
> Je voyais une chasse tandis que je montais
> Et l'ascenseur s'arrêtait à chaque étage
>
> Entre les pierres
> Entre les vêtements multicolores de la vitrine
> Entre les charbons ardents du marchand de marrons
> Entre deux vaisseaux norvégiens amarrés à Rouen
> Il y a ton image
>
> Elle pousse entre les bouleaux de la Finlande
>
> Ce beau nègre en acier
>
>   (Apollinaire, 1956, 179)

(You went for a walk in Leipzig with a slim woman disguised as a man / Intelligence for there's an intelligent woman for you / And we shouldn't forget the legends / Dame Abund in a tram by night in the heart of a deserted quarter / I saw a hunt while going up / And the lift stopped at every floor / Among the stones / Among the many-coloured clothes in the shop-window / Among the burning coals of the hot-chestnut seller / Between two Norwegian ships moored at Rouen / There is your image / It grows among the birches of Finland / That handsome negro in steel)

In the first two lines of this extract, the poet reminisces fairly coherently about a woman he knew who struck him as being intelligent. The reader is thereby given to understand that one thing will lead on to the next: whereupon Apollinaire changes the subject, switching to the idea of legends, then introducing the fictional creature Dame Abund (Dame Abonde was, it seems, a good fairy in French mythology, but I am assuming that the English reader possesses no such information), and placing her on a nocturnal tram. Is there some connection with the intelligent woman of line one? The scene changes too rapidly for any underlying implications to become evident, for next minute the poet goes up in a lift and witnesses an unexplained hunt. Next, the text becomes preoccupied with locating an apparently obsessional image, which might be seen amid stones, in a shop-window, in the coals of a hot-chestnut seller's brazier, in the harbour at Rouen, in the Finnish landscape. The image is identified as being '*ton* image', which might mean the image of an unspecified beloved, or else – in accordance with Apollinaire's practice elsewhere and with my assumption that the opening *tu* represents the poet addressing himself – the poet's own image. Why in the latter case he should be so obsessed with his own image is anybody's guess, unless one reads the last line, 'Ce beau nègre en acier', as a semi-ironic description of himself – a tough (*acier*) outcast (*nègre*). This final phrase constitutes a singular example of Apollinaire's technique of 'indeterminate determination' as Philippe Renaud has called it (Renaud, 1969, 344): the apparently irrational conjunction of *nègre* and *acier* is lent a spurious air of plausibility by the demonstrative *ce*: '*that* handsome negro in steel'. We have no prior knowledge of this creature, yet the poet airily assumes otherwise, and since we cannot stop and ask him, he goes on with his story without explaining anything.

There are signs of formal regularity in the lines introduced by the repeated preposition *entre* (which carries the sense either of *among* or of *between*). However, there is no regularity about the allusions: what do stones, coals and birches have that might remind the poet about himself? We have no way of guessing what the connection might be, nor indeed is it entirely certain that this particular connection is an appropriate one for the reader to be thinking about. The lines are so teasingly *underprovided* in respect of link words like 'therefore' or 'because' that the reader is obliged to parse the sentences for himself, inserting punctuation and imagined conjunctions that will lend them some semblance of continuity. But as I remarked of the poem by Reverdy, it may not be legitimate practice on the reader's part to inscribe his annotations on the poem. For one thing, they may be accidental and so subjective as to seem silly when he comes upon them on a later occasion. For another, they do disservice to the open spirit of the text, in that they dissuade him from other potential responses, other parallel constructions of sense. For instance it might be worthwhile to take the last line 'ce beau nègre en acier' as a phrase in apposition not to 'ton image' two lines before, but to the immediately preceding 'la Finlande'. Taken thus, the lines permit the association of that country with ideas of beauty, dark strangeness, toughness. The capacity to cater for such alternative readings is perhaps the whole *raison d'être* of 'Arbre'. After all, the poem consists of a series of unlabelled moments, and we are at liberty to scan up and down the lines, pausing, like the poet in the lift, at each level of the structure. We cannot guess at the purpose of the structure as a whole, unless it is to function as a puzzling denial of normal expectations of sequence and consequence. Even if we guess that the text contains certain echoes of the poet's actual experience (Apollinaire once visited Leipzig, though to my knowledge never went to Finland), it is undeniably the case that the way the text may be said to 'act' is as a mechanism that plays with words rather than experiences drawn from life.

The opening of John Ashbery's poem 'Clepsydra' is evidence of a similar strategy of denying continuity while communicating a sequence of propositions. Here, however, the dominant feature of the discourse is its rather dogmatic tone, which is such that the speaking voice seems to be explaining a situation to the 'you' of the poem in a most unequivocal manner. Ashbery's method is to posit an event which is unspoken, and then to explain it with apparent authority, all the while using terms which slide away from clarity. In the absence of a context, the reader feels himself being led through an argument which he can only follow bemusedly. It is rather like trying to pick up speech in a language which one understands only imperfectly.

> Hasn't the sky? Returned from moving the other
> Authority recently dropped, wrested as much of
> That severe sunshine as you need now on the way
> You go. The reason why it happened only since
> You woke up is letting the steam disappear
> From those clouds when the landscape all around
> Is hilly sites that will have to be reckoned
> Into the total for there to be more air: that is,
> More fitness read into the undeduced result, than land.
> This means never getting any closer to the basic
> Principle operating behind it than to the distracted
> Entity of a mirage. The half-meant, half-perceived
> Motions of fronds out of idle depths that are
> Summer. And expansion into little draughts.

> (Ashbery, 1977, 27)

The poet pitches us magnificently *in medias res* with a query about the sky to which the reader can only respond with a counter-query: 'Hasn't the sky?' — 'Hasn't the sky *done what*?' We are allowed no clue as to the action in question, and cannot therefore assess whether or not it is something which the sky might be expected to have carried out. In any event, do people normally ask questions about the sky's actions? Does the sky normally 'do' anything? The ensuing phrases provide two possible indications as to the sun's putative action: the past participles 'returned' and 'wrested' may be taken as completing the interrogative sentence 'Hasn't the sky . . .?' Not that this takes us very far. What could it mean to be asking whether or not the sky has 'returned from moving the other / Authority recently dropped'? The only direction of interpretation that leads to any obvious sense might be that the sky is being envisaged as 'returning' to our sight after the removal of another power which has 'recently dropped'. Possibly this is a reference to rain-fall, for after rain has finished dropping, the sky and indeed sunshine do return. There may be a comic exaggeration here in referring to rain as an 'authority', given that this authority is undercut by the play on the word 'dropped': one drops one's authority, and rain also drops. All the same, these considerations do not represent a particularly signifi-cant advance towards illumination of the passage. We still have no idea what part the sky is playing in the poetic argument. That there *is* an argument here appears to be our one certainty, given the presence of explanatory phrases which introduce the various sentences. 'The reason why', 'that is', 'this means', these are the stock phrases used when someone purports to set out a series of facts or to present an analysis of a situation. The first of these explanatory comments purports to elucidate the event which occurred after an unidentified 'you' woke up: this event may or may not be the return of blue sky and sunshine after a shower of rain. What we are invited to attend to, is not so much the event itself as its *timing*: we are informed that 'it happened only since / You woke up'. Would the situation have been dramatically altered if the event had taken place before or during 'your' sleep? we may ask. The poem remains mute on this point. And we are in no posi-tion to force the question, given that no reader has access, can have access to explanations *outside* the context established by the text. We cannot simply induce explanations by artificially introducing a context not motivated by the words proper. In this instance, the explanation has to do with the steam disappearing from 'those clouds'. As with Apollinaire's *'ce* beau nègre', we are provided with a confident determi-nation of something which at the same time has never been mentioned before, and therefore lacks all grounding within the space of the poem. Our attempt at elucidation continues with a weird allusion to a process of calculation which needs to reckon 'the landscape all around' into a mysterious total in order to establish the possibility of 'more air'. This is hardly a calculation we can make sense of in normal terms, though we may have vague associations of land-surveys or meteorological assessments. Furthermore, there is little encouragement to press for a clear-cut view of the operation, given that its result remains 'undeduced' – unresolved, impenetrable – and hence of no help to us in clarifying the problem posed at the outset.

By now we, as readers, are beginning to appreciate the poem as a sequence of explanations which lead us by painful degrees towards a meaning that, we suspect, is never *actually* going to materialise. By this stage in the poem, after construing some nine lines, we have no sense of who 'you' or the narrator may be, nor what their concern is with weather conditions or the shape of the landscape. It is as though the poem were intent on offering itself as a set of mock explanations which are comically inadequate to elucidate the poem's obscurities: or rather, the explanations are gestures towards meaning, but gestures deliberately stifled so as to fall short of meaning. The concluding lines of the extract might be read as a commentary on this very process, and thus as a general caveat to readers of poetry of this frustrating type. To read 'Clepsydra' and poems like it entails quite literally 'never getting any closer to the basic / Principle operating behind it', given that the poetic principle here is precisely that of preventing the reader from getting close to the operative 'meaning'. The point of the poem is to shrug off genuine sense, and to offer the reader only 'the distracted / Entity of a mirage'. The intriguing thing about Ashbery's poetic game is that the illusion of meaning can still be strong enough that we are enticed into trying to grasp his 'half-meant, half-perceived / Motions of fronds'.

The poem 'Clepsydra' has indeed the deceptive, alluring motions of a plant in a stream, apparently unfolding its tendrils towards our world of light and air, yet kept from us by the strict boundary of the water's surface. It would be idle to pluck these fronds and expect them to continue to sway and delight us: just as it would be idle to explain such poetry in a cut-and-dried way and expect it still to attract us. All we can hope for are a few 'little draughts' of meaning, a few hints passing up from the depths. This is what passes for meaning and what seduces us into reading on.

The 'meaning' of such a poem may therefore be said to reside in its compactness as an ensemble of lines whose disparate segments are tied together by metre and syntax: that this merely formal continuity is all the while belied by disparities and *non sequiturs* at the semantic level suggests that the poem is posed all the while on the brink of incoherent nonsense. Some readers may well refuse to place themselves in the potentially dangerous situation of giving credence to such mirages: others again will, I am sure, take pleasure in being teased, enjoying the poem even though it might turn out to be a fraud. Already though, my argument has gone far enough to show that unreality can be attractive, and that the poem which courts meaninglessness may not be all mumbo-jumbo.

Poetry of the type I have been examining may be said to move away from a position of relevance to the real world and towards what I will call the 'logological extreme'. I borrow the term 'logological' from the painter Jean Dubuffet who, in his recent work, has tried to shake clear of the context of his previously representational or textural paintings.[5] In turning to 'unnatural' materials such as polystyrene and epoxy, and in creating out of these artificial substances structures which have no equivalent in the material universe, Dubuffet has hoped to institute a realm of pure forms that have no connection with outside reality. His conception of artistic invention implies 'the notion of a logos to the second degree, which, ceasing to be a code referring to the phenomena and objects of the world, starts to proliferate from out of its own resources' (Dubuffet, 1973, 425). Such a code, be it visual or verbal, would constitute a supreme act of defiance in the face of the mimetic requirement normally laid down by public taste. It would imply that art can be nurtured by its inner resources alone: that its forms may owe nothing to an external context but draw sustenance from themselves like some self-reproducing organism.

The logological extreme has been more and more of an attraction to poets since the Symbolist period. We have seen that Mallarmé wanted language to be granted its autonomy, so that words could be respected not as referents but as entities in their own right. Rimbaud and the Surrealists approached language as the medium of unreality and the destroyer of presuppositions. One of the Surrealists, Robert Desnos, was particularly drawn to experiments in sound permutations and puns, whereby he allowed words to negotiate their own relations rather than have them imposed from outside. His encouragement of a kind of verbal algebra, in which words broke down into constituent syllables which then re-formed themselves as fresh words, resulted in the crazy epigrams of 'Rrose Sélavy' or the garbled quipping of the following poem:

Vos bouches mentent,
vos mensonges sentent la menthe,
Amantes!

Cristaux où meurt le Christ
reflétez la froide beauté
de Kristiana.

Nos traditions?
Notre addition!

(Desnos, 1953, 66)

(Your mouths tell lies, / your lies smell of mint, / Loving ladies! / Crystals wherein Christ dies / reflect the frozen beauty / of Christiania. / Our traditions? / Our bill, please!)

There are statements here whose logic can only be defended in terms of sound values, but not of meaning. To suggest that 'lies smell of mint' is only defensible because of the shared syllable in the French words *mensonge* and *menthe*. Again, *cristaux* and *Christ* have no semantic relation in ordinary parlance. They come together only because Desnos has heard an echo which normal discourse ignores as irrelevant to the composition of meaning. The last association he offers is that of a woman's name, *Kristiana*. To the extent that there is a suggestion of a Scandinavian spelling, with possible connections with *Christiania*, the former name for Oslo, it could be argued that the word gives rise to the connotation *coldness*. If so, then the phrase 'froide beauté' is legitimised; moreover, the connotations *coldness* and *perfection* may be said to be in tune with the notion of *crystals*. Further, *Kristiana* embodies the word *Christ*, and acts as a point of attraction for the various phonic and semantic associations in these lines of the poem. Now whatever pleasure the reader may derive from all this is very much a matter of private taste: there are no objective criteria for evaluating puns. All the same, it seems unlikely that there is much satisfaction to be derived from the last lines, with their play on *traditions / addition*. It falls flat, I think, because the rhyme is ponderous, and all too facile within a language where nouns with the same Latinate ending are a commonplace.

Desnos's poem is a very slight one, yet it serves to illustrate the possibility that a writer might find himself more receptive to assonance and paranomastic (punning) combinations of words than to the considerations of normal sense-making. One writer who went further than most in prospecting the phonic resources of language was Raymond Roussel. He managed to compose whole stories and long poems which are almost entirely logological constructs. One device of his will exemplify the sort of verbal algebra he loved to play with. Roussel's story

'Chiquenaude' evolved from a linguistic game in which an opening phrase is repeated in scarcely modified form at the close of the text, in such a way that the intervening material persuades the reader to accept the two occurrences of the phrase as transmitting quite different meanings. Thus 'Chiquenaude' begins with the phrase 'vers de la doublure dans la pièce de *Forban talon rouge*'. As one reads on, one can appreciate this as a reference to the lines (*vers*) spoken by an understudy (*doublure*) at a performance of a play about a devil named Forban who has red heels (*talon rouge*). At the end of the story, the phrase returns in the form 'les vers de la doublure dans la pièce du fort pantalon rouge'. This time the phrase is intended to carry the sense that there are mites (*vers*) in the lining (*doublure*) of a pair of tough red trousers (*fort pantalon rouge*), a statement which we are supposed not to baulk at, given the way the intervening story has been built up (Roussel, 1963, 39-48). The game is perfectly gratuitous, even rather silly; yet Roussel was to spend many years on similar sports – his masterpiece, *Nouvelles Impressions d'Afrique*, is a monstrous compendium of verbal procedures, whose 1,276 alexandrine lines took him thirteen years to complete. (See Roussel, 1932.)

Among the most recent heirs to this tradition of loyalty to language as a system of logological permutation are the writers of OULIPO, the 'Ouvroir de la littérature potentielle'. Of these, Georges Perec is certainly the most tenacious experimenter in the combinatory potential of language. His novel *La Disparition* achieves the feat of running to 312 pages without the letter *e* being used once! (Perec, 1969). A specialist in the palindrome – a text which is the same whether read frontwards or backwards – Perec holds what may well be the world record with a piece over 5,000 letters long (about five printed pages). Such a text is the product of abnormally rigid constraints, and these conduce to a situation of violently reduced comprehensibility. For although the rules of the game prohibit the invention of non-existent words, the phraseology Perec is forced to use is worlds away from normal French, as is quite evident from this extract taken from the centre of the text, i.e. at the point where the two mirrored halves fold together.

Fi! Marmelade déviré d'Aladine. D'or, Noël: crèche (l'an ici taverne gelée dès bol . . .) à santon givré, fi!, culé de l'âne vairon.

Lapalisse élu, gnoses sans orgueil (écru, sale, sec).
Saluts: angiome. T'es si crâneur!

* * *

Rue. Narcisse! Témoignas-tu! l'ascèse, là, sur ce lieu gros, nasses ongulées . . .

S'il a pal, noria vénale de Lucifer, vignot nasal (obsédée, le genre vaticinal), eh, Cercle, on rode, nid à la dérive, Dédale (M . . .!) ramifié?

(Oulipo, 1973, 103-4)

(Fie! Marmalade unwound from Aladdin. Golden, Christmas: crib (the year here tavern frozen as soon as bowl . . .) with frosted figurine, fie! backing from the wall-eyed ass. / Lapalisse elected, wisdoms without pride (unbleached, dirty, dry). Greetings: tumefaction. You're a proper swank! / * * * / Street. Narcissus! You were witness! the ascesis, there, on that gross place, ungulated eel-pots . . . / If he has stake, Lucifer's venal bucket-hoist, nasal periwinkle (obsessive, the oracular type), eh, Circle, they're running in, nest adrift, Dedalus (Mr . . .!) branching out?)

The restrictions imposed on the writing are such that normal explanations become impossible. Verbs, articles, conjunctions — these are indispensable in ordinary discourse, but can only be rarely allowed within the palindrome, since they do not bend easily to the exercise. Instead, isolated nouns and single-letter words are frequent. Statements are governed no longer by a properly articulated syntax, but by a phantom syntax of commas, brackets and full stops. These are the only things that can group the separate words into units of meaning, and often they fail to do more than juxtapose a few items of sense — leaving it to the reader to guess at the connections. Admittedly Perec achieves an incredibly high score of sentences that are syntactically defensible; but often he has had to fall back on single-word sentences ('Rue.') or scarcely meaningful interjections ('Fi!') in order to mop up unused syllables. The reader's reaction to such a text may well be one of admiration at the feat: to have managed to introduce complete idiomatic statements such as 'T'es si crâneur!' (possibly a gibe aimed by Perec at himself?) is an impressive feat, even though we may feel that its obverse formulation 'Rue. Narcisse! Témoignas-tu!' is too constricted and arbitrary to support any genuine meaning. What the text conveys is a sense of its own grotesque uniqueness as a monument to useless effort. That is, we admire Perec for his crossword-puzzler's ingenuity and patience, rather than savour his prose for its occasional felicities and coherences. The 'meaning' of this language object is that it exists at all.

After such an extreme example of arbitrary constraint, it may be appropriate to turn for a final example of logological experimentation to a poetry of exuberant lawlessness and disregard for sense. The Zürich Dadaists were in many ways the supreme anarchists of linguistic revolt. Written expressly to be performed — and hence heavily reliant-on initial impact rather than on gradual perusal — their poetry took many forms: poems made up of disjointed phrases, usually comical or absurd; poems that tell inconsequential anecdotes; 'simultaneous poems' with lines intercut in different languages; poems accompanied by drummings, noises and gestures; poems composed of numerals or repeated single letters; and poems made out of words clipped from newsprint and jumbled in a hat, according to a celebrated recipe of Tristan Tzara. One extreme of Dada anarchy was reached in the sound poems of Hugo Ball. These are no longer a direct attack on meaningful discourse in the sense that they seek to disrupt ordinary meanings by displacing, modifying, negating or otherwise tampering with phrases that have some measure of meaning in the first instance. Rather they are sequences of completely invented words, chosen to look least like orthodox speech. The result is a poetry of perfect meaninglessness, a nonsense verse which has not only abandoned all reference to external reality but equally ignores all those linguistic features — vocabulary, syntax, etc. — which normally channel meaning. They spring forth as specimens of pure logological spontaneity. One of Ball's poems begins thus:

gadji beri bimba glandridi laula lonni cadori
gadjama gramma berida bimbala glandri galassassa laulitalomini
gadji beri bin blassa glassala laula lonni cadorsu sassala bim
gadjama tuffm i zimzalla binban gligla wowolimai bin beri ban
o katalominai rhinozerossola hopsamen laulitalomini hoooo
gadjama rhinozerossola hopsamen
bluku terullala blaulala loooo

(Quoted in Schifferli, 1963, 69)

There is clearly a case for saying at once that such poetry yields no meaning. There are letters set out in groups which, when voiced, give rise to phonic units which it is convenient to call 'words' — but these are not the words of any known language, nor do they form part of a code which could in theory be transliterated into accessible meaning. They are arbitrary combinations of sounds, devoid of all denotative impulse.

To drop the poem at this point might seem the most sensible response, but there are two other aspects that deserve comment. First, there are, after all, one or two recognisable elements among the neologisms. The coinage *rhinozerossola*, for example, looks suspiciously like a whimsical modification of the familiar word *rhinoceros*. And Ball's *hopsamen* could suggest a German compound noun, *Hopfensamen* = hop-seed. (Or it might be a compound of the English words *hops* and *amen*, suggesting a hiccup and a prayer!) The phrase 'zimzalla bim' is nonsensical, but may be traced to a magic word used in some German fairytales. There may indeed be other echoes of actual words in the text which prolonged study might pick up. Now, does this suggest that there is a case for saying that the poem edges, however reluctantly, towards saying something intelligible? Probably not, to the extent that the words we half-recognise are very much isolated. They glimmer through an ambient haze of senselessness, and their connotations are not weighty enough to impose any real coherence. The rhino and the hop-seed are therefore droll lapses in an overall continuum of meaninglessness and as such they simply enhance the general impression of babbling nonsensicality.

A second aspect of the text raises a more subtle issue. There are in evidence certain regularities which conduce to a sense of rhythm and even of rhyme. The opening phrase, 'gadji beri bimba', contains three prefixes which give rise to analogous phrases in the next three lines, creating an effect of theme plus variations: 'gadji beri bimba / gadjama-berida-bimbala / gadji beri bin / gadjama-binban-bin beri ban'. This sounds rather like a phrase in a foreign language being recited through different declensions or conjugations. Furthermore, significantly long words, like *laulitalomini* and *rhinozerossola*, are accurately repeated, and there are internal rhymes such as *-assa*, and the end-of-line rhyme *hoooo / loooo*. Closer analysis could well disclose a whole internal structure of phonic permutations. If it did, the poem would assert itself not as an arbitrary jumble of sounds, but as a true *pattern*, analogous to a musical composition in its deployment of a limited number of sound units within a more or less stable rhythmic framework. None the less, the logological construct would still retain its autonomy: like music, it would not refer to anything outside itself.

4 OCCULTATION AND ENIGMA

In its exploration of alternatives that countermand our habitual approach to things, poetry can operate on a number of fronts. First, it may
voice a challenge to the empirical determinations which govern our
physical existence. That is, it may summon up an unreality characterised by its willed non-conformity to the world of shared physical relations and tested human expectations, that reliable world in which ripe
apples drop from trees, and old age is accompanied by grey hair. Such
a refutation of natural order may take many forms, ranging from the
comparatively cautious modifications of a Sitwell investing the mainland opposite the Great Skellig with an intensity of unnatural green to a
Rimbaud's absolute subversion of the physical properties of known
objects by inducing spectacular changes in their colour, size, position
or movements. A second mode of poetic contestation arises as a corollary of the first, and occurs when a poet steers his language away from
all the conventions of literary representation, thereby contesting the
assumptions we have about the way literature should go about treating
reality. For while I have, for simplicity's sake, been suggesting that the
poetry of strangeness and derealisation can represent a refutation of the
empirical world, it would be more strictly accurate to say that it is a
refutation of the way we *perceive* the world, and more specifically, of
the way we are accustomed to perceive it when looking through what
Victor Hugo called the 'focusing mirror' of art.

A third stage of withdrawal from the real comes when poetry shifts
its field of operation completely away from distorted versions of the
world and dedicates itself instead to its own self-generation, speaking
in a pure discourse with itself, proud and isolate, so as to delineate
what Blanchot said Mallarmé's poetry was, 'a unified space which is
sovereign and autonomous' (Blanchot, 1955, 138). At this logological
extreme, yet another assumption begins to erode, namely the one
whereby literary activity is thought to be an act of simple communication from writer to reader. For when poetry moves into this uniquely
self-absorbed space, it becomes more and more difficult to understand.
Of course it is a commonplace to say that much modern poetry is
'difficult': writers like René Char, Paul Celan and others use styles
which are frankly antagonistic to facile comprehension. It is also quite
obvious that, despite some family resemblances, modern poets require

individual attention, and that there exists no master key with which to unlock all their secrets. In this chapter, I want therefore to offer not so much an all-purpose thread allowing unimpeded movement into and out of the labyrinth of modern poetry, but simply a number of suggestions concerning certain postures and strategies adopted by poets as they travel towards the limits of comprehension. This may help us grasp the general shape and nature of our inability to understand, even if this is all we can grasp.

It is in Stéphane Mallarmé that we encounter the most unabashed champion of obscurity as an essential component of true poetry. 'There must always be enigma in poetry' (Mallarmé, 1961, 869) is a trenchant announcement of the poet's determination to align creativity – the development of original poetic insights – with mystery – the occultation of those insights. Mallarmé justified his own obscure style by saying that art is as sacred an enterprise as any religion, and accordingly to be protected from the damaging incursions of the uninitiated: 'Every sacred thing which desires to remain sacred shrouds itself in mystery' (Mallarmé, 1961, 257). Seeing poetry as a medium of Orphic knowledge, the poet argued that writing was a process akin to magic ritual, and the act of putting pen to paper took on for him the character of a secret ceremonial. He took enormous pains over the typography of his printed texts and went so far as to organise a facsimile printing of his poems copied out in his best handwriting in purple ink. In one text, Mallarmé associates the creative impulse with darkness rather than with the crystal clarity that we might ordinarily attribute to the successful illumination of an idea. The secret of poetic revelation lies paradoxically in the zone of blackness metaphorically represented as a droplet of ink or the shadows of an unlit room.

> L'encrier, cristal comme une conscience, avec sa goutte, au fond, de ténèbres relative à ce que quelque chose soit: puis, écarte la lampe.
>
> (Mallarmé, 1961, 370)

(The inkwell, crystalline as consciousness, with its droplet, deep down, of shadows which are a condition of something emerging into being: then, thrust the lamp aside.)

The pursuit of black traces inked upon the white surface of the paper seems to have haunted Mallarmé as an image of the idea that creative discovery involves the writer in a deepening of obscurity. The poetics of dispelled clarity which arose from these ideas led him to concoct those two dozen sonnets which are his dense masterwork.

The best of these are too complex to be easily adduced here: I have chosen to illustrate the discussion with the relatively slight poem 'Petit Air'.

PETIT AIR

Quelconque une solitude
Sans le cygne ni le quai
Mire sa désuétude
Au regard que j'abdiquai

Ici de la gloriole
Haute à ne la pas toucher
Dont maint ciel se bariole
Avec les ors de coucher

Mais langoureusement longe
Comme de blanc linge ôté
Tel fugace oiseau si plonge
Exultatrice à côté

Dans l'onde toi devenue
Ta jubilation nue.

(Mallarmé, 1961, 65-6)

The title 'Petit Air' suggests a lighthearted little piece, but the reading of the poem will probably give rise to an immediate impression that the words are not arranged in a casual fashion. The average reader will immediately realise that he is confronted with a rather difficult poem, even a wilfully difficult one.

The text is obscure for a number of reasons, of which the first manifests itself as soon as we try to read it as a sequence of linked statements. If we know something about versification, we will accept that the form of the octosyllabic sonnet inevitably poses constraints on the disposition of words: we are prepared to accept that the poetic text will be syntactically rather crabbed in contrast to a passage of prose. But Mallarmé's syntax is crabbed in a special way, and we need to reconstruct his word order radically before we can arrive at a fluent reading of his sentences. In this poem, an inversion at the very outset places the adjective 'quelconque' (referring to 'solitude') in the dramatic first-word position, an odd effect of highlighting inasmuch as the word itself is basically mundane (it means 'any whatever', 'commonplace', 'unexceptional'). Later, the natural continuity of the noun phrase 'regard de la gloriole' is disrupted by the interpolation of the clause 'que j'abdiquai/ Ici', so that the phrase 'de la gloriole' floats on its own, apparently unlinked to anything else in the sentence. The phrase 'Haute à ne la pas toucher' may make us baulk, not so much because of the archaic positioning of the pronoun *la* as because of the construction '*à* + infinitive' attached idiosyncratically to the adjective *haut* – not a feature of ordinary French.

In the latter part of the sonnet we are obliged to seek out a subject for the verbs *longe* and *plonge* and though we may reach the conclusion that the phrasing is inverted and that the subjects are, respectively, 'tel oiseau' and 'ta jubilation', we still find ourselves staring at the line on the page 'Tel fugace oiseau si plonge', which encourages the erroneous possibility of reading *oiseau* as the subject of *plonge*. Mallarmé's abstruse syntax tends to force such errors upon us, so that the process of working through to a proper parsing of what Malcolm Bowie calls 'these studiously disjointed texts' (Bowie, 1978, 17) is punctuated by recurrent experiences of false trails and red herrings.

By this stage we are ready to consider an English version of the text in which some of the syntactical difficulties of the original have been resolved:

'An unexceptional solitariness / With neither swan nor embankment / Mirrors its disuse / In the look which I renounced / Here from the phoney glory / So high as to be untouchable / With which many a sky is painted / Along with the sunset golds / But langorously skims past / Like white linen pulled off / Some fleeting bird if there plunges / Exultant at its side / Into the water you embody / Your naked jubilation.'

Once the reader has elected a syntactical pattern in which he can organise the words, he is then faced with a second set of obscurities. Mallarmé uses various techniques of indirectness which make the basic *semantic* content of the poem difficult to establish. Direct reference is constantly supplanted by indirect allusion, achieved by a range of stylistic devices. Thus metonymy (the attribute in lieu of the thing proper) is apparent in the nouns *solitude* and *désuétude*, which appear to be representations of the river scene in which the poem is set; that is, the qualities of isolation and disuse take the place of any direct mention of the unfrequented stretch of water. In the phrase 'Ta jubilation nue', there is a transferred epithet: the adjective 'nue' ought rightfully to refer to 'toi', the woman in the poem. Instead it is attached to her jubilation (which is in turn a metonymic substitution of an abstract quality for a concrete entity, the woman's body). We are not referred to the woman so much as to her emotional state. The synecdoche (the part for the whole) whereby the poetic word *onde* (wave) stands for the water of the river at large is a commonplace in French poetic style, and should not therefore pose any problem.

We may trace hyperbole in the usage 'les ors de coucher' which, if we take this to be an allusion to the effect of the setting sun, sets off a panoply of grandiose associations about bright gold, riches and so forth. The simile 'comme de blanc linge ôté' appears to refer to the way the bird flies past; we may imagine that its feathers flash white in the same way that white undergarments might flash if speedily removed. But since the woman alluded to in the last lines seems to have stripped before plunging into the water, the reference to white linen might equally be taken as a literal statement rather than a figure of speech. The ambiguity here is deliberate, and reflects a typically Mallarméan procedure of interlocking the two parts of a metaphoric figure in such a way that each becomes an image of the other — the bird is like a woman, the woman is like a bird. Finally, we can identify a species of ellipsis in the omission of any direct reference to the woman, whose textual presence rests only on the words 'toi' and 'ta' and a couple of adjectives in the feminine.

By this stage, we have reached at least some measure of clarity, and can begin to imagine that the poem is the account of an incident which occurred when the poet went walking by a deserted riverbank one evening and saw a bird flash past while his mistress took a dip. At the same time, we have reached a point where the poem's obscurity may be said to reassert itself. Let us suppose that the poem began as the record of a simple event (a woman diving into water just as a bird flies by). This basic 'anecdote' has been draped round in a specially coded language, whose syntactical and stylistic procedures we have analysed. The poem then constitues a package: anecdote plus wrapper of obscurity.

What we glimpse when we remove the wrapper of superficial obscurity, is a poem which is still curiously difficult, but now in a different way. This time the poem is obscure because its final import eludes us: we now have to interpret what is *intended* by this story, this colloca-tion of anecdotal fragments. Our effort to demystify has, so to speak, led us to a point where we can now look properly at the true mysteries. In the present instance, I have no wish to reduce Mallarmé's poem to a final single meaning, since I feel it has enough vigour to permit a multi-

plicity of readings. So for simplicity's sake, let me say that the simultaneous sighting of the woman-like bird (which we may imagine skim-
ming the surface of the river just as white underwear skims the surface
of a woman's skin when she pulls it free) and of the bird-like woman
(who dives into the water, exultantly exchanging one element for
another) has set off in the poet's mind a feeling of joy, a sense of poetic
epiphany. From this, one might go on to speculate that this synchron-
icity is emblematic of some higher intuition of inter-relatedness in the
universe; that the slipping-off of garments is an image of revelation; that
the dive into the water is an image of re-veiling, whereby the nakedness
is once more hidden after being momentarily disclosed; or that the
poetic event evoked here corresponds to an intuition of beauty as a
rare and ephemeral flash of perfection, a privileged moment which can
only be verbally sustained by wilfully indirect allusion. But these are
only suggestions, my point being that the poem's 'meaning' is that it
leads us to endless speculation upon the mysteries of its final implications, which are manifold. Thus the epiphany itself is mysterious, and
so is the occultation in which it is enshrouded. The basic message of
these obscurities is that 'there is more here than meets the eye'. Naturally Mallarmé intends that we should never feel we have fully 'seen
through' the enigmas of the text.

A case could be made for obscurity being an inherent feature of
poetic language at large in as much as the kinds of messages on which
poets are intent are incompatible with the modes of clear communication which we associate with prose. Coleridge once wrote that 'poetry
gives most pleasure when only generally and not perfectly understood'
(quoted in Hawkes, 1972, 52), which suggests that poetic expression
is most effective when it does not seek to function as a sequence of
accurately aimed signals which trigger off clear-cut responses in the
reader's mind and reduce uncertainty and ambiguity to a negligible
minimum. Poetic language, as we know, is not the language used in
such situations as the composing of an industrial report or a military
plan of attack, situations where the message formulated and the message received must tend towards absolute identity, with no residue of
uncertainty, no unspoken implication, no variant readings. But precisely because it has more to say than the 'block language' which we use
to cope with inflexible, literal ideas (cf. Wheelwright, 1960, 3-4), poetic
language operates by way of subliminal appeals to the reader's imagination, a process of suggestion rather than reference, an evocation of
meaning which may be said to reside in what *underlies* the text rather
than what lies on the surface.

A classic example of a poet who deals in hermetic allusion is Gérard de Nerval. The sonnets of *Les Chimères* are a group of poetic messages in which what is most central remains unformulated and even what is 'given away' comes to us as a begrudged concession. How is the reader new to Nerval even to begin to make sense of the following heavily coded text?

ÉRYTHRÉA

Colonne de Saphir, d'arabesques brodée
— Reparais! — Les *Ramiers* pleurent cherchant leur nid:
Et, de ton pied d'azur à ton front de granit
Se déroule à longs plis la pourpre de Judée!

Si tu vois *Bénarès* sur son fleuve accoudée
Prends ton arc et revêts ton corset d'or bruni:
Car voici *le Vautour*, volant sur *Patani*,
Et de *papillons blancs* la Mer est inondée.

MAHDÉWA! Fais flotter tes voiles sur les eaux
Livre tes fleurs de pourpre au courant des ruisseaux:
La neige du *Cathay* tombe sur l'Atlantique:

Cependant la *Prêtresse* au visage vermeil
Est endormie encor sous *l'Arche du Soleil*:
— Et rien n'a dérangé le sévère portique.

(Nerval, 1960, 14)

(ERITREA: *Column of Sapphire*, decorated with arabesques, / — Come back! — The *Ring-doves* weep, seeking their nest: / And, from your azure foot to your granite forehead / The purple of Judea unrolls in long folds! / If you see *Benares* leaning on its river / Take your bow, and put on your breastplate of burnished gold: / For here is the *Vulture*, flying over *Patani*, / And the Sea is flooded with *white butterflies*. / MAHDEVA! Let your veils float upon the waters / Surrender your flowers of purple to the current of the streams: / The snows of *Cathay* are falling over the Atlantic: / And yet the *Priestess* with rosy cheeks / Still lies sleeping below the *Arch of the Sun*: / — And nothing has disturbed the frowning portico.)

At first reading the poem seems to proclaim its own obscurity. Its title is opaque, and the body of the text bristles with italicised words which insist on being treated as foci of significance in an almost intimidating way: for the reader will surely have no immediate idea how to connect these meanings and construe the urgent telegram 'Column of Sapphire / Ring-Doves / Benares / Vulture / Patani / white butterflies / Cathay / Priestess / Arch of the Sun'. Yet if he can survive this first intimation, he may pluck up courage to peruse the sonnet more carefully. What he will find is a series of exotic references, some recognisable and some not. He will perhaps know that Cathay is an old word for China, but will not necessarily remember in what country Benares is located; he will probably draw a blank on Patani. As he ponders the references to the places he does know, he may be struck by how disparate they are. The poem is confused in its geography: what on earth does it mean to say that snow from Cathay is falling over the Atlantic? The line looks like nonsense, or at best a contrived message in a very private code. Moving on, the reader might find a certain stability in the notion that the poem is in large part an address to the mysterious figure of Mahdeva, who is being asked to come back to fulfil some obscure purpose. Is it the case that Mahdeva is equated with the sleeping Priestess? There is no syntactical evidence to confirm this. All we are explicitly told of Mahdeva is that he or she is like a column, wears a cloak, and later veils and flowers, and has a bow and breastplate to hand as if in readiness to do battle. Not the person, but the person's attributes are highlighted. Several items in the inventory are ornate or rare: the column is of sapphire decorated with arabesque woven patterns, and the cloak of rich-sounding Judean purple. The ring-doves are foregrounded in the text by means of a capital letter and italics: they must be special birds, and their separation from their nest is fraught with significance.

And so it goes on: as each allusion occurs, the reader feels obliged to attribute importance to it, yet without knowing why. He begins to feel like a visitor to an exotic kingdom, bound to salute the authority of the place and yet totally ignorant of the import of local custom and ritual. The allusions emerge almost line by line in the poem, as in a formalised and stately procession. Birds, butterflies, flowers, rivers, the ocean: these natural references merge smoothly with the cultural allusions, as if all derived from one common source of meaning. The poem exhibits a certain agitation in the use of exclamation marks and the hint of violence in some of the actions; yet it closes on a note of grave stability with the priestess asleep on the undisturbed portico, and this seems to throw over the poem a retrospective aura of changelessness, underscored by the heavy ceremoniousness of the rhythms. The poem seems to embody a kind of inevitable immutability, and this (perhaps) is its final import.

In recent years scholars have tracked down many of Nerval's preoccupations in such areas as ancient myth and religion, alchemy, astrology, genealogy and the like, as well as elucidating the biographical basis of many of his writings. It is thus open to us to turn to learned studies of Nerval's sources in order to chase the likely object of a given allusion. To gather in such intricate textual annotations is however simply to attach to the poem proper a kind of extended exegetical footnote rather than to understand *the way the poem actually functions*. Thus to discover from such and such a scholar that Patani may denote the new Jerusalem, or that the line 'La neige du Cathay tombe sur l'Atlantique' correlates allusions to Tibet and to Atlantis and thus has to do with the vision of a spiritual reunion of the Orient and the Occident, is to gain in erudition what one loses in mystery and poetic pleasure. In terms of the poetic effect which I imagine Nerval was aiming at, it is surely a defensible position to try — at least in the first instance — to attend seriously to one's initial *uninformed* responses to the text. These are indissociable from the reality of the poem as an experience of reading.

'Érythréa' is first and foremost an exercise in making enigma. By maintaining a majestic tone of indisputable seriousness while yielding a minimum of explicit information, the poem succeeds brilliantly in rousing our interest without actually communicating anything very much at all. Yves Bonnefoy writes that it creates 'a troubled vagueness in the air. Something you cannot grasp, something black and formless within the crystal's purity' (Bonnefoy, 1970, 212). For this poetic effect to be successful, the poet must strike an exact balance between the poles of crystal clarity and black opacity. A true poem of Enigma is one which entices us in, mesmerising us with promises of deeper meaning, and releasing what André Breton, in a different yet not irrelevant context (he was in fact speaking of the enigmatic appeal of Oceanic masks) called a 'perfume from beyond this world' (Breton, 1953, 180). As with the fascination with unreality, so with the fascination with the obscure: it catches us, gives us pleasure, in those moments when we experience the sensation of moving swiftly across great distances.

There are a few rare poets whose writing can affect us with the uncanny force of an obsession or spell, something which magnetises our faculties long before any glimmer of intellectual understanding comes forth. The almost alarmingly gnomic late manner of Friedrich Hölderlin, for example, gives the impression of a sort of underlying vibration of meaning, while the words proper lie immobile and grand upon the page, impervious to the reader's initial scannings.

The poem 'Patmos' opens with these hieratic lines:

Nah ist
Und schwer zu fassen der Gott.
Wo aber Gefahr ist, wächst
Das Rettende auch.
Im Finstern wohnen
Die Adler und furchtlos gehn
Die Söhne der Alpen über den Abgrund weg
Auf leichtgebaueten Brücken.
Drum, da gehäuft sind rings
Die Gipfel der Zeit, und die Liebsten
Nah wohnen, ermattend auf
Getrenntesten Bergen,
So gib unschuldig Wasser,
O Fittige gib uns, treuesten Sinns
Hinüberzugehn und wiederzukehren.

(Hölderlin, 1953, 173)

(The God is near / And hard to grasp. / Yet where there is danger, flourishes / Also that which saves. / In the darkness dwell / The eagles and fearlessly / The sons of the Alps tread away over the abyss / On flimsily-built bridges. / Therefore, since all round are piled / The peaks of time and the best-loved / Dwell close by, exhausted upon / The most separate mountains, / Give us water without guilt; / O give us wings, that we might with truest mind / Go across and then return.)

The poem starts up with two paradoxes: there is a God who is close, yet he is hard to grasp; there is danger, yet also a power which can save from danger. The import of these aphorisms is unclear, and all we can be sure of is that they establish a tone for the poem, one of portentous meaning, the suggestion of a dark but powerful order of things. These more or less abstract propositions are the opening moves in a sequence which now shifts into the evocation of concrete realities, which are rather easier to cope with. The poem sketches a topography, with mention of the Alps, the home of eagles and fearless men. The early reference to danger seems to be picked up here, for the men are able to tread boldly across fragile bridges over abysses. By now the poem has made use of two devices that create puzzlement: the gnomic aphorism and the incompleted story. Both are formulated in the third person. In

the fourth sentence there arises a new tone, with a first-person appeal
on behalf of an unspecified 'us'. Presumably the voice speaks for the
community of those who dwell in the Alpine heights. They seem to be
in a situation of difficulty, for there are distances that need to be trav-
ersed and the landscape is stern and unyielding. The voice speaks of
water and wings, but these make good sense in the context of a landscape where streams and eagles are natural features. But several things
remain to puzzle us. If water and eagles' wings are natural features in
this setting, why must they be asked for? And who is being asked to
supply them — the Christian God? What symbolic resonances are intended by the poet when he attributes the human quality of innocence to
the material element of water? What significance attaches to the peaks'
being categorised as 'the peaks of time', surely intended as a lofty and
attention-demanding formulation in the way it elevates a material
entity onto the plane of the immaterial, the abstract? Is there something paradoxical in the association of mountains, often thought of in
terms of their immutability, and time, which connotes change?

Our reading of the poem is one in which practically each line contributes a new question to this list. Since we lack a context or a glos-
sary of allusions, we are being asked to construct meaning by way of
patient listings of the points we do not understand. And gradually the
effort of formulating the questions begins to pay off, as connections
and regularities begin to emerge from the text. The proximity yet
ungraspability of the deity seems to be echoed in the nearness of the
best-loved ones, who at the same time appear to be 'exhausted upon /
The most separate mountains' — hence not really near at all. The
ambiguous correlation of danger and rescue is likewise taken up in the
image of untrustworthy bridges across chasms and the appeal for safe
wings with which to traverse the dangerous terrain.

Cultural knowledge is a further aid to elucidation. The title of the
poem offers some orientation to the reader who picks up the reference
to Patmos as the name of the bleak island off Asia Minor where, traditionally, the evangelist Saint John was shipwrecked and composed the
Biblical book of Revelation. Since this is a visionary and obscure work,
Hölderlin's title may read as an announcement that the ensuing poem is
to be a symbolic account of things supranormal; this will then shape the
reader's response to his terse, oracular style.

All in all, the opening of 'Patmos' is an example of an obscurity
which does not rest on syntactical convolutions *à la* Mallarmé or
heavily-coded allusions *à la* Nerval. The sentences are simply constructed, albeit with some elliptical turns of phrase (as in the first sentence,

where the oddly short line 'Nah ist' floats unexplained until we read on
and discover that its subject, 'der Gott', is simply being kept back to
the end). Semantically, there is little that is problematic, for nearly all
the vocabulary is commonplace. What remains obscure is the resonances
which the poet imparts to the words. The austere, rugged manner of
the prosody and rhythms shapes the language into a series of lofty
statements which demand to be pondered as containers of deeper
meaning. The reader's task will be to stick with the poem long enough,
until such time as his questions are resolved by admissions or supposi-
tions in the unfolding text. Since I have cited only 15 out of the total
225 lines of 'Patmos', there is a reasonable chance that the attentive
reader will be able to establish connections to confirm or modify the
tentative reading he has initiated and lead him towards a sense of the
poem as an interconnected whole. He has a long way to travel before
such a work becomes fully accessible, however, for Hölderlin remains,
despite his apparent simplicities, essentially a poet of oracular darkness,
the author of a poetry which is at once 'near / And hard to grasp'.

Some poets declare that to write obscurely is a necessary strategy if
one is to take issue with areas of intuitive experience which defy intellectual analysis and presentation. Once a poet decides that he wishes to
deal with mysterious experiences, an enigmatic manner may be entirely
appropriate to the task. Jacques Dupin is one of those modern French
poets whose obscurity is a function of their dedication to a nigh-impos-
sible aim, that of deciphering a non-acquiescent reality. 'Tant que ma
parole est obscure il respire' (Dupin, 1971, 120) (As long as my word is
obscure he will breathe), he asserts cryptically, seeming to suggest that
he, the poet, is only able to breathe easily if his language is abstruse
enough. It is as though he needs to compound zones of obscurity so as
to work through to certain fringes of meaning. The result of all this is a
poetry of shadowy encounters and almost conspiratorial secretiveness.

N'être plus avec toi dès que tu balbuties
la sécheresse nous déborde
le cercle de tes bras ne s'entrouvre que pour mieux
ne rien dire
selon l'heure et le parfum
et quel parfum se déchire
vers le nord, l'issue dérobée . . .
peut-être ton visage contre le mien,
quand bien même tu me mènerais,
encapuchonné, sur ton poing,
comme aux premières chasses de l'enfer

(Dupin, 1971, 99)

(To no longer be with you once you stammer / dryness overwhelms us / the circle of your arms only half-opens the better / to say nothing / according to the hour and the perfume / and which perfume is torn / towards the north, the exit withheld . . . / perhaps your face against my own, / even though you might lead me, / hooded, at your wrist, / as on the first hunts of hell.)

There are various sorts of obscurity here. We may assume, as with almost any poet, that certain allusions refer to private associations or memories to which none but the poet can, in the nature of things, hope to have access. The references to perfume in this poem, for instance, may have an affective resonance for Dupin which he has not actually written about in his work and about which we as readers must therefore remain ignorant.

Where an allusion we do not immediately understand turns out to be one which occurs in other poems by the same author, we can however begin a collection of slightly differing contexts and thus move towards the meaning of the reference by pinning it down, as it were, from different sides. Here, the allusion to being led 'hooded at your wrist' makes sense in conjunction with allusions in other of Dupin's poems to the blindfolded hawks used in hunting. Significantly, this image reveals itself to be an image of the very process which the poet is engaged in. It is a self-conscious image whose meaning, I believe, is that the poet sees himself advancing, like a hooded hawk being led towards its prey, through a space of darkness which may only at the very last turn out to contain a capturable meaning. The examination of other poems than the present one thus helps us cope with its particular densities of allusion: as I suggested of Hölderlin, obscurity diminishes to the extent that one is prepared to keep on reading.

It is characteristic of Dupin's poetic imagination that he should feel himself drawn to images that are ambiguous or uncertain. Indeed anything too clear-cut seems to him lacking in authenticity. The woman to whom he refers in the present poem is depicted at one moment with half-open arms, ready to embrace him, and later she has her face next to his: and yet this same figure seems to treat him as her slave, leading him to the hunt as the obedient hawk. The ambiguous co-existence of contrasted motifs or moods is typical of Dupin's manner: his intuition of poetic 'truth' seems to rest upon the sense of a vacillation between opposites — contact and distance, control and panic, tenderness and aggression. At one point the poet seems to find in the curious image of the 'torn perfume' some sort of token of discovery in that it seems to announce a way forward 'vers le nord'. And yet a moment later, this promise of advance is cruelly curtailed, since the way is blocked — 'l'issue dérobée'. The motions of the poem seem to correspond to a struggle to escape from darkness and a concomitant delight in darkness. Even when the woman starts to speak ('dès que tu balbuties'), the poet hesitates and withdraws, sensing that it is better that nothing be said ('ne rien dire'). If this reading is valid, it makes of the poem a kind of allegory of the poetic quest, portraying it as a particularly intense pursuit which is not satisfied with facile solutions and instead aims at some ultimate revelation which can only be arrived at by crossing a territory of intense darkness. Again, the virtue of the poem lies not in its being merely 'hard to grasp', but in the conviction and intensity it conveys *notwithstanding* the reduction in communicability.

Difficult poems are not necessarily so sombre in tone. The early poems of Tristan Tzara are characterised by a racy tomfoolery that instils a sense of fun, even if this is the only 'sense' we can construct upon the text. This is the opening of his poem 'Saut Blanc Cristal':

sur un clou
machine à coudre décomposée en hauteur
déranger les morceaux de noir
voir jaune couler
ton cœur est un œil dans la boîte de caoutchouc
coller à un collier d'yeux
coller des timbres-postes sur tes yeux

partir chevaux norvège serrer
bijoux vers tourner sèche
veux-tu? pleure
lèche le chemin qui monte vers la voix

(Tzara, 1975, 113)

(on a nail / sewing-machine decomposed vertically / to disturb the bits of black / to see yellow to flow / your heart is an eye in the box of rubber / to stick to a necklace of eyes / to stick postage stamps on your eyes / to depart horses norway to squeeze / jewels towards to turn dry / will you? weeps / licks the path which rises towards the voice)

Tzara prided himself on writing poems 'in the form of errata' (Tzara, 1975, 569), and this brief text illustrates the disjointed stuttering that typifies his early style. The inconsequential opening of the poem introduces objects without explanation: a nail, a broken sewing-machine, unexplained black fragments, a rubber box. We become aware of a person addressed in the second person whose heart is equated with an eye. The curious phrase 'voir jaune' ('to see yellow') may be a wilful distortion of the usual idiom 'to see red', and it is possible that the verb *couler* ('to flow') coming directly after is a corruption of the noun *couleur* ('colour'). It is evident that the text is in part generated by phonic associations: there is a whole constellation of words beginning with the letter *c* (*clou / coudre / couler / cœur / caoutchouc / coller*), within which can be traced the close paranomastic association of the set *couler, coller* and *collier*. Words similar in sound are here obliged to 'make sense' in one another's company, as if Tzara were forcing language to play a special sort of charade.

The text is syntactically awkward, consisting largely of truncated phrases or even free-floating items of vocabulary. Thus the title 'Saut Blanc Cristal' is made up of two nouns, presumably linked appositionally, with a central adjective which might be taken as belonging to either (hence the readings 'White Leap, Crystal' or 'Leap, White Crystal'). Ambiguity is a natural result of Tzara's principle of disruption and disorder. A preponderance of infinitives, as against more specific verb forms, tends to negate any notion of subject or object: the verbs tend not to initiate sentence formations wherein events might take place, and so create an effect of pure logological energy without application or purpose. The last four lines of the quotation read like a telegrammatic reduction of a thrilling story about an urgent departure on horseback to Norway, a journey which the second person in the poem appears to find upsetting ('veux-tu? pleure'), and which culminates in a route towards a possibly significant encounter with an unspecified voice ('le chemin qui monte vers la voix'). The lines are parodic in that they are mere remnants of normal discourse, linguistic bits and pieces without the usual guidance provided by articles, verb endings, conjunctions and the like. They form a kind of daft telegram which we, as recipients, must construe as best we may, in ignorance of the distant circumstances which motivated its being sent.[6]

It seems unlikely, though, that this is a poem whose difficulty arises from its being a cut-down version of a text which started out making sense: it is not that Tzara erased any pre-existing meaning so as to produce the puzzlement we feel, but that he wrote with no prior intention of articulating or communicating meaning. His poem is a pure experiment in the aleatory collocation of language fragments, and while there are a few wisps of coherence (as in the hint of an emergent 'theme' in the allusions to *eyes* and to *travel*, isotopes which suggest to me, at least, the context of a romantic love story), the general effect of the text is to set off a manic swirl of chattering nonsense.

Tzara's poems are notable for the sensation of reckless *speeding* which they induce, a sensation which carries a special pleasure for the reader who learns to adjust his expectations to the situation of not understanding. Further, the poems achieve the odd result of being shrill and purposeful, as though voicing some urgent need, while maintaining a brusque impersonality of manner. Once again the reader is thrown on his own resources and must decide for himself how seriously he is prepared to take such writing and in what direction and with what instruments (dictionary? encyclopaedia? chronology of Tzara's private life?) he is going to grope towards meaning, in the absence of any authorial guidelines.

In their different ways, the poets I have discussed in this chapter are drawn to obscurity because this is something inherent in their aesthetics and in some cases in the metaphysical or existential attitude they have chosen to adopt. Hence we have such 'modes' of difficulty as the cramped occultation of Nerval, the oracular densification of Hölderlin, and Tzara's jocular derailment of vocabulary from the accustomed track of referentiality.[7] It remains to cite one final example, that of a poet whose work takes on a closed appearance inasmuch as it constitutes the record of mental experiences which are so private and strange as to preclude their formulation in any easily communicable form.

The work of Georg Trakl bears the imprint of a progressive psychopathological disorder which carried him from neurosis through to a full-scale psychotic collapse.[8] A creative world such as his is almost by definition an inaccessible realm, for we are hardly likely to feel attuned to the expressions of a sensibility so far alienated from the shared reality of other people. I suggested earlier apropos of the poem 'Untergang' that we can derive a certain perverse pleasure from looking at the surfaces of Trakl's later poems, with their glacial tonality, their sharp disjunctions of style, their air of remoteness and unrealness; but we can hardly expect to acclimatise ourselves to this poetic world on the strength of such tentative skimmings. Rather than detail all the aspects of Trakl's writing which make his work difficult (context, theme, style, etc.), I want to concentrate on one particularly striking feature which has established Trakl as something of a test-case in an ongoing general controversy about how critics should go about reading works of imagination. It is Trakl's ingrained *inconsistency* of allusion.

Now, critics usually feel that once they have committed themselves to reading a poet whose work is occulted, they are entitled to expect that, at the very least, the poet will behave *consistently* in the way he goes about his occultation. My approach to Hölderlin's 'Patmos' rested on the rather comfortable assumption that one could eventually ease into his poetic world by virtue of noticing the consistent patterns that inform it. But Trakl is not a consistent writer, his work seeming to flaunt even this last surviving clause in the implicit contract between writer and reader.

To illustrate the point, I shall take the example of colour allusions. The more poems one reads by Trakl, the more one finds that references to colour not only lack plausibility (like Rimbaud, he enjoys painting things the wrong colour — black snow, purple sun, etc.) — but are apparently totally unsystematic. Thus an adverbial usage of the colour word *silbern* (the adjective 'silver') will in one poem have connotations of repellent sliminess:

Silbern weint ein Krankes
Am Abendweiher,
Auf schwarzem Kahn
Hinüberstarben Liebende.

('Abendland', in Trakl, 1972, 76)

(Silver weeps something sick / By the evening pool, / Lovers pass over to death / On a black boat.)

The context of sickness, blackness and death cannot but demand that we identify the word *silbern* as belonging within a constellation of negative references. The reader accustomed to expect regularity will feel that silver is, for Trakl, symbolic of gloom and depression: it is a chill and sickly colour. But then, in the very next poem in the volume, he will come across the selfsame word in a totally different context.

Grünlich dämmert der Fluss, silbern die alten Alleen
Und die Türme der Stadt. O sanfte Trunkenheit
Im gleitenden Kahn und die dunklen Rufe der Amsel
In kindlichen Gärten. Schon lichtet sich der rosige Flor.

('Frühling der Seele', in Trakl, 1972, 77)

(The river at dusk gleams greenishly, and silver the old lanes / And towers of the town. O sweet tipsiness / In the drifting boat and the blackbirds calling darkly / In the gardens of childhood. Already the rosy garland is brightening.)

These lines from a poem which, after all, announces itself to be about the 'springtime of the soul', evoke a mood of wonderment and nostalgia associated with memories of childhood days. Set within this context, *silbern* can only carry positive connotations: it becomes a warm, seductive colour.

Given that such a word as *silbern* has shifting significance for Trakl (there are even cases where he switches colour connotations from verse to verse of the same poem), it appears that our response to such a word is going to be governed by each individual context in which it appears. The correct critical approach would seem therefore to be to try to establish the dominant mood in a given poem and then see the colour word as a *reflection* of that mood rather than suppose that each colour is univocal and *sets* the mood. In this sense, we must treat each poem separately, as establishing its own unique mood and context.

The implication of this is that our reading of Trakl will necessarily be localised, tentative and personal, based on subjective response and personal hunches rather than any quasi-scientific procedures involving statistical counts of vocabulary across all the poems, or other types of 'objective' literary analysis. Arguably, the only way to become sensitive to the original import of his poetic style, would be to familiarise oneself with it totally by projecting oneself into the mental and emotional states whence it arose. Ultimately, only a kind of 'psychotic criticism' could be expected to empathise fully with this most alienated style of writing, and this is something that the normal reader can hardly be expected to achieve.

My assessment of Trakl's discrepant manner is that in his writing he was wrestling with psychic material that caused him anguish and which he found it impossible to articulate rationally and consistently. While he still made use of words from the collective idiom, he found himself forcing them into hitherto proscribed areas of meaning. In the end, a given word would itself become 'alienated' from the norm. His word *silbern* is no longer the word we can check in the dictionary or usefully compare with its appearances in the work of other poets. It is not unthinkable that Trakl himself finally lost touch with language as an intentional instrument and began writing sentences which even he could not understand. At this point the poem slips beyond the last bounds of intelligibility – the message is meaningless not only for its notional recipient but also for its transmitter! At this extreme, the words on the page are quite literally blank signs emptied of any referentiality or shape. The poem then represents an enigma which is absolute.

In general we have seen that the poetry of Enigma arises when the writer is, whether by choice or involuntarily, bound by certain constraints. Poets who write obscurely are as likely to be serious and dedicated to their art as any poet communicating in unequivocal terms. It is simply that their approach to expression is not easy for them and involves them in difficulties with their medium; or to put the point in another way, they engage with meanings which are, by their very nature, problematic.

At this stage we might draw some provisional conclusions about an appropriate stance on the reader's part. Now, it seems pointless to make recommendations about poems which a reader finds that he simply 'cannot read' at all, in the sense that he can find nothing to get hold of and feels no inclination to give the text a second chance. I think there is no argument against the sensation of total apathy when that is *all* that a poem instils. What I think we *can* talk about is the situation where a poem is impenetrable on first reading and yet still manifests itself as some sort of puzzle or challenge to which the reader feels not only entitled but actively stimulated to pursue. If an abstruse text at first resists being understood yet at the same time succeeds in sustaining our interest, we can, I think, make the assumption that it will *eventually* have something to say to us. The rationale for this is that when we are 'caught' by a poem we cannot rationally comprehend, it is because the poem has *already* begun to speak to us, albeit at a level below that of ordinary reason. In this sense one could say that the enigma poem *par excellence* is one which transmits its appeal at the emotional level while frustrating us intellectually. The situation might be compared to that of an attractive woman who snubs an admirer: in love as in poetry, an initial rebuff can be the catalyst of passion.

Reading one's way into an enigma text and gradually uncovering its hidden virtues can be an exhilarating and enriching experience. It must presuppose a tolerance to perplexity, since the mind must first accept that its normal skills are inappropriate to the task in hand. What is necessary is not that the reader should immediately exert himself magically to transform the darkness into blinding light, but that, as Hugo Friedrich remarks of the reader's approach to Mallarmé, he should 'himself enter into the Enigmatic' (Friedrich, 1956, 121). It is a paradoxical approach, this attempt to align one's mental processes to processes which are by definition foreign. Yet this slow adjustment of the eyesight to the darkness can be a prelude to aesthetic pleasures all the more intense for our awareness of the paradox.

René Char has a dark aphorism, probably originally intended to serve some other purpose, but sufficiently ambiguous in expression to be worth citing here as a motto for readers about to venture into the regions of obscurity:

> Amis, la neige attend la neige pour un travail simple et pur, à la limite de l'air et de la terre.

> (Char, 1967, 97)

(Friends, the snow awaits the snow for a simple and pure piece of work, at the limit of air and earth.)

My interpretation of this secretive sentence is that the link between air and earth, between the space of transparency and the space of opacity, will be established by snow falling on snow, that is: by a process of layers gently covering earlier layers. The inference is that the boundary between light and darkness is defined by repeated attentions from the former − each falling snowflake is like an exquisitely soft gesture of understanding, of contact. Yet each equally contributes to covering over again that which has been touched. For each moment of revelation, there is a concomitant reveiling, just as, in Mallarmé's 'Petit Air', the baring of the woman's body is at once followed by its submersion in the dark water. To simplify the lesson: the reader of occulted poetry must learn to accept the darkness, to move around within it, and not to try to drag the poem back into the daylight. For once a secret is stripped of its veils, it will forfeit its fascination and its value.

Part Two

COMING BACK TO THE REAL

5   THE POEM OPENS UP TO THE READER

We have so far looked at ways in which poems assert themselves as verbal microcosms which distantiate themselves from empirical reality and delineate a more or less autonomous counter-reality. Such poetry appears to be fundamentally escapist, a means for the poet to enact a grand gesture of solipsistic defiance of the rest of the world. To write punningly or elliptically, to invest energies in gratuitous formulation rather than cogent thought, to invent enigmas or chimerical forms bound by purely artificial constraints, these would seem to be activities calculated to discredit the normal practices of literary communication and eventually to alienate all possible readers. How else than as idle provocation can we understand Wallace Stevens's remark that 'personally, I like words to sound wrong'? (quoted in Ehrenpreis, 1972, 114). Surely no sensitive poet would want actually to sabotage his own message and thereby ruin all communication?

Let us think about why there should be an objection to Stevens's remark. Evidently we are making an unspoken assumption, namely that language is an idiom shared by writer and reader and which the former is expected to manipulate in a responsible manner, in order to transmit certain ideas or values which the latter is capable of receiving and appreciating. But is this assumption really justified? Why should we expect poets to furnish us with something accessible and palatable? The language of prose is more adequate to this function. Can we not allow that poetry may have other purposes and more subtle meanings to prospect? Anyway, why shouldn't Stevens enjoy foxing his reader, as his quip seems to imply? But Stevens is more serious than this: what he wants from a word which rocks the literary boat by 'sounding wrong' is not just that it should alarm the reader and make him feel uneasy. Rather, it is that it should awaken him to meanings to which ordinary prose and ordinary thinking have tended to make him impervious. In making the remark, Stevens is not just being an impish flouter of commonsense or a flabby refugee from the harsh reality of direct speech; instead he is an ardent seeker of fresh perspectives on the world, which he hopes to open up by disrupting the *status quo* of language. In other words, the poet of strangification and derealisation is not an escapist but a revolutionary.

It may well be, then, that the poetic strategy of withdrawal from engagement in actual facts and responsible contact with others is, in the long term, a means to transform attitudes to language and thereby to the way we talk and think about the world. To tamper with language is simply the poet's natural way of querying the ways we perceive reality. In shunning normal speech habits, he is in effect preparing himself and his reader for acts of new expression which will facilitate new perceptions. 'The freshness of transformation is / The freshness of a world. It is our own. / It is ourselves, the freshness of ourselves . . .' writes Stevens elsewhere (Stevens, 1955, 397-8). Which is to say that poetic writing at its fullest pitch represents a straining away from habit, an effort to break with reality as it has unfortunately become – stagnant, stultified, a thing paralysed by stock definition and standard rhetoric. Making words 'sound wrong' is simply a means to revive their latent energies, to lend them an intensity which will allow them to mediate the new ideas, the 'right ideas'.

What I am now arguing for is a reorientation of the perspective pursued in Part One. What I there described as techniques of strangification, verbal algebra, dark incursions into language which lead to the brink of incommunicability, I shall now want to see as manifestations of a desire for change, a desire channelled through words, a desire concentrated into words, but a desire no less deeply *felt*. The verbal experiment which modern poetry seems so frenziedly to pursue is not just playing with unreality for the fun of it. Rather it reflects a solemn quest for a new reality, or of reality renewed through fresh perceptions.

Robert Duncan underlines the point that escapism is not enough when he writes: 'Working in words I am an escapist; as if I could step out of my clothes and move naked as the wind in a world of words. But I want every part of the actual world involved in my escape' (Duncan, 1971, v). The poet's paradoxical claim must be stressed to the full: it is that when poetry rushes into unreality, it does so precisely in order to attack the old reality. What I have thus far expounded in terms of withdrawal or derealisation or puzzle-making, must now be seen in terms of advance, transformation and illumination. It is the purpose of this chapter, and thereafter of the rest of the book, to explore the view that poetry is not a shunning of reality, but a simulated retreat which subsequently reveals itself to be a fresh and celebratory advance. So far from turning away into its own shell, the poem now opens up.

Like the horizon, the logological extreme can never be reached. There is simply no way in which the love of the unreal can lead to the permanent establishment of a poetic domain pure of all contamination from the world of sticky fact. As Valéry remarked of *poésie pure*, 'nothing so pure can co-exist with the conditions of life' (Valéry, 1962, 1275). How is this so? Why should it not be possible to follow Mallarmé's lead and create language objects based on the erasure of referentiality and the severance of links to extra-verbal experience?

A fascinating text by Novalis called *Monolog* sketches an answer to this question. It begins by an apparent underlining of the logological principle in that it insists on recognising the self-reflexive nature of verbal expression. But the text goes on to make the astonishing assertion that if language *is* abstracted from reality it must in fact – *because* of this very abstraction – tend to mirror aspects of the natural world. world.

> It is a silly thing, actually, about speaking and writing: true speech is a mere word-game. One can only wonder at the laughable error whereby people imagine that they speak for the sake of things. Nobody seems to know that the most characteristic thing about language is that it is concerned solely with itself. And this is why it is such a wonderful and fertile secret: for when someone speaks simply for the sake of speaking, he expresses the most beautiful and original truths . . . If one could only get people to grasp that language is analogous to the formulae in mathematics, – they constitute a world in their own right – they simply play amongst themselves, expressing nothing other than their own singular nature: and yet precisely for this reason, they mirror the strange interplay of natural relationships. It is only thanks to their freedom that they are components of nature and in their free motions alone does the World Soul find expression, making them the delicate measure and blueprint of all things. And so it is with language also.   (Novalis, 1962, 323)

The modern reader will feel hesitant about accepting these propositions wholesale. He will probably have difficulty coping with the allusion to Schelling's mystic-sounding concept of the World Soul, and the Romantic picture of nature as a harmonious system attuned to the human spirit and, by extension, to human language. Yet Novalis's thinking moves on an illuminating track, and it is my belief that his idea of a secret homology between human language and natural phenomena represents a fundamental poetic tenet which has, with modifications, survived until the present day. In a later chapter I shall examine the Romantic conception of reality as a coded script, and try to show its relevance for the modern poetic sensibility. For the time being, let me simply draw from Novalis's text the essential point that undirected discourse has a spontaneous tendency to acquire form and meaning, almost despite the intentions of the one who speaks or writes. Given this proposition, it follows that unchannelled nonsense will tend to surge into sense, and, by extension, that deliberate contortions of syntax, fragmentation of references, the choice of 'wrong' words, the occultation or strangification of texts, will also eventually furnish meaning. Within the chaos of uncertainty and perplexity, a significance may begin to assert itself. As Novalis implies, language has a secret loyalty such that even in its most freakish and wild moods, it will not disown its responsibility to the world we live in. We are close here to finding a deeper meaning to Éluard's dictum that 'Words don't lie'.

There are three main reasons why poems must always tend to furnish meanings even when they may seem recalcitrant in the face of the reader's expectation. The first is that words continue to secrete referential tendencies even when poets feel tempted to suppress their referential potency by using them as neutrally as possible. For however much the poet may strain towards the logological extreme, it remains necessarily the case that words are *signs* and, as such, are inevitably going to point *at* something rather than lie listless and apathetic upon the page. The second reason is that these signs are never the dry and univocal mechanisms which linguistic theorising often seems to insinuate them to be.[9] Words always mean more than just one thing: they *denote* but they also *connote*. And *a fortiori* words as used in poetry, that is, words set out in ways which give them the opportunity to maximise their connotative powers. Thirdly, the words we encounter in a poem do not come to us limply, without assertion. We recognise them at once as being *special*, as embodying something more than casual remarks. I have already pointed to the quirky authoritativeness of John Ashbery's style, or again, the flamboyance of Nerval's italicised words, studded like rare jewels upon the velvet obscurity of the rest of the text. Even the undirected idiom of the Surrealists comes across to us with an aura of potential surprise which at once requires that we pay special attention to it.

Poetic language, then, always reaches us with an implied stress, as if ringed around with the reminder 'This is something to be read carefully.' And words which are stressed leave a special imprint on the reader's consciousness. They have impact. By virtue of their self-assertiveness and their wealth of connotations, they enter the reader's mind in a way which stimulates his associative responses. The receptive reader does not glance at a poem in an offhand way, but opens himself up to nuance and suggestion, allowing the patterns on the page the chance to expand within his participating consciousness.

This participation represents nothing less than the implementation of the reader's private resources, the mobilisation of his hidden sensibility. Day-to-day prosaic communication rarely touches on this; only occasionally do experiences in the physical world activate it. But poetic language is singularly endowed with the capacity to strike notes that echo through to the deeper levels of our being. When this happens, the language of the poem may be said to come truly alive. As Octavio Paz says, 'There is no poem *in itself*, only *in me* or *in you* . . . Without a text there is no reading, and without a reading there is no text' (Paz, 1974, 162). The act of reading is a collaborative one in which the reader brings to fruition the act of calling forth meaning which the poet has started. Such reading is not mere 'reading-off' of meanings, but a fertile engagement in the processes of exploring meaning which lie at the heart of all poetry. Holbrook Jackson writes thus: 'Reading becomes an experience, and although it may begin by prolongation through the imagination of the author's experience, it ends by becoming a part of the reader's consciousness, by a process of absorption' (Jackson, 1946, 27). I hope to show that the apotheosis of the poetic process occurs when the poem, having elicited the involvement of the reader, begins to take shape for him as an experience which is not merely literary or intellectual, but which partakes of the savour and depth of experiences in real life.

In an article which examines some of the extremes of logological writing in modern German literature, Richard Brinkmann comes to a conclusion similar to mine when he maintains that at the extreme pitch of withdrawal from referentiality, poetic language continues to be subject to some form of semantic determination. Only if the poem veers into sheer noise can the connection between poetry and the world be said to be entirely severed.

It is a strange paradox that the most spiritual of the arts, the one which seems most intimately wedded to the logos, remains inseparably tied to the concreteness of the shapes of the human world. Concreteness certainly does not mean only that which is visible and can be touched with our hands. It includes also the realm of feeling and thought, also the realm of dreams and archetypal visions. But it is always, in the broadest sense, something shaped according to the images of our experienced world.   (Brinkmann, 1965, 134)

As I suggested, I am now committing myself to the righting of a stress which, during the preceding chapters, I deliberately pressed in one direction only. My strategy has been to acknowledge the attractions of unreality and the tendency of modern poems to pull away from the world and even the reader. I have put the case for the logological extreme as a suppression of referentiality, and the enigmatic absolute as the final extinction of understanding. But now I want to correct this perspective and say that in poetry, the world and the reader are never irredeemably spurned. Precisely by virtue of those resources which the reader brings to the occasion of reading – namely, his intelligence, his emotions, his personal memories of life and his more or less extensive experience of literature – the poem will have something to appeal to, a chance to bridge distances, a space within which meanings can unfold. It would be tiresome for me to review every single case examined above, and so I propose to sketch the counter-argument to the gist maintained hitherto by way of a brief re-opening of a few typical cases. In arguing that these selected cases do, in spite of what has been said so far, implicate the reader and his sense of reality, I hope that the general focus of this book can be adjusted in an important and more truthful way.

We should now be more fully able to appreciate how Sacheverell Sitwell goes about those fantasy modifications of reality which I discussed in Chapter 1. They involve in the first instance a recourse to *language*, the most active word in Sitwell's textual game being the word *unreal*: 'The wild mountains were of unreal green . . . [The mainland] had, therefore, not only the appearance of a vision, but, as well, its unreality and intangibility'. Implicitly Sitwell is asking the reader to join in the literary game of conjuring up a fantastic image in the mind's eye. The word *unreal*, I would suggest, makes its impact only if the reader 'plays the game'. It can only make full sense if the reader's intellect follows the sign to its referent and then sets the abstract notion of unreality against his own imaginative experience of the unreal. At this point the co-operative reader will 'see' (or at least momentarily accept the plausibility of seeing) the abnormal greenness of the mountains: whereupon the text will stimulate a particular sort of pleasure. But the point is that what is 'unreal' for the reader can only have meaning to the degree that he can implicitly measure it against what is real. In this case, he will implicitly be testing the unreality of the mountains described in the text and now held as an image in his imagination against his memories of real mountains – or, more likely, his memories of the unreal appearance which mountains in the real world often assume

when seen from a distance. In Chapter 1 I considered the view that the
pleasure imparted by the fascinating image or illusion depends on the
percipient's recognising the discrepancy between it and his accustomed
sense of what is real. The successful literary evocation of blatant unrealities by poets such as Breton and Rimbaud is in fact reliant on the
reader's willingness to set the reading experience in the context of his
literal awareness of the occasional odd behaviour of reality when he is
not reading. The naked woman conjured up in Bousquet's fantasy and
conveyed to the reader in the form of a verbal equivalent would forfeit
her trembling beauty if the reader were unable to counterbalance her
unreality with images from his own memory which are instinct with
the desire that such images should be real. Reading, like imagining,
means to invest something with reality, not to censor its potential for
becoming real. Éluard once complained that 'imagination is often used
as a convenient term to differentiate man from the world which sur-
rounds him, to create for him an abstract, egoistic universe in which he
finds himself isolated' (Éluard, 1968, I, 541). But like imagination,
reading is neither abstract nor solipsistic. The appeal of textual unrealities lies not in their invitation to jettison the real world *per se* and to
enter into a purely delusional realm: rather it lies in their revolutionary
demonstration that the phenomenal world may itself be subject to the
transformations which the poet can exercise through language. The
message of the 'hallucination of words' is not that it is possible to displace the real universe by a verbal abracadabra, but that by entertaining
images of unreality alongside our perceptions of the real universe, we
can learn to grasp its realness in an enhanced way. We may then discover that the world is not something prosaic but rather something
poetic. But I am anticipating my later explorations and must first
ground my argument on the revised analysis of earlier examples.

I have begun to argue that the reader of poems is able to negotiate
meanings by reference to perceptual images. Similar processes operate
where a reader is faced with texts shaped in the light of what might be
called the 'poetics of strangeness'. In the case of Li Shang-yin's poem,
which turned out to be about a bride abandoned by her lover, I suggested that, for the English reader ignorant of its cultural connotations,
the text acted as a powerful source of mystery (cf. Chapter 2). The
effect of strangeness was a function, then, of cultural distance as much
as of the author's use of a gnomic style. None the less, the poem does
have impact on the English reader and can create certain patterns of
meaning for him. The fundamental experience of the poem is of course

that it provides an excursion into strangeness. But more intricately, the poem takes us through a sequence of stressed impressions which, despite our ignorance of their intended significance (or rather, *because* of this ignorance), cannot but impose themselves upon our consciousness, and thereby begin to fashion a meaning valid for us.

>Phoenix tail on scented silk, flimsy layer on layer:
>Blue patterns on a round canopy, stitched deep into the night.

A reader of some sensitivity will, when his intellectual faculties are not engaged, listen in to the non-rational workings of his mind. A poem without surface argument can make some sense at the level of pre-conscious association or reverie. Li Shang-Yin's reference to a bird's tail may set off mental images involving the delicate mesh of threads which constitute the feathers on the sweeping tail of an exotic bird: these arise alongside other images prompted by the reference to scented silk, which has parallel associations of delicate textures and sweeping motions. The poet's reference to the patterns in conjunction with a canopy may elicit thought about embroidery being patiently stitched — by whose hand? It is easy to import the idea of a girl from the later stages of the text. The reader then imagines this girl stitching 'deep into the night'. The English phrasing here (whether or not it is an accurate rendering of the original Chinese is immaterial to my argument about the way I respond to the text before me) can give rise to either a temporal or a spatial interpretation. That is, the girl may be working *until* late at night: or she may actually be stitching *into* the night, i.e. the night is envisaged as a species of fabric itself. Whereupon the round canopy with its blue patterning becomes an image for the night sky, one reading leading on to further dimensions of imaginary participation. Flurries of associations may follow: the sky's blue canopy bears images which represent birds or patterns of stars; layers of scented silk waft like immaterial layers of atmosphere across space; the reference to scent creates the fetishistic suggestion of a woman's perfumed robe; and so on.

What is happening here is that I am following up associations that are released by the stimulus which these lines provide for my imagination. Where Kugel suggests that poetic strangeness means providing 'a direction for the reader's imagination without offering it a means of satisfaction', I would say that while the poem offers the direction, it is up to the reader to follow his own path to satisfaction by giving full rein to his imaginative responses. The associations to which I feel myself led may indeed be perfectly plausible ones, as when I associate the word 'stitching' with the activity of a girl at her embroidery; or they may be illogical ones, the product of sheer idiosyncrasy. The latter are naturally the ones least defensible in objective logical terms; not everyone will want to accept the notion that these lines evoke the night sky seen as a decorative panoply. There is indeed an *a priori* objection to this reading, for strictly speaking the patterns are defined as being *blue* — and constellations of stars are not that colour, even if the sky may be.

In the present instance, I will find that having established a pattern of meanings which makes sense *to me*, I must read on into the next strange lines and see whether they conflict or comply with the interpretation I have begun to develop. Luckily, I will come in the next line upon a reference to 'the fan's sliced moon', which will tend to confirm my interpretation of the poem as elaborating an analogy between the image-nexus *embroideress* (scented silk, stitching, fan) and that of *sky* (night sky, moon). My reading of the poem may thus far seem justified, even though I cannot be sure that other readers will concur. I have not yet determined a meaning for the reference to the *phoenix*: but I must be content to have only some elements of meaning clear in my mind, rather than expect all the enigmas to fall patly into place at once.

The danger of obscure poems is that the reader who constructs his own version of their meaning may end up inventing something totally remote from what the author intended. Dupin has written of the dangers of solipsism in this connection.

> Absorbed in your reading, crossed by the lightning which shoots down from a cloud of signs, as if to sanction their lack of reality, you are condemned to wander between the lines, to breathe only your own smells, a labyrinth to yourself.   (Dupin, 1971, 140)

What Dupin is suggesting is that some poetic texts may be so abstruse as to lack all semblance of reality, all purchase on collective experience. The reader who then tries to 'read between the lines' may find himself trapped *between* their meanings, rather than confronting them face to face. He will end up wandering in a labyrinth which has nothing to do with the poem proper, condemned to contemplate the significance of his own fetid exhalations. Or to put it more suavely: he will be treating the text as an opaque mirror in which to read off reflected images of his own creation. The answer to such an objection, perfectly valid in theory, is that in actual practice texts are rarely so opaque, and that one's subjective associations are never so idiosyncratic as to lead to acutely distorted readings of a poem. The point is that words do refer, and they do refer in fairly consistent ways: so that the reading of the same poem by different readers will tend to move along similar lines, since those different readers may be expected to have access to at least the basic shades of meaning which a given set of words may be assumed to carry. Here I am aware that I am making a somewhat rough and ready apology for the 'objectivity' of subjective interpretation: but exactly what criterion of correctness or incorrectness could one establish where enigmatic poems are concerned, if it is assumed that our reading is to take place without benefit of critical guidance? The reader can be assured, I believe, that he is on some sort of right lines if, first, he takes pleasure in his reading, and, secondly, if that pleasure derives not just from a single detail (a reference to scented silk, say) but from an overall sense that the meanings he is establishing are moving towards cohesion. Positivists or formalists might find different structures in a poem than the ones I intuit: a Marxist critic might organise his analysis on very different premises. To them I would say that their approach is not an authentic way to respond to the potencies of lyrical language, and that what is most important about the poetry of strangeness is that it calls upon responses which cannot be programmed or mechanically measured. Scientific rigour, far less partisan presuppositions, are irrelevant to Li Shang-yin's poem. What does matter is the ability to lower one's intellectual guard and to listen in to one's emotional, subjective associations as one reads the words on the page. When this really happens, the poetry of strangeness can take up its rightful space in one's consciousness, flowering intimately within the mind. Further, this accession to intimacy will tend to demonstrate the surprising fact that obscure poems do not necessarily negate the relevance of sensory and emotional experience to the mental processes of reading. Rather, the lack of specificity in the text will be even more likely to engage the reader in terms of his extra-intellectual faculties. I have no doubt that a silk fetishist would be especially delighted by the present poem: more seriously, I have no doubt that the poem, in the moment of its successful re-creation in the receptive consciousness, makes of each reader a silk fetishist – as well as a star-gazer, a lovestruck dreamer, and a connoisseur of patterns of imagery.

If I can experience these responses to Li Shang-yin's graceful poem, in what way can I claim to be touched in my deep sensibility by that chattering text of Péret's which I quoted in Chapter 2? I spoke then of the poem as an unreality machine capable of generating an endless stream of aberrant associations after one initial input, the mention of 'my head'. One line is sufficient to remind us of Péret's manner.

Ma tête de papier de verre frottant tant et plus sur une coupe de
    cristal

Almost certainly the impression registered by the intellect is one of
extreme incongruity. The sequence 'head / glass-paper / crystal glass'
has no rational consistency. At the level of reason indeed, Surrealist
statements of this sort always tend to provoke immediate intellectual
short-circuits. If he reads the poem at normal speed (and there are
another fourteen lines to come in this poem, 'Sais-tu'), the reader is
unlikely to be able to cope with the jaunty inconsequentiality of the
signals coming off the page at him, and his mind will seize up or
become numb from the strain. Possibly this will seem like a good time
to abandon the text. But I would contend that this numbness of the
intellect may only be the superficial effect of Surrealist writing. At a
deeper level, inconsequentiality has a different impact: for to the non-
rational sectors of the psyche, sequential and associational coherence
are of no great importance. As Anton Ehrenzweig maintains in his book
The Hidden Order of Art, the unfocused scanning carried out by subliminal vision is able to apprehend series of items which logic would
categorise as totally disparate. 'Undifferentiated perception can grasp in
a single undivided act of comprehension data that to conscious perception would be incompatible' (Ehrenzweig, 1970, 46). How this all
works is not something that can be crisply defined, since any discourse
upon the subliminal must incline to an evocatory rather than an analyti-
cal mode of description. What I am advancing here is, in the nature of
things, only an approximation of what goes on when I try to let Péret's
line 'make sense' for me. But let us see what happens. First, I let the
references sink into my mind as deeply as possible. Secondly, I try to
scan the manifold associations released by each element in the text in
the hope of finding common denominators that might justify links
being inserted to tie together the various elements in the line. The single
nouns *verre* (the substance 'glass') and *coupe* (the artefact 'a glass') are
obviously semantically close, but I have trouble setting the noun phrase
papier de verre (glass-paper) in relation to *coupe de cristal* (crystal glass,
champagne cup). Glass-paper is roughly textured and is normally used
to smooth down a solid primary substance such as wood; crystal glass,
on the other hand, is a finished artefact of great delicacy and value. The
suggestion that the one should rub against the other is incongruous and
also irritating: I can imagine the tactile and acoustic sensations promp-

ted by that harsh surface scraping the fragile rim of a champagne glass. This irritation seems to be partly mental, but also partly physical – it sets my teeth on edge.

Now this suggestion of irritation might be the fruit of the Surrealist intention, which Péret is certainly pursuing in this poem, of subverting the security of the reader. It might also be said to be the superficial effect of almost any of the poems of strangeness we have examined. But I think my present irritation goes deeper than this. My irritation is not just exasperation *with* the text, but something I can situate *within* the text, where it constitutes something akin to a theme. That is, the sense of irritation derives from an intimate contact with the line, not from a superficial glance at it, and in this way I can feel justified in my reader's stance.

In a curious way, the strangeness of the initial reading remains, yet now the text has become familiar to me by virtue of my having explored it in the light of my personal associations and responses. At its most successful, Surrealist poetry can achieve this dual enlightenment whereby the reader appreciates his personal resources as a legitimate complement to the resources of the text proper. Even if it remains jaggedly irrational, a Surrealist poem may eventually attain a quite surprising semblance of 'logic' in that its oddity, the shapes of its strangeness, will be seen to be defined in a necessary relationship to the realm of logical structures and tested congruences which it flaunts.

In these recent pages I have been proceeding on the assumption that the reader can and does turn not simply to his intellectual knowledge of what words denote, consulting as it were a mental dictionary of their definitions, but to the implications or connotations which they stimulate when they are set alongside the full resources of the low-level sensibility, compounded of his emotions, his desires and fears, and his sense of physical reality, which is built up of a complex web of remembered perceptions and acquired instincts. When I read about glass-paper rubbing against a champagne glass, I imagine the contact which the words articulate by way of an appeal to images in my visual and tactile memory. The verbal formula thus prompts a response – the sense of something grating on my senses – which is channelled by the workings of my personal sensory preferences. Mysteriously, I feel able to assert that an actual occurrence of this sort would cause me some measure of distress, whereas simply to evoke this encounter inside my imagination seems to provide me with a perverse sort of pleasure. No doubt this takes me back to an earlier notion, that the fascination of the poetic image can lie in its vacillating between reality and unreality.

In claiming that language literally partakes of sensation, I would be pressing towards an unjustified hyperbole, for it is presumably axiomatic that no literary terminology exists for inducing genuine physiological sensations. However intensely Rimbaud dreamt of creating a language capable of reaching out to all the physical senses, it remains the case that no arrangement of words upon a page can be the vehicle of literal sensations (other than that of its visual appearance as a typographical unit, black on white). Borges's poem of the tiger never traps the animal pacing through the jungle. Poems are not the things of which they speak, no more than a sign is that to which it points. Strictly speaking, all a poet does is to create for the reader a chance of *reconstructing* certain sensations he has had in the past: when this occurs, the text may be said to be the verbal trigger of the memory-trace of a sensation. Since a time-lapse is involved, the text is clearly very distant from the original sensation. And in any case, the reconstructed sensation will tend always to be a conglomerate of different sensory memories, which again diminishes the possibility of direct replication of an authentic single sensation.

All the same, and this is the virtue of the best poetry, there do occur verbal formulae which have the capacity to seduce the reader into supplying the act of reading with a context replete with all the colour and detail which imagination and the memory of past sensations can provide. When this happens, the reader tends to stand on the divide between a figurative and a literal response. He may apprehend a given set of words as a figure of speech, but often his private sensibility will be so activated that he experiences it as something *all but physical*.

Further, one could argue that the act of reading does not just revive old memories, but can involve present sensory awareness. Reading a poem attentively can lead to quite literal physical effects: nerves tense up, the muscles of the throat may move as in speech, the hands may be clenched, the lips bitten. Reading a poem aloud naturally increases such effects. While it might not be legitimate to lay claim to these effects as final proofs that literature reaches out to influence our physical being, all the same they can complement in powerful ways the images which language calls forth within the imagination, whether these images be visual, acoustic, tactile, olfactory or gustatory, to a point where some readers may be tempted to think that they are not virtual but real.

I spoke in Chapter 2 of Mallarmé's 'nul ptyx' as a purely notional object, something defined through its failure to exist at all. In fact, though, the perfect emptiness which Mallarmé dreamed of evoking never really came into focus in his poetry except in terms which the reader tends to refer back to existence. Let me explain. When he tried to formulate verbal signs of total absence, Mallarmé found himself unable to progress convincingly except by degrees, gradually filtering off substance from his allusions, and thus derealising the poetic structures bit by bit. In the end, the postulate of an absolute vacuity remained an ideal: his actual poems consist of allusions to objects which we recognise in their *movement towards extinction* rather than as absences. And if we do register the final abolition of the object, this is, I am sure, as much an imaginary disappointment of the senses as an intellectual act. The idea is, so to speak, accompanied by a neural twinge.

Let us re-consider two other texts which, in Chapter 3, I suggested were language objects lacking in consistency or meaningful referentiality. First, let us look again at a few lines from Apollinaire's 'Arbre'.

Entre les pierres
Entre les vêtements multicolores de la vitrine
Entre les charbons ardents du marchand de marrons
Entre deux vaisseaux norvégiens amarrés à Rouen
Il y a ton image

Elle pousse entre les bouleaux de la Finlande

If we continue to accept my earlier reading of the passage as a set of bizarre associations accruing to the poet's own image, then the lack of immediate congruity would perhaps confirm that the poet is uncertain as to where he should best locate that image. We might, without too much stretching of the imagination, see the poet's problem as one of finding places in which his personality can feel at home. A list of such places would, perhaps, furnish some minimal information about him, providing a stable frame for his image, which presently seems to be lacking in contour and dimension. Scanning the allusions once again, the reader can begin to 'place' Apollinaire. The poet's image is first imagined as being 'among the stones': his being is indeterminate, floating, it merges into its background just as a single stone merges into the mass of stones around itself. The next situation is more detailed in its specification and we might be justified in visualising an actual picture (*image*), or even a photograph of the poet, being placed amid the bright clothes on show in a shop-window. Apollinaire might here be thinking of his public image as one which imperfectly matches his true identity. Next, his image is located among the coals of a hot-

chestnut vendor: the reader will probably take this as a fantasy, whereby the poet imagines gazing at his own image in the glowing embers. (I
am reminded here of Gaston Bachelard's remarks on glowing flames as a
medium of creative reverie, as in such texts as *La Flamme d'une chandelle*.) Then the poet associates his images with two foreign ships tied
up at a French port: I know of no obvious reason why Apollinaire
should choose *Norwegian* ships, though we may surmise (this time by
reference to what we know of Apollinaire's biography) that this might
be an allusion to the poet's characteristic sense of not belonging in
France, his nagging feeling of being an alien in his chosen country.
Finally Apollinaire sees his image firmly located among birch trees in
Finland. Have we implicitly voyaged on Norwegian vessels from Rouen
to the Baltic? The allusion to Finland suggests a remote and inclement
setting, in that Finland is commonly associated with cold and snow.
However the words here suggest an almost spring-like locality, since
there are birch trees growing, and indeed the image itself is said to be
growing: 'Il y a ton image / Elle pousse'. The connotations here strike
me as indicating a potential for growth and self-assertion, a regained
confidence. The poet has, in these images, moved from the depressed
landscape of stones to the inspired landscape of young trees. In a sense
he has moved through a crisis of self-confidence, expressed in the form
of a passage through images.

It would be wrong of me to insist on the above interpretation as
being absolute; I am mindful of my earlier warning that it does no
service to poetry of this kind to interpolate subjective associations
which tie the lines up into a neat but artificial system and thereby stifle
the natural openness of the text. On the other hand, to have no desire
to marshal one's responses is to be pitifully unenterprising, and if the
reader finds that the lines exercise an appeal for him, he can hardly be
acting wrongly in seeking some underlying consistency (in my case, the
theme of self-searching) that will 'justify' the diverse allusions. Without
any attempt to consolidate his responses, they will in any case collapse
back into the undifferentiated levels of pre-consciousness and all purchase on the meaning of the poem will be relinquished.

The other example I want to return to is Hugo Bell's poem, of
which the opening three lines are a sufficient reminder (cf. Chapter 3).

gadji beri bimba glandridi laula lonni cadori
gadjama gramma berida bimbala glandri galassassa laulitalomini
gadji beri bin blassa glassala laula lonni cadorsu sassala bim

I suggested at first that this Dada sound poem could create an effect of meaninglessness and communicative anarchy. But I went on to point out the presence of phonic regularities in the text — in this fragment, for example, each line opens on the same syllable *gadj-* — and to argue that, almost totally innocent of semantic reference though the text is, it does make some form of 'sense' by virtue of its rhythms and repetitions of sounds, and thereby bears comparison with a musical composition. Now, anyone who takes the trouble to read Ball's poem out aloud in a serious spirit will find it lends itself readily to a chanting delivery; he will undoubtedly also experience an odd physical power at work in the fabric of the syllables and their rhythms. It is important to remember that Ball's poem was written to be spoken, not silently read. Its first performance was at one of the Dada evenings in the Café Voltaire in Zürich, with its author dressed up as a 'magical bishop' in a huge cylindrical hat and with flapping cardboard wings. The complete poem is fairly long, and as he read, Ball found that the only natural way to sustain a tone of seriousness, even of solemnity, was to intone the text like a priest reciting mass, all the while slowly waving his wings up and down. In his diary of the Dada days, Ball records that after performances such as this, people would go away with nonsense formulations imprinted on their consciousness so deeply that they remained obsessed by them for the rest of the week. Ball ascribes this hypnotic effect to the power of language to generate formulae tantamount to magicians' spells (cf. Schifferli, 1963, 28). The Dada poets, it seems, were invoking powers dormant in the verbal utterance, bringing into play subliminal responses within the listener. Totally unintentionally, Ball and his friends had hit upon a crucial discovery, namely that the more a poet may retreat from conventional forms of communication, the more he may unleash the power of words to address our unconscious being. Perhaps such an example gives some backing to Novalis's contention that the free motions of language are expressive of the World Soul which moves through all creation.

Lastly, let us return to two examples of poetic obscurity examined in Chapter 4, which may now be seen not as instances of the reader being rejected as of his being subtly invited in. Nerval's 'Érythréa' is an impregnable text on first reading, yet while it withholds exact information about its allusions, it does supply several sensory cues for the reader. I suggested he might be dumbfounded by the geographical inconsistency of the line 'La neige du Cathay tombe sur l'Atlantique', yet the words do also supply him with an image of undoubted visual appeal — white snowflakes falling upon deep waters, each flake vanishing as it touched the surface. To this may be added the connotations of sadness and loss motivated by the contemplation of its ephemeral beauty.[10] Once the reader is launched on this sort of interpretation — based, as I have stressed, not on clarifications offered by scholarly exegesis but on his personal resources — he may find other pointers in the poem which will confirm or modify the direction of his musings. The line 'Et de papillons blancs la Mer est inondée' may now come into focus as an image analogous to that of snow on the ocean. The parallelism in the falling both of white butterflies and of snowflakes tends to legitimise the sense of sadness and loss, and the pathetic realisation of the ephemerality of beauty. Even if the reader is still none the wiser about Mahdeva, he can at least respond to the plea that that figure should let his or her veils float upon the water and abandon his or her purple flowers to the streams: do not veils and flowers thereby reveal affinities with the butterflies and snowflakes, all of them being scattered over water? Associations build up: the reader may now think of exotic ceremonies of lament in which wreaths or silk scarves are tossed into rivers, of snowflakes that spread over fresh ice like a white veil cast on the darkness, of white or purple butterflies fluttering helpless as petals in the wind, of the poignancy of all these images in their fragility and ambiguous status at the fringes of imagining, as all-but-abstract virtualities . . .

The sense of alienation created by the techniques of strangeness may therefore be a temporary phase. The reader can move from perplexity to creative participation, provided he does not insist on instant literal communication and is prepared to allow his analogical faculties to scan for the underlying associative patterns.

Such indeed is the strategy to be recommended in approaching any work of art which at first seems arbitrary, nonsensical or obscure. But what of a work which is occulted in an apparently total way? In speaking of the poetry of Trakl, I drove my argument to its limit in suggesting that his writing tended more and more to an autistic extreme whereby each poem was a separate entity dissociated from the rest of his work, and where in the end, his very vocabulary was 'alienated' from all context in the sense that a verbal signifier might not correspond to anything remotely like the signified we might expect. Trakl's poems appeared to Rilke 'as impenetrable as the space within a mirror'. But this view now needs revision.

In theory, a text written by a person in a state of extreme psychosis would seem logically to resist all interpretation by a sane reader. It would be like reading a text in an unknown language without a dictionary and with no knowledge of the subject matter. However, in practice, it appears that even extreme psychopathological processes tend to generate texts which move in the direction of sense.[11] This is because, despite the weird distortions that may occur in terms of syntactical aberrations, neologisms and abstruse symbols, the psychotic normally does still have recourse to the vocabulary shared by other people. Theoretically, as I have said, we have no guarantee that when the psychotic says 'river' he will mean what *we* mean by that word: the signifier may point to a signified to which we have no access. But once we read our way into the psychotic text, we are more than likely to find that the patterns of relations between the signifiers still maintain a connection with the patterns we attribute to the signifieds. For example when the schizophrenic poet Ernst Herbeck writes

blau ist der Strand der Donau

(Navratil, 1977, 59)

(blue is the beach of the Danube),

we may assume that the poet has taken the cliché 'the blue Danube' and subjected it to an arbitrary revision, transferring the colour from the water of the river to the beach along the riverside. But to do this is surely not just to play with words in the abstract: that Herbeck is able to supply the word *beach* after thinking of *the blue Danube* is surely to be explained in terms of a true visualisation of the river. To put it another way, the image is startling, but not *startling enough* to throw us out of all sense of there being a stable referential context on which the poem draws. The power of vocabulary to refer is not, I think, something that the psychotic ever really suppresses: hence to read his text should not create so radical a despair in the interpreter that he feels all persistence in reading to be doomed.

In returning to Trakl, I can now make the case that his poetry does not in practice equate to my earlier model of a series of blank signs deprived of all referentiality and dimension. In my discussion of his erratic colour allusions, I suggested that the shift from connotations of pain to connotations of pleasure in the single semantic unit *silbern* could be an index of a discrepancy at the level of both expression and existence, and that such discrepancy is not something to which our ordinary experience of literature or of life prepares us. At the same time, such discrepancy, once registered by the reader, may be identified as a theme and taken as seriously as any other theme in literature. This

can be a beginning of communication, once we are able to recognise in
Trakl someone who uses words to a purpose.

I also indicated that an effort of patient concentration on individual
poems could be a way forward. What we should do is to attend lucidly
to what is special about each poem as it is placed before us. When I
selected the two extracts from Trakl for my examples, it was because
I had been forcibly struck by the distinctive flavour of each text.

Silbern weint ein Krankes
Am Abendweiher

and

Grünlich dämmert der Fluss, silbern die alten Alleen
Und die Türme der Stadt. O sanfte Trunkenheit . . .

are couplets whose tone or atmosphere emerge unequivocally as being,
on the one hand, depressive, and on the other, cheering. Such an iden-
tification of mood seems to occur quite spontaneously and has immediate power to shape subsequent impressions. And this is how, in the
actual practice of reading, we find that we *can* cope comfortably with
words like *silbern*. For instance, no sooner has the sensibility registered
an emotional nexus in the first example — weeping, the 'sick thing', a
pool at evening — than the associative spectrum of the word *silbern* is
scanned, with strong connotations of deathliness and decay pressing on
the mind. The pool, by association, becomes visualised as having a stagnant slime on its surface or round its rim, which gleams with a dank and
repellent silveriness. Conversely in the second example, despite a reference to dusk, the general climate is so much one of 'sweet tipsiness'
('sanfte Trunkenheit') that the silver which shines from the towers and
the old lanes (or, by extension, from the roofs of old buildings along
the lanes) seems to radiate in a positive way, reflecting the warm light
of a lingering sun, and thus encouraging us not to entertain the possibility of negative connotations accruing to the preceding reference to
the greenish gleam of the river at dusk. The mood remains agreeable,
and even euphoric. Such involvements as these convince me that while
I am a long way from fully adapting myself to Trakl's world, I can feel
confident that it does have something to offer me, and will not turn out
to be a blank and inanimate space.

In summary, then, I am saying that the hints released by the semantic
thrust (even the inconsistent or incoherent semantic thrust) of words in

a poem will tend to open up immediate directions to the reader's imagination, which will thereby rapidly place a putative construction upon the text. The imagination is often so quick off the mark that the intellect has scarcely started to grapple with the poem before a mood or connotative field has strongly asserted itself. Whereas the reading of a straightforwardly informative piece of prose — a newspaper report, a lawyer's letter, an instruction leaflet — is an intellectual activity which can proceed smoothly because it is not interrupted by promptings from the other faculties, the reading of a poem is a far more complex procedure wherein the intellectual apprehension of syntactical and semantic configurations is supplemented and sometimes even supplanted by non-rational impulses, active right across the psychophysical system at large. The scanning that allows us to elicit patterns of meaning in all this is finally not so much a scanning of the words on the page as of the subjective responses vibrating within the wide connotative field which the reading of those words has activated.

The full participation of the reader in the poetic process thus presupposes that there is a fertile supply of responses emerging from his extra-intellectual circuitry. Where these responses are not forthcoming, his reading will be bleak, lifeless, unpleasurable, and the text might as well be dull prose. Reading a poem as though it *were* no more than prose is indeed a singularly pointless enterprise (unless one is deliberately trying to startle oneself into visualising the statements therein as being literally *true*, like reading Carroll and trying to accept that in real life a postage stamp might at any time be mistaken for an albatross). The effective way to read a poem is to approach the activity as a fertile living experience, not as a cut-and-dried conceptual exercise.

6   THE POEM OPENS ONTO THE WORLD

In stressing that the reader's apprehension of a poem is the fulfilment of the creative gesture initiated by the poet, I am envisaging the poem as the centre of a *relation* which constitutes the bond, however momentary, between the transmitter and the recipient of the poetic message. But the poem is not just one relation, it is a whole cluster of relations. Within its own immediate sphere, there are those verbal units we call words, all of which interrelate at the level of syntax and semantics. Moving beyond the boundaries of the text, we can perceive that these patterns relate to the world of meanings that lies outside the literary artefact. In viewing a poem by Reverdy as, in the Cubist perspective, a free-floating verbal microcosm, I suggested that the literary structure was intended as something decontextualised, distantiated from contingent reality. Now in a straightforward sense it is indeed the case that a poem cannot contain any literal residue of the material and emotional world we inhabit. Words are arbitrary signs without initiative in themselves: only human convention sustains their referential power. So that if we were to look at a text in a deliberately cold and indifferent way we might indeed see it as an entity which, if it had any spatial dimension at all, would be the locale of an absence. But reading is not like this: reading is an *intentional act*, one which channels the verbal signs towards signification, lending them direction and life, summoning up the language object to manifest itself as meaning, as presence.

In a strange way, then, it is the privilege of literary artefacts — 'fictions' we may call them — to be intrinsically empty, and yet liable to come across so powerfully when they are read that firm relations between sign, substance and reader come into being. Remembering Giacometti's sculpture *The Invisible Object*, we may now appreciate that work more fully as an allegory of the dynamism of figurative form. The hands of the woman delicately enclose what appears to be a void: the object she clasps with such mesmerised dedication is invisible, absent. And yet so intense is her concentration, her projection of emotional value upon this invisible object, that we are able to imagine it as something which, if literally empty, is figuratively full. The invisible object is, on this reading of Giacometti's work, the perfect emblem of the figure of speech. It represents those verbal forms which we call images, or when they are extended, whole poems. As an absence which an act of imagination calls forth marvellously into a presence, the invisible object is a sign of the capacity of poetic speech to conjure up certainties of visible and tangible realness. In a flat-footed sense, a poem is exempt from exterior contact; in a logological perspective, it even shuns links to the world. But in the mature perspective which I hope by now to have established, a perspective which might roughly be called 'phenomenological', the poem is seen as an intentional appeal to the real world, and may even be said to *demand the context of reality* for its full and final realisation.

A poem by Rainer Maria Rilke offers an alternative illustration of this idea. 'Die Rosenschale' explores the modernistic theme of refusing external reference in the interests of a purely aesthetic apotheosis. The theme is rendered through the symbolic presentation of a bowl of roses, each of which appears as a perfectly self-contained emblem of the beautiful. But then the paradox is uncovered: the state of 'self-containment' does not signify the hermetically-sealed emptiness of cold aesthetic form.

> Und sind nicht alle so, nur sich enthaltend,
> wenn Sich-enthalten heisst: die Welt da draussen
> und Wind und Regen und Geduld des Frühlings
> und Schuld und Unruh und vermummtes Schicksal
> und Dunkelheit der abendlichen Erde
> bis auf der Wolken Wandel, Flucht und Anflug,
> bis auf den vagen Einfluss ferner Sterne
> in eine Hand voll Innres zu verwandeln.
>
> (Rilke, 1955, 554)

(And are they not all like this, containing but themselves, / if self-containment means: to take the world out there / and the wind, the rain, the patience of spring / and guilt and unease and masked destiny / and the darkness of the earth at dusk, / even the changings of the clouds, their flight and drift, / even the vague influence of remote stars, / and to transform all this into a handful of inwardness.)

Far from being ideal Mallarméan roses, figures of virtuality or absence, these flowers have an active role as the foci of a poetic vision. In a marvellously evocative list of aspects of the outer world, which includes human emotions along with physical phenomena like rain, clouds and stars, Rilke draws together the sweep of all creation into a single 'handful of inwardness', the poetic intuition of a unity within multiplicity, and the coincidence of consciousness with the plenitude of the cosmos. The rose bowl positively sucks all reality unto itself, and as such becomes a representation of Rilke's aesthetic ideal, the poetic text which is an autonomous object at the same time as it demands comparison and contact with the orders of sensation and emotion.

In proposing that poetry is no longer to be seen in antithesis to direct experience of the world, I am adopting the view of William Carlos Williams when he writes that

> The province of the poem is the world.
>   (Williams, 1963, 99)

This is the view that there is a special affinity between the verbal plot which is the poem, and the universal ground of reality at large, and that poetic experience is what reveals the relation of the one to the other. That is, the savouring of a decisive line of poetry can be an affirmation of an expressive channel which links word to world, and thereby consciousness to reality. True poems should be seen as organisms which breathe the air of the world, not as dead letters: theirs is an energy which impels them towards existence, and through our reading of poems we can hope, in certain moments of felicity, to transcend our normal limits and gain through their mediation a sense of startled participation in the manifoldness of life.

Now, to speak so lyrically may not seem appropriate in a book which deals with generic issues concerning the values and ambitions of poetic writing. But can one remain detached and sober on such a subject? Jacques Dupin does not censor his enthusiasm when, in an ostensibly 'critical' introduction to the poetry of Char, he executes an impetuous slide from the idea that poetry deals in figures to the idea that such figures have literal force.

> The poet does indeed believe in the reality of language, and in its power to seize and transform reality. He knows that the words which represent fire and signify burning, are capable of setting off a real blaze; that it is not necessary to describe a flower in order to convey the smell of its glory and fragility; that language can not only stigmatize the tyrant but also strike him down; that death, evoked flippantly, can rise up and pounce at the turn of a phrase ... The poem gathers up and destroys the mobile totality of the reality of the world and of language so as to institute their fusion.   (Raillard, 1974, 157)

It seems preposterous for Dupin to claim literal magic efficacy for poetic language. The word 'flame' can be written on paper, for instance, without the paper getting scorched. It would be superstitious to believe otherwise. The word 'flower' has no fragrance, and political slogans are not in themselves the material weapons of an insurrection. It appears to make no sense to take Dupin as literally as he seems to demand to be taken. But let us seek to grasp the procedures of communication within which he is operating. In effect, Dupin is relying on a special kind of pact with his reader whereby the poet will make the hyperbolic claim to be stating the literal truth and the reader will agree to allow these statements to have maximum impact on his mind. And in a peculiar way, which I surmise to be bound up with the whole secret of poetic efficacy, I, as reader, do find myself persuaded that Dupin is saying something valid, while agreeing with the objective riposte that his manner of argument is in conflict with literal material fact. Dupin states that a poem should lift up and destroy material reality and language — destroy in the sense of abolishing their differences? — and then fuse them into one. This seems to be a proposition demanding to be translated into plainer terms before we can at all adjust our understanding to it. But the statement stands, and to water it down risks betraying the author's intention. We are obliged to take the proposition at face value, and to try to grasp the 'truth' of the metaphoric union it advances. It may be over-hasty for me to ask at this stage that we give Dupin our trust: but at least, as I understand him, he intends that we should grasp the implausible though infinitely exciting notion that poetry and reality are in some magical way equivalent. In fact what is happening is that the manner of Dupin's speech and what he says are dual aspects of the same principle: he is asking us to accept that metaphoric discourse (poetry) and external reality (the realm of the literal) should be acknowledged as contiguous, or better: intimately joined, even interpenetrating. Essentially this relation is analogous to the relation we normally recognise between literal and figurative usage in ordinary speech. Except that here, we are being asked to take Dupin's statement both literally and figuratively at once.

Let us turn to easier ways of justifying the view that poetry is grounded within a context of reality, ones which involve less of a strain on the reader's willingness to give credence to figurative discourse as a medium of literal truth. Yves Bonnefoy states the relation of the poetic to the material domain in a more cautious way, suggesting that it is a matter of our verifying the former by testing it against the latter: 'La poésie se poursuit dans l'espace de la parole, mais chaque pas en est vérifiable dans le monde réaffirmé' (Bonnefoy, 1970, 213). (Poetry is pursued within the space of language, but each step taken can be verified in the world, which is thereby re-affirmed.) Poetry is validated, then, by being set *in relation* to reality, an operation which can only be carried out if the reader has participated fully in the poem and can therefore project the illumination it offers onto the world around him. Once he does so, Bonnefoy claims, that world will itself be illuminated and so given a fresh validity, a 're-affirmation'.

Much the same point has been argued apropos of the paintings of the Impressionists. Pierre Mabille, for example, writes that the characteristic features of a canvas by an Impressionist such as Monet – the way sunlight is refracted by foliage and plays in flickers of nuanced colour on a girl's cheek, the surface of a river, etc. – were absorbed by the public in such a passionate way that afterwards they found themselves actually *seeing* the same phenomena in the natural world, which previously had passed unnoticed.[12]

Mabille goes on to contend that for a later generation Surrealist painting similarly opened up perspectives onto landscapes hitherto unnoticed, though no less real for all that. Here, though, the development is more complex in that these new landscapes are 'inner' landscapes, i.e. Surrealist art affords insights into the realm of the unconscious, lighting it up so to speak in order that we should witness its reality – and therefore its contiguity to the world of conscious experience (Mabille, 1949, 186-7). The drift of Mabille's argument here fits nicely into my earlier discussion of the way Surrealist poetry affects the sensibility. Far from being an escape from 'normal' reality into a remote realm of fantasy, the Surrealist imagination proposes the exploration and eventual appropriation of areas of experience hitherto kept in the dark, or categorised as unreal. Just as Monet made the diffusion of light real to us, so Surrealism makes the interconnectedness of the unconscious real to us. Both sorts of artistic transmission are in a sense metaphoric (Salvador Dali, for instance, did not literally 'photograph' his unconscious, as he claimed): and yet both attain validity for us by virtue of our willingness to verify them against our immediate experience. What we might term the concrete potential of a work of art is thus the capacity of a creative work, born within the limits of the formal or the figurative, to radiate with such an intensity that the observer is convinced that its illumination continues beyond those limits and into the world beyond. In this sense, any 'absence' in the aesthetic domain becomes a movement towards presence, the abstract tendency of the intellect being countered by a revivifying concreteness.

It seems to me that art which refuses to countenance the test of
reality must become desiccated and ultimately self-condemning. The
poet, painter and sculptor Hans Arp used to like to see his so-called
biomorphic sculptures — stone forms which are not literally representational, yet which seem directly to echo Nature's typical shapes and
rhythms — erected in a wood or on a hill, so as to demonstrate that
they could stand comparison with the natural world. Or rather: to
demonstrate that in the end there is no need for comparison, since
both carved stone and natural site participate in the same fundamental
processes. Each mirrors the other: each is a figure of its counterpart.
Why not then imagine placing one of Arp's poems up against nature
too?

les pierres sont remplies d'entrailles. bravo. bravo.
   les pierres sont remplies d'air.
   les pierres sont des branches d'eaux.

(From 'L'Air est une racine', in Arp, 1966, 103)

(the stones are full of entrails. bravo. bravo. the stones are full of air. /
the stones are branches of waters)

To read the written text against the greater text of a landscape would
be to attempt a practical test of the reciprocity of word and world. It
could lead to the attestation, counter-signed by the participating sensibility of the reader-observer, that verbal patterns do indeed lead to a
new appreciation of natural patterns, and vice versa. This is at least the
theory I am proposing; it still needs fuller examination.

One of the fundamental values offered by the poem which can measure up to reality is the sense of *contact*. Meditating on a pebble held in
his hand, the critic Raymond Jean expounds the idea that contact has
become a central theme and indeed ambition of modern art. We are no
longer concerned with the thing *as thought about*, nor the thing *as
represented*, but with the thing *given* (cf. Jean, 1965, 14-15). In other
words, we may have reached a point in the history of reading where
what we demand of a poetic text is no longer that it should propose to
us a distant demonstration of pleasingly articulated gestures, but that it
should present us with an experience of direct participation in those
gestures. It is perhaps this triumph of immediacy, the abolition of all
distance between the defining word and the defined sensation, which is
caught in Rimbaud's elliptical announcement

L'air et le monde point cherchés. La vie.

('Veillées', in Rimbaud, 1960, 281)

(Not a pursuit of air and the world. Just life.)

As I read it, this is a declaration of an immediate apprehension of reality, an assertion of the power of words to become 'accessible to all the senses', and as such a flat contradiction of Rimbaud's other phrase, 'elles n'existent pas', which was examined in Chapter 1.

The certainty of contact is unfortunately a very subjective matter. The responses which determine that a pattern of verbal signs shall enter into my mind with such force that I literally shiver, are impossible to monitor exactly, let alone replicate within other sensibilities. Let me at least cite a text which has had such an effect on me, in the hope that something of its impulse can be communicated in illustration of my point. It is a short prose poem by René Char.

FRÉQUENCE

Tout le jour, assistant l'homme, le fer a appliqué son torse sur la boue enflammée de la forge. A la longue, leurs jarrets jumeaux ont fait éclater la mince nuit du métal à l'étroit sous la terre.

L'homme san se hâter quitte le travail. Il plonge une dernière fois ses bras dans le flanc assombri de la rivière. Saura-t-il enfin saisir le bourdon glacé des algues?

(Char, 1967, 23)

(FREQUENCY / All day long, collaborating with the man, the iron has pressed its torso to the fiery mud of the forge. Eventually their twin hocks have made the slender night of the metal burst from its narrow location below ground. / The man, without hurrying, leaves his work. One last time he plunges his arm into the darkened flank of the river. Will he at last be able to grasp the icy bell of waterweed?)

For hours on end on a hot summer's day, the blacksmith has been the slave of his forge. Hammer and furnace have strained to the task, but it has been a noisy, inhuman struggle to summon forth the miracle of metal. The first half of the poem establishes a mood of stifling heat and muscular effort. My response to this is not particularly intense, but I do register a distinct atmosphere, and it is against this that the second half of the poem will introduce the shock of fresh sensation. The man comes to the end of his work, and prepares himself for rest. Through the day, he has been able to experience momentary escapes from the infer-no of the forge by dipping his hot arms in the cool river. Now he carries out this ritualistic act for the last time, this time reaching so deep down as to come close to grasping the waterweed on the riverbed. It is the rendering of this moment which, for me, occurs with such immediacy as to create the effect of a sensation. The sensation is not raw, of course, it is mediated through language, and within a context built up by the connotations to which my consciousness has acceded. I first elect to take *bourdon* to mean a large bell (the meaning seems more productive than the word's other meanings, which include 'humble-bee' and 'organ bass-pipe'; here, the semantic choices seem as plentiful at the level of denotation as they normally are at that of connotation!). I then see the image 'le bourdon glacé des algues' as on one level a peri-phrase for a clump of weeds growing on the icy riverbed, and on another as a symbolic allusion to some secret quintessential power with-in the archetypal element of water, which the poem so clearly establi-shes in contrast to fire. My mind is already moving towards further connotations and patterns. But my point here is a simple one, and I shall forgo fuller rumination on the poem in order to highlight what Char achieves in this reference to the arm plunging into the icy depths. There is here a sudden concentration of semantic impulses such that I almost feel the sensation of cold water on my own skin. The fact that I feel in all honesty bound to say 'almost', that is, to conceptualise what I feel as a meta-sensation, a mental *frisson* which approaches but never literally attains physiological status, this does not detract from the singular force of Char's evocation as I experience it.

What Winifred Nowottny calls 'studied erosion of the boundary between figurative and literal' (Nowottny, 1962, 183) is a poetic procedure which can lead to effects akin to hallucination. Certain poe-tic structures are capable of generating eidetic suggestions sufficiently strong that the unreality of the text takes on material form. The para-doxical result of the Surrealists' experiments in verbal automatism, seemingly oriented towards the total denial of physical reality, was the discovery that words can become concrete. During the 'period' of sleeps' evoked in Louis Aragon's *Une Vague de rêves*, the Surrealist poets did nothing but scribble all day long and finally reached a pitch of physical and mental exacerbation which conduced to hallucinations every bit as stunning as those of Rimbaud:

We would see a written image which at first presented itself with the character of something fortuitous, arbitrary, reach our senses and

there shed its verbal aspect in order to assume that phenomenal
reality which we had always believed it impossible to provoke, as
something fixed, outside of our imagination.   (Aragon, 1924, 18)

In later life, Breton was to comment on the dangerousness of the first
automatic text *Les Champs magnétiques*, claiming that at least one
image produced by the automatic method, that of a 'Jesuit in a blond
tempest', took on a spurious and yet frightening consistency such that,
Breton insists, he began literally to see the threatening swaying of the
Jesuit's robe as it came closer . . . (Breton, 1970a, 9). In a different context again, I will quote a couplet by Ingeborg Bachmann which similarly asserts a belief in the sensory immediacy of purely imaginary
entities.

Nebelland hab ich gesehen,
Nebelherz hab ich gegessen.

> (Bachmann, 1956, 35)

(I have seen fog-land / I have eaten of fog-heart.)

Here we can safely say that the thing the poetess claims to have tasted
is an unreal substance without natural parallel. It is indeed a paradoxical substance in that *fog* is impalpable while *heart* is tangible; the two
concepts are fused into what can only 'exist' as an imagined synthesis.
Reason alone will reject the image, but if the reader allows the substance some credence and brings his imaginative awareness to bear upon
it, it is not impossible that he will elicit the soupçon of a taste. My personal responses to the image lead me into synesthetic associations (e.g.
the taste of the fog as a misty shade of purple) — associations which for
all their subjective character give me a pleasure which I cannot accept as
being uniquely self-induced and without relevance to Bachmann's
actual words.

Novalis once observed that 'genius is the capacity to discuss imaginary objects as though they were real ones, and indeed to treat them like
real ones' (Novalis, 1962, 343). A truly empathetic reading of works of
imagination will depend on the reader's capacity not just to toy with
them as virtualities, but to make *contact* with them as realities. The
means to ensure this are simple to describe, though I cannot claim that
it is easy to effect them. They consist in first becoming conscious of the
verbal creation as it takes shape in its imaginary space, as a figurative,
unreal entity; and then in nourishing that shape with all the resources

of the creative imagination so that it starts to flourish as something real. To entertain the figure of speech as something verging on the literal means attributing to the words, hitherto seen as 'intransitive', a new and exciting *transitivity*. The figure of speech then begins to direct intentional energies into perceptual space. Breton's slogan 'the imaginary is that which tends to become real' is echoed in Williams's scarcely less provocative proclamation that 'the work will be in the realm of the imagination as plain as the sky is to a fisherman' (Breton, 1966a, 100; Williams, 1970, 102). It is as though in its ostensible cultivation of unreality and hermeticism, poetry has been gaining time, gathering strength, so that it can now burst forth on the reader with maximum impact.

These are giddy claims, and I cannot expect them to be ratified by my reader's intellect alone. At this point in the discussion, I would feel happier if I could introduce some persuasive influence into my text which would induce the kind of sympathy necessary for him to appreciate what I am saying. Short of trying to cast my own verbal spells, let me at least turn to a fresh example of creative participation which may add weight to my assertions.

J.A. Baker's book *The Peregrine* describes a man's attempt to participate in the non-human experience of a wild creature. The peregrine falcon hunts its prey by swooping down from immense heights, and its most remarkable characteristics are its skilful and varied flight – it can hover, glide, jink, stoop, stab and so forth – and the uncanny alertness and power of its eyesight. In order to study this creature of the upper air, the writer calls upon his own physical faculties – his eyesight, his ability to move – and supplements them artificially by means of powerful binoculars and a bicycle. But these are imperfect instruments, and as he trains his vision on the swerving bird in the sky, he needs also to apply his imagination in order to comprehend the exact meaning of its actions. The book has what may be termed a 'realistic' intent, and yet to fulfil that intent Baker is obliged to go beyond objective observation.

> In my diary of a single winter I have tried to preserve a unity binding together the bird, the watcher, and the place that holds them both. Everything I describe took place while I was watching it, but I do not believe that honest observation is enough. The emotions and behaviour of the watcher are also fact, and they must be truthfully recorded.   (Baker, 1970, 11)

If Lefebve is right in saying that 'to give way to fascination is to surren-

der to that which is *other*' (Lefebve, 1965, 123), then the author of
The Peregrine is one who falls in love with that which is alien *because* it
is alien. Much of his passion seems bound up with his difficulty in pic-
turing to himself the way the countryside must look from hundreds of
feet up. Often he chases after the gliding hawk on his bicycle, clutching
a map, striving to recreate by way of an imagined animation of the flat
signs on the paper, the way the landscape must appear to the bird.
Months of patient pursuit create in him a sense of intimacy, even com-
plicity with the peregrine. Shunning other men, he enters into a pact
with the wild creature and becomes a hunter who kills through his
familiar. Although there are passages in the book which suffer from an
over-straining for stylistic effect, Baker generally manages to translate
his empathy with the hawk into remarkable reconstructions of what it
sees and how it experiences its world of air and wind and space. And in
rare moments of perfect coincidence, he finds himself coming close to
apprehending the actual perceptions of the hawk:

> He saw it all, as he swung and swayed round the glittering gun-sight
> of his eye's deep fovea, and watched for a flash or spurt of wings at
> which to aim his headlong flight. I watched him with longing, as
> though he were reflecting down to me his brilliant unregarded vision
> of the land beyond the hill.   (Baker, 1970, 116)

The 'as though' in the last sentence here can be seen as the pivotal
point in the operation of imaginative participation. It is the transitional
moment where imagined vision, metaphoric and thus unreal, becomes
actual vision, literal and real. The 'as though' can function rather like an
intransitive verb which we suddenly discover may be used transitively.
To the extent that the book is powerful in its evocations, and offers
convincing evidence that a human being and a bird have indeed established a kinship, the formal reservation announced by Baker in the
figurative marker seems to be constantly overruled by a kind of pressure towards the literal. In other words, the involved reader will tend to
read the passage in a way that imparts transitivity and ignores the 'as
though'.

I cannot help sounding impressionistic here, for an isolated quotation cannot amount to a convincing demonstration that Baker actually
succeeds in conveying a 'real' sense of the peregrine to myself as reader.
But whether or not the example is conclusive, I think it offers a clear
enough allegory to communicate my point about the tendency of the
imagination to veer towards the true field of the real. What I am driving

at is this: after the man has studied the peregrine in the sky he looks at his map and finds it possible to *bring that map alive* by implementing his intuitive understanding of how the landscape must look to the bird. Now the same thing can happen with the reading of a poem: viewing the text from the ground level of cautious objectivity the reader will see only flatness, a system of conventional signs without depth or colour. But if he can create for himself an imaginative perspective equivalent to that of the man projecting his vision into that of the soaring hawk, he will perceive the text no longer as a statement *about* reality, a pale reflection of the facts, but as something which focuses directly upon and even *coincides with* the actual world. In short, just as the map is potentially a landscape, so the poem can merge into that reality of which it speaks: its verbal topography will be seen to coincide with the topography of the real world, much as, in one of Borges's fantasies, an emperor has a map drawn up to the scale of 1:1, so that it ends up covering his entire empire point for point, eventually merging indiscriminately with the landscape it represents, in a magical union of sign and substance (Borges, 1975, 131).

Once we accept that the poem takes on meaning by a process of absorption through all the faculties — intellect, emotion, sensory awareness and the rest — it clearly becomes something more than an arrangement of signs. One might dramatise the transformation by speaking of the poetic figure of speech as representative of what happens to the total poem when it is thus read. First, let us suppose that we are faced with a verbal proposition in the form of a simile, that is, a proposition whose status is designated by the marker 'as though' (whether or not this is actually verbalised or is simply implied by the surrounding context). Such a proposition is clearly being projected as a hypothesis, something less than real, and will be a disappointment to the reader who hates his poetry to be escapist. (Stevens writes bitterly of 'the intricate evasions of as' (Stevens, 1955, 486).) But what really counts is *how we read* the simile, not its apologetic label. What we must do is to take 'as though' not as an invitation to ease up, but as an invitation to concentrate the imagination. If we are bold, we will begin to read the simile as a metaphor, calling up its potencies and ignoring its hesitations. The full latent energy of the words is now released, as the trope asserts itself as literal statement and suddenly impinges on the reader's sensibility rather than his intellect alone. At this point, engagement is complete. And in just the same way that the single image strikes home, so the total poem can come alive. Like the map which becomes a landscape, it passes from the status of inferior simulacrum to that of double. By this I mean that the poem, in its ultimate flowering, takes on the character of a reality on a par with other realities, defined specifically as *that which it articulates*. In other words, what the poem says is at once (a) a statement *about* some aspect of reality, and (b) an entity *within* the real life of its reader. What we witness here is nothing less than the commingling of the signifier and the signified. Both the verbal object and the experiential complex it embodies end up as doubles, each mirrored in the other, with the reader, so to say, as the medium of this reciprocity.

Since Romanticism there have been poets who consciously apply themselves to the task of articulating a concord which they intuit between the inner world of mental and emotional experience and the outer world of material experience. Some might term this a mystical search, a quest for the reconciliation of the alienated consciousness with the seemingly resistant objects outside it. The ideas about reading which I have been sketching in recent pages correspond closely to the ideas associated with this poetic quest, so much so that I am tempted to say that my argument is a recommendation that the reader turn himself into a poet, appropriating the mystical posture of those who strain towards oneness with the non-self, and thus moving towards oneness with the poem. And in the end, there is no great difference in the two postures, beyond the fact that the reader is limited by the text before him (since I am not actually asking him to re-write that text); whereas the poet is presumably free at any time to alter his focus and switch from object to object in his search for contact with the outer world.

Where do these non-rational experiences take us? Are we completely adrift in an area of faith? Can intelligence have any part of all this? Let us not feel alarmed. I want to endeavour to show that the direction in which we are moving does not lead to a situation in which we will end up splashing around in a spill of arbitrary responses. On the contrary, I see these experiences as being governed by a special logic and necessity. But to make quite sure that our sense of balance is not affected, let me go back briefly over some of the terrain covered earlier.

In the first chapter of this book I spoke of poetry as creating un-reality, an antithesis to what we might call surface reality. I there suggested that there might actually be a certain pleasure, even, in witnessing the patent difference between the one and the other. Rimbaud's whispered commentary on the dreamt-up flag of bleeding meat and arctic flowers that 'they do not exist' emerged as a device to intensify poetic excitement by underlining the illusory nature of the objects fashioned in words. But can it be satisfying in the long term to remain at the point of intersection where unreality and reality are so firmly dissociated? Pierre Reverdy has said that he finds it unpleasant to be caught in this 'difficult and often perilous position, at the intersection, with its cruelly acute cutting-edge, of the two planes of dream and reality' (Reverdy, 1968, 18). Thus it may turn out that it is painful to differentiate between private unreality (dream) and existence (reality). I would extrapolate from Reverdy's statement and say that poets do not in fact want to consign their fantasies to an alternative and hypothetical realm where what they say can be easily disregarded by people who prefer to set their sights on the real world. That whispered comment of Rimbaud's might in fact be highly sardonic: 'I'm telling you they don't exist, those flowers, because, dear reader, I know that's what you like to hear. I'll play along with you, because it amuses me to see how you lap up my reassurance that poetry is mere fantasy. But just you wait: poetry will catch up with you yet.' What Rimbaud and the other makers of unreality may in fact want is to find readers for whom poetry is *meaningful within life*, and not an escapist indulgence or an aesthetic frisson within brackets. Poets are people who have direct experience of both the seductions of language and the attractions of certain aspects of material life, and they tend to dream of an osmosis of subjectivity and objectivity, of pleasure in prolonged encounters rather than in wistful partings. What now of Bousquet's dream woman, 'so much a presence that you had no need of light to see her'? Was she not a reality to him? Here we may turn back to Lefebve also, who confirms that the fact of the matter is that those images which stress their illusory character can suddenly, by virtue of a mysterious reversal, come across to us with all the plenitude of actual appearances.

> There is a moment when the image affirms itself *as* image and appears, exactly as in a dream, to be separated from our life, existing as the sole guardian of a time and a space proper to itself alone; it is at this very moment that the quality of unrealness, which had initially condemned it as being the merest trickery, suddenly takes on the consistency of being, of true reality, of the absolute.   (Lefebve, 1965, 69-70)

Where Joë Bousquet is concerned, the evidence is that in general he did not trouble to pass through this procedure, for he admits quite coolly that 'I have never known very well where reality begins'

(Bousquet, 1934, 131) — nor, I might add, where unreality stops. For such a poet, the intersection of the planes of fantasy and literal experience is a line that can be crossed at will, so that there is no need even to mark it out. For others, a more painstaking effort is necessary in order to achieve an accommodation of the demands of surface reality with those of poetic invention. Their investment of energies in this quest is immense, but the effort seems worthwhile because of the marvellous promise that, in the end, the poet may not just cross the border from time to time, but will actually erase that border and so arrive at Bousquet's enviable position. The ultimate fusion of the verbal and the material of which Dupin speaks must be nothing less than a dialectical process, one which does not simply yoke one to the other, but creates out of their union a third and new entity which can be called poetic reality (or deep reality, absolute reality, etc.).[13]

These transactions between interior and exterior states, between figure and reality, form the subject matter of many of Wallace Stevens's poems. I want to quote a representative meditation on poetry and its functions, taken from the lengthy 'Notes towards a Supreme Fiction'. It describes the poet's impressions while sitting in the park one day. As a regular manufacturer of artifice, a long-established director in the 'Theatre of Trope', the poet at first sees his surroundings in terms which deny their naturalness and turn material things into poetic symbols. (The reference to swans may remind us that Mallarmé often did much the same thing.) But as he continues to sit and absorb impressions from the outer world, a state of grace descends upon him, and a rather different vision ensues:

A bench was his catalepsy, Theatre
Of Trope. He sat in the park. The water of
The lake was full of artificial things,

Like a page of music, like upper air,
Like a momentary colour, in which swans
Were seraphs, were saints, were changing essences.

The west wind was the music, the motion, the force
To which the swans curveted, a will to change,
A will to make iris frettings on the blank.

There was a will to change, a necessitous
And present way, a presentation, a kind
Of volatile world, too constant to be denied,

The eye of a vagabond in metaphor
That catches our own. The casual is not
Enough. The freshness of transformation is

The freshness of a world. It is our own,
It is ourselves, the freshness of ourselves,
And that necessity and that presentation

Are rubbings of a glass in which we peer.
Of these beginnings, gay and green, propose
The suitable amours. Time will write them down.

(Stevens, 1955, 397-8)

The poem begins with a denial of sensation: catalepsy is precisely this, a suspension of all sensation and consciousness. Here, though, the bench in the park is still the locus of residual consciousness, since the poet sitting there continues to witness externality. His mind however seems mechanically to turn all things into artifices or tropes. The swans on the lake become 'artificial things' and exist only in the mode of simile (*'like* a page of music', etc.) or of metaphor ('swans / Were seraphs'), finally to become simply 'changing essences', presumably lacking in real identity. On the face of it, the poet's apprehension of the park seems fit to turn it into a frozen unreality, a capricious array of analogies without substance. But fortunately, the natural world is not a state but a field of living actions. Impressions pour into consciousness. The poet intent on derealisation is now obliged to cope with the motions of the swans which come curving in on the wind, making the eye strain ('iris frettings') to focus them against the empty sky ('on the blank'). Sensation is no longer in abeyance, and indeed, retrospectively, how could it have been excluded from the poetic operation, inasmuch as the poet has always been a percipient of the scene before him? The water of the lake which had at first seemed to him 'like a page of music', that is, an artefact patterned by subjectivity, now appears to owe its patterning to the impact of a natural force: 'The west wind was the music, the motion, the force . . .' Far from remaining the smug creator of an autonomous unreality, shaped by fantasy, the poet is now obliged to accept what happens outside him as being meaningful in its own right. The external world is both 'volatile' and 'too constant to be denied'. It has its own powerful ways of behaving, based on constant movement, none of which can be regulated by the subject. Yet if the poet is called back to earth and forced to recognise the inalienable *thereness* of the lake, the swans and so on, he is not necessarily being forced into a posture of passivity or defeat. For Nature might be herself 'a vagabond in metaphor', that is, a capricious dealer in tropes like the poet himself. And when Nature's eye suddenly catches the poet's own, the glance they exchange seems to communicate a sense of mutual recognition. All at once the world shapes itself into clarity and poetic meaningfulness. 'The casual is not enough' – it is true that the moment is something the poet must concentrate upon for it to arise perfectly. Yet when it happens, the state of grace is absolute. It unites consciousness and world to a point where it is impossible to know quite whether it is the poet who has revealed Nature to himself, or Nature which has disclosed the poet's own 'freshness'.

This is a marvellous fusion of brute perception and imaginative vision, subsumed in the one 'will to change' which comprises both *natural* change, i.e. literal transformations of the situation, such as the swans flying away (with all their poignant associations for the poetic sensibility), and *poetic* change, in the sense that the sweep of the imagination has opened a new perspective on things, lending them a freshness which resembles aesthetic purification, yet which continues to honour the specificity and irreducibility of natural fact.

All of this takes place within the poet's consciousness, and at the close he seems to indicate that what has taken place is an experience which still remains to be articulated. It will take him time to write down a text keen enough to match the freshness of those 'beginnings, gay and green'. Yet in a sense, the text *is* written, and it is the poem we have before us. In this sense, the poetic epiphany is available to us as readers, and it is now our turn to respond. Looking closely at the text, we may note that there is a slide from the pronouns *he* to *we*, corresponding to the poet's realisation of his epiphany. On the face of it, this signifies the joining of the poet, *he*, with the world, making *we*. Yet we the readers may feel ourselves implicated in the dialectic also. We are persuaded that what we are reading is happening to us, that the words before us are *our* words. 'The freshness of transformation is / The freshness of a world. It is our own, / It is ourselves, the freshness of ourselves . . .' The fact of reading provides us with an entry into the exciting process of articulating the epiphany. Or perhaps we can even say that our reading itself *creates* the epiphany, given that the revelation is structured by the words *as we read them now*, not on the supposition that it all took place outside the poem, a long time ago.

Freshness, transformation, a sense of the marvellous unification of self and world – these are themes equally central to the poetry of Octavio Paz, a specialist in images and illuminations who constantly

probes towards some kind of central luminosity, instinctively identified
as being the essence of the deeper reality.

> El día
> Es una gran palabra clara
> Palpitación de vocales
>   Tus pechos
> Maduran bajo mis ojos
>   Mi pensamiento
> Es más ligero que el aire
>   Soy real
> Veo mi vida y mi muerte
> El mundo es verdadero
>   Veo
>   Habito una transparencia

('Contigo', in Paz, 1971a, 162)

(The day / Is a great clear word / Palpitation of vowels / Your breasts /
Ripen beneath my eyes / My thought / Is lighter than air / I am real / I
see my life and my death / The world is true / I see / I inhabit a transparency)

The experience evoked here is an almost mystical one, completely by-
passing reason. The poet finds himself as the ecstatic percipient of a
world to which he at last fully belongs — belongs in the act of finding
himself, and of expressing that finding. There is a reference to a woman,
whose beloved body is invested with a privileged sense of fertility and
perfect beauty, and reflects the freshness and plenitude of the world at
large. Poetic consciousness here achieves full coincidence with its objects. The natural world of events and things becomes transparent
before the poet's gaze: he sees through to the heart of the truth, and his
expressive response to what he sees is so instantaneous that it is as
though it were not the poet but the day itself which speaks, clear and
vibrant: 'El día / Es una gran palabra clara / Palpitación de vocales'.
Reality speaks so luminously that the poet's transmission of its utterance is cast in the simplest words: clear, real, true, transparency. This is
a basically abstract vocabulary, and yet the breathless buoyancy of the
poetic delivery is such as to carry us beyond any sense of a dry philoso-
phical discussion of subjectivity and objectivity, even if there were not
also physical allusions (breasts, eyes, air) which bring the senses alertly
into play.

If we look closely at the last three lines of the quotation we can see that they enact a marvellous synthesis of opposites. First, the objective world offers itself to the poetic perception as a totality in which delusion has no place: 'El mundo es verdadero'. Secondly, the focus turns the other way, towards the subject, who proclaims his discovery of pure vision: 'Veo'. Finally, the syntax correlates a concrete verb and an abstract noun, the resulting sentence expressing the union of subject with object: 'Habito una transparencia'.

This experience of the immediacy of vision, of the poetic opening of reality to a consciousness which equally opens to it, is pinpointed in the last word *transparencia*, which carries full force as the climax of the mounting ecstasy expressed in these lines. This transparency becomes present to us as readers in a dual manifestation: both as a *place* — the midway point between materiality and the subjective imagination, that is, the locus of exchange between outer and inner worlds — and a *state* of poetic rapture. Now this state may be said to synthesise the two moments of mental apprehension. For on the one hand, it admits of *contact*, in that the poet is genuinely in touch with the actuality of things about him. And on the other, it sustains that clarity of apprehension which under less passionate circumstances we associate with intellectual *distance* from things, as when the consciousness takes as it were a step back from immediate data, the better to scrutinise them. In Paz's poem, there is no stepping back, nor indeed any need to step forward. There is neither separation nor numbness. The poet inhabits a simple transparency; he is psychically and physically attuned to a known world.

In the last pages, I have tried to give some measure of critical form to what I have suggested to be an almost unverifiable notion, that words written down in certain ways are capable of achieving a genuine purchase upon, and illumination of, the reality around us. The poets I have quoted seem to have no trouble in shifting from statements concerning sensory experience, i.e. statements which point to attested existents like birds in flight or a woman's body, to statements which imply the recognition of a deeper level of being. This level, we have seen, can be immediately accessible to the poet, and the hypothesis he wants to test is that it is also expressible and therefore communicable.

The ideal reader will go along with this expression of deeper reality, this absolute of poetic vision, and take a phrase such as Paz's 'Your breasts / Ripen beneath my eyes' as an observation which was real in the thinking and the writing, and now becomes real once more in the participatory act of reading. However, in practice many readers are not always inclined to follow in the poet's literal footsteps and give unhesitating credence to everything he says. Readers are, I suppose, at liberty to withhold support from the poetic enterprise, to close off their sensibility and maintain a steady stare of intellectual disapproval. For such readers, there is little point in my continuing to argue: by now we should already have gone our separate ways. But, for the reader who does feel the urge to make himself available to poetic meanings, I will offer a final account of what I believe to be an appropriate reading stance.

The mode of reading I recommend amounts to nothing other than maintaining a proper awareness of the way poetic language behaves, as at once a highly figurative discourse *and* a discourse dedicated to profound truths, which it seeks to render actual, shareable, literal. We have, then, the paradox of a figurative discourse which lays claim to literal meanings. Our mode of reading should simply seek to fit into this situation. Let me explain myself by way of an image. If art can be said to hold up a mirror to reality, in such a way that what goes on within the space of the mirror is a figurative version without substance, while on the other side of the glass everything is literal and substantial, then we should, as creative readers, establish our observation post neither on one side nor the other, but along the intersection of the two confronted realms. This means camping in the narrowest of zones, the mid-mirror position.[14] And yet from this tricky position everything becomes transparent for us. On one side we can observe reality in all its unfathomed immediacy; on the other, we can contemplate the artistic process as it seeks to press its attentions upon that world. Perched within the glass of the mirror, we can witness what happens when a statement takes shape inside a poem which purports to have a bearing on the world on the far side of the glass. It is that the figure of speech draws breath and presses towards the mode of literality. A verbal image which has value is one which vibrates through the glass to affect the world of sensation and become an experience in people's real lives. From our mid-mirror position we can truly feel its passage as it reverberates through us.

I must now add the rider that the reader will sometimes need to adjust the stress of certain tropes, transposing them into terms relevant to his experience, as when we 'come to terms' with extravagant or irrational images. Often though, as we have seen, it is precisely those words which meet with resistance at the intellectual level, which in fact set off the richest resonances at the deeper levels. We should therefore avoid a rigid, literalistic reading of poems: this will either lead to an impasse, since the intellect cannot swallow what it sees as patent untruth, or else it will reduce the poetic statement to a single narrow meaning which may fall flat when set against the shifting complexities of real life. A flexible mode of reading must allow the language of metaphor the fullest scope, savouring now its impact as a direct and urgent appeal, now its enigmatic swaying-toward-sense, the release of dark clusters of connotations which must be given time to align themselves into a coherent meaning.

In this process, the reader must be aware of his responsibility as the mediator of meaning. If he at all honours the text before him, he should recognise a duty to treat all figures of speech with equal solemnity, and to lend them, through the resources of his whole sensibility, the energy that will carry them through the glass and into the dimension of literal impact. What might be called 'transparent reading' would be just this, a mode of participation which, within the limits of individual competence and sensitivity, would seek to attend to what the poem is saying and to respond to it directly as though to an important object in the natural world. Reading transparently means arranging one's sensibility to facilitate to the maximum this passage from the figurative to the literal, from word to fact. Only when the reader gives of himself fully can the poem be truly said to open up, through him, onto reality.

Part Three

SIGNS OF THE POETIC

Poetry advances where the real world intensifies its claims on the imagination. 'There are', writes Baudelaire, 'moments of existence when time and space take on extra depth, and the feeling of existence is immensely amplified' (Baudelaire, 1961, 1256). At such times, the world seems to welcome the percipient consciousness: there is a con- cordance of imagination and perception, a harmony between mind and external reality. What Proust calls 'privileged moments' are those giddy instants of awareness when the mind experiences its delicious integra- tion into the material environment. And the poetic is precisely this: the mysterious quality or value which derives from such intuitions or, alter- natively, which impels the poet to envisage his relationship to the real world as one in which there is no interruption of continuity between intentions or expectations and the space within which they operate.

Moments of charmed awareness are among the most irresistible stimuli to poetic writing. Occasions which seem to proclaim the desire of the world to reveal itself to human consciousness are moving experi- ences which demand to be recorded. The experience of waking in an unfamiliar place, for example, can be conducive to a sense of magical participation in outer reality. Robert Bly describes such an awakening in a poem whose unadorned brevity understates and thereby authenti- cates the intensity and fullness of the event.

IN A TRAIN

There is a light snow.
Dark car tracks move in out of the darkness.
I stare at the train window marked with soft dust.
I have awakened at Missoula, Montana, utterly happy.

   (Bly, 1962, 47)

The poet is on a long rail journey in winter and, apparently, has slept overnight. As he wakes, he first registers the simple fact of an external world changed by a coating of whiteness; then he notices the contras- ting darkness of rails and shadows. His gaze focuses on something closer to, the dust on the window. This dust is seen to be 'soft' — the slightly unexpected choice of adjective concentrates our awareness of a whole process of softening, whereby the harsh wintry world outside becomes as one with the warm and cosy space of the train compartment. Aware by now of having achieved a simultaneous focus on outer and inner space, the poet declares his sense of felicity, and records it so to speak in his private log by pinpointing the exact location of the poetic occasion: the township of Missoula, in the state of Montana, alliterated names which at once take on themselves a poetic fragrance.

A similar enchanted awakening occurs in a poem composed nine centuries previously by the Chinese Sung poet Su Tung P'o. It also describes someone emerging from sleep, not quite knowing where he is, and finding external space full of meaning.

SOUTH HALL

Sweep the floor, burn incense, close the door to sleep;
A mat marked like water, curtains like mist.
I dream a guest comes, wake wondering where I am,
Prop open the west window on waves that meet the sky.

(Source unknown)

The place where the poet sleeps seems already strange as he prepares for the night: the floor needs to be swept, incense to be burned before it can become homely. The mat and curtains are described in similes which anticipate what will be seen on awakening, the lake view outside with its water and mist. Finally asleep, the poet has a dream about an unexpected visitor, and awakes having lost all sense of place. To situate himself, he opens the window, and looks out on an immensity of space in which the waves of the lake stretch from window to sky to form a continuum so absolute that it overwhelmingly draws the little room and its occupant into its undifferentiated vastness. As Ezra Pound observed, Chinese ideograms are peculiarly suited to an evocative style of writing. They represent singular units of meaning and a poem is simply a collection of such units which fit together without any of those connecting words which in English make manifest the relations between parts of speech. It is up to the reader to supply the connotations that will link the ideograms into sequential meaning. The process of translation into English is one in which ellipsis has to be expanded into something more explicit. This process can be observed even without reference to the original Chinese text if we turn to a second English version of Su Tung P'o's poem. Kenneth Rexroth's version is twice as long as the one quoted above, and thus represents an articulation of some of the implications which Rexroth found in the Chinese.

THE SOUTHERN ROOM OVER THE RIVER

The room is prepared, the incense burned.
I close the shutters before I close my eyelids.
The patterns of the quilt repeat the waves of the river.
The gauze curtain is like a mist.
Then a dream comes to me and when I awake
I no longer know where I am.
I open the western windows and watch the waves
Stretching on and on to the horizon.

(Rexroth, 1956, 83)

In fact Rexroth's version more or less embroiders on the basic equations identified just now. His text reiterates the analogy between curtain and mist, but goes on cleverly to insert the parallelism between the
closing of shutters and of eyelids. The dream visitation (Rexroth
declines to mention a person as such) announces the movement towards
privileged vision. Emerging from this unreal sleep, the subject experiences a heightened perception of reality: opening his eyes, then the windows, he focuses on an external immensity which somehow seems
accessible as his gaze sweeps out over the water to the horizon. Of
course it is *my* embroidery if I add that this moment is one of ecstatic
revelation, the opening up of the subject's inner vision in response to
the material perception.

The theme of a watery environment and a mind merging into it is
explored at some length in Jean-Jacques Rousseau's *Les Rêveries du
promeneur solitaire*. Exiled on an island in a large Swiss lake, Rousseau
devotes himself to solitary ramblings in which pragmatic observations
of nature are balanced by introspective meditations on his own being.

I used to fling myself alone in a boat which I would take out to the
centre of the lake when the water was calm, and there, lying outstretched on the bottom, my eyes turned skywards, I would let myself drift slowly wherever the water took me, sometimes for long
hours, plunging into a thousand confused yet delightful reveries ...

(Rousseau, 1960, 67)

Lying on a level with the water and gently swayed by its lapping motions, Rousseau experiences a transcendent joy as both mind and body

are absorbed into a timeless sensation of pure existence, from which he only gradually surfaces to a consciousness of his surroundings, unable for a while to distinguish what is subjective daydream from what is perceived reality.

The impulse to conceive of poetic certainty in terms of a laying-hold of space seems typical of much modern poetry. Rimbaud described himself memorably as one who was 'pressé de trouver le lieu et la formule', 'in a hurry to locate the place and the formula', his poetic endeavour being to situate the poetic in a special 'place', identified by perception and confirmed in a verbal formulation (Rimbaud, 1960, 278). Yves Bonnefoy takes up the theme at length in his book *L 'Arrière-Pays*, where he describes his poetic yearning for that 'vrai lieu' or true place of poetic experience. Rather like Nerval, he enjoys toying for a while with exotic place-names – Capraia, Caucasia, Tibet, Appecchio, Brindisi, Venice – in the hope that remote places on the map could literally be the sites where he will catch up with the poetic emotion he is pursuing. Later he realises that this emotion doesn't have to do with a real place *per se*, but with the relation between that place and the consciousness which perceives it. He discovers that the sensation of the poetic has as much to do with expectancy as with certainty, with yearning as much as with triumphant apprehension. There are, after all, places which are poetic when seen from afar yet which lose all their charm once you actually set foot in them.

In isolating the emotion of yearning as a key ingredient in poetic experience, Bonnefoy skates close to an idealistic position whereby nostalgia is highlighted in a position superior to direct apprehension. There are times when he comes close to relinquishing the world of sensation in favour of an attachment to an ideal world which has an abstract and unearthly beauty about it. Yet Bonnefoy eventually reasserts his faith in real external space as the necessary locale of the poetic. The union of *here* (the immediate space of consciousness) and *there* (the distant space of the world outside) is enacted at one of those elective sites which represent a kind of paradigm of poetic fulfilment. Bonnefoy describes the magical synthesis of near and far which he at last achieves when, on a visit to India, he stands on the lofty terrace at Amber and looks out onto a circle of ramparts so constructed as to coincide perfectly with the skyline, thus permitting him a half-perceptual, half-imaginative apprehension of the total space beyond him (Bonnefoy, 1972, 51-5).

Poets often like to locate poetic experiences in specific sorts of places. André Breton feels that castles are 'elective places' possessing a

poetic magnetism of their own: the enigmatic profile of gaunt battle-
ments and turrets, the tantalising idea of secret panels and hidden
passages, the half-echoes of ancient deeds of arms and forgotten pas-
sions, these create for him an atmosphere conducive to marvellous
emotional and mental adventures (cf. Breton, 1928, 150-1). In the
prose poem 'Le Point', Paul Claudel relates a visit to a Chinese ceme-
tery on a site strictly delimited by water and muses on the poetic
'opening of the Earth' to which the place seems to gesture, the glimpse
of a path leading uninterruptedly away from life into death (Claudel,
1973, 355-6). Francis Ponge devotes the whole of his *Carnet du bois de
pins* to the description of a copse, a description which, though it breaks
down into a series of half-failed attempts to hit on the right figures of
speech to express certain features of the copse (the pine needles resemble hairpins, the branches and trunks are like the swaying masts and
rigging of ships in harbour), is sustained by an underlying harmony so
pervasive that one must conclude that for Ponge this little wood is the
exact locus of the poetic. (Ponge, 1947). A similar sense of intimate
intensity is conveyed in the poetic evocations of woods in J.A. Baker's
The Hill of Summer, though here the sense of enigma is foregrounded:
'The interior of a wood is forever beyond our reach, so sunlit and complete, brimming with its own secret life' (Baker, 1969, 52). Maurice-
Jean Lefebve suggests that the attraction of thick woods lies in their
being spaces which open up to us, then close behind us, shutting off the
light and thus utterly transforming our sense of reality. The multiplicity
of perspectives created by the way the trees shift as we advance creates
an uncanny atmosphere in which the call of an unseen bird can constitute 'the perfect manifestation of the strange and the impenetrable'
(Lefebve, 1965, 133). The experience of entering such a dark, fragrant
space, capable of such transformations of perception and appeals to
imagination, may be readily equated with that of entering a poem in
the act of reading.[15]

All these experiences have to do with the poet's readiness not simply
to receive impressions from the world outside, but to meet it halfway
with imaginative impulses that themselves shape perception. What
Gaston Bachelard has defined as the 'material imagination' is that practice of imaginative penetration whereby consciousness projects itself
into meaningful contact with the elements of physical reality. In a
whole series of books, Bachelard has plotted the types of the material
imagination, which he sees as corresponding to the elements of earth,
air, fire and water. Matter, he argues, is the substance on which reverie
thrives, and daydreaming about such sensations as touching stones or

'the exact locus of the poetic'

Paul Nash, *Wittenham Clumps*

Source: Carlisle Museum and Art Gallery

feeling wind on the skin can be creative of intimate encounters between mind and matter and thus annul the distance that separates
consciousness and the world (Bachelard, 1960, 149-50).

Coleridge had already seen imagination as the faculty which links
perception and consciousness, and converts sense data into symbolic
meanings and images. In this sense, the poet is someone who does not
simply observe but who *imagines* the universe. Those who cannot
accept that the universe can be apprehended otherwise than by objective observation will not sympathise with this approach, but poets from
Blake to Robert Duncan have insisted that they cannot proceed otherwise. The latter it is who exclaims: 'How shall we explain that seeing,
touching, smelling, hearing, are all mere and that desire moves us
toward more — and the imagination is of this more. All that is merely
sensible objects to or yields to the urgencies of ours to dream the
world' (Duncan, 1968, 103). This is to say that the poetic is the quality
with which poets engage by way of acts of imagination propelling their
sensibilities into creative contact with things. Poetic reality is thus
reality enhanced; poetic perception is perception channelled by imagination, which Novalis calls 'the wondrous sense which can supplant all
senses for us' (Novalis, 1962, 459).

I propose to examine some of the natural elements to which different poets are drawn, and which represent elective pathways leading
'through' sensation and into contact with poetic realities. Bachelard's
studies of the four elements are simply a convenient way to group the
myriad elective affinities of the poets of whom he speaks. And it would
seem axiomatic that each individual poet should have his own preferences and hence his own distinctive ways of handling poetic experience.
Given the endless range of possible material, I have chosen three arbitrary examples from poems which have to do with three types of weather: fog, rain and snow. I hope these will furnish a sampling of how
different poets react to specific elemental stimuli, and also give us some
idea of the general process whereby a given set of external circumstances may be summoned into poetic significance by virtue of the perspective applied by the creative imagination.

The first example is the opening of George Barker's poem 'Battersea
Park', which sets the stage for what will be a long (and somewhat melo-
dramatic) journey into Barker's emotions. What I want to illustrate is
the way in which a more or less drab setting, a city park by the river,
can be invested with a special meaningfulness.

Now it is November and mist wreathes the trees,
The horses cough their white blooms in the street,
Dogs shiver and boys run; the barges on the Thames
Lie like Leviathans in the fog; and I meet
A world of lost wonders as I loiter in the haze
Where fog and sorrow cross my April days.

(Barker, 1957, 89)

The scene is witnessed at the point where autumn turns into winter,
when the air becomes cold and dark and breath turns to white vapour.
Factually, it is the time when dogs do indeed shiver and boys run to
keep warm. Emotionally, the poem is propelled by the poet's realisation of his ageing and the irrecoverability of youthful happiness: April
days are now available only in the form of memories. Finally, in poetic
terms, the poem can be situated at the meeting-point of the actual and
the emotional. On the one hand there are objective data, trees in the
mist, coughing horses and barges on the river. On the other, there is the
poetic response to these data, and their consequent extension into the
realm of emotional meaning: the mist thus becomes a wreath, the
horses' breath suggests white blooms, and the barges are grandly associated with Leviathans. These associations mingle pleasure with sadness:
the world of poetic vision is 'a world of lost wonders'. The investment
of real data with emotional colour creates a sense of yearning and a
recognition of the inevitability of passing time. Present sorrow disrupts
the reveries of April days. But the most important feature of the verse
is the *fog* which drifts through everything, acting both as literal guarantee of the time and place (it *is* likely to be foggy in November down by
the Thames at Battersea Park) and as the medium of poetic intensification: it is the element which poeticises the scene, and imparts emotional
immediacy.

Let us next consider a prose poem about rain. It is by Julien Gracq,
a writer always drawn to exceptional and even apparently unreal
experiences. For him, rain is the bearer of images and marvellous illusions of perception.

L'AVERSE

Voici le monde couvé sous la pluie, la chaleur moite, le toit des
gouttes et des brindilles, et les molles couvertures d'air aux mille
piqûres d'éclaboussements. Voici la belle sur son lit d'eau, toute
éveillée par la soudaine transparence fraîche, toute coïncidante à

une pure idée d'elle-même, toute dessinée comme l'eau par le verre. Dans l'air où nagent les balbutiantes étoiles de l'eau, une main d'air sort de l'alcôve verdissante aux parfums d'herbe et suspend à l'embrasse de lianes les courtines emperlées et l'arithmétique crépitante du boulier de cristal.

(Gracq, 1958, 36)

(THE SHOWER / Here is the world nestling under the rain, the moist warmth, the rooftop of droplets and twigs, and the soft covers of air with their thousands of splashing pinpricks. Here is the beauty on her bed of water, fully roused by the sudden fresh transparency, coinciding perfectly with a pure idea of herself, completely delimited as water is by a glass. In the air where swim the stammering stars of water, a hand of air emerges from the alcove turning green with its grassy scents, and hangs up on the loop of lianas the pearly curtains and the crackling arithmetic of the crystal abacus.)

On one level, the text describes the characteristic atmosphere, agitation, and eventual cleansing of things caused by a shower in the country. On another level, each successive perceptual notation has been dressed up in analogies to create an overall sequence of purely imaginary forms. There is in the centre of the text an extended image derived from the phrase 'lit d'eau' − riverbed. Having thus made a 'realistic' reference to an actual phenomenon, Gracq goes on to infer the presence of an imaginary woman lying on this bed. This is of course a poetic conceit, and an example of distortion equivalent to a deliberate swerve towards unreality, even abstractness − as is confirmed by the beauty's being equated with 'a pure idea of herself', a phrase with distinctly Mallarméan overtones. Yet this feminine presence − the incarnation of water itself − does not absorb the poet's attention for long. Rather than lose himself in an unreal allegory, he turns back to the objective appearance of raindrops falling from twigs and foliage once the main shower has passed, and observes with scrupulous accuracy the way in which they form a kind of curtain of droplets ('les courtines emperlées') all along the edge of a dark wood ('l'alcôve verdissante') and the way these dribblings finally become identifiable as single droplets that can be counted one by one ('l'arithmétique crépitante du boulier de cristal'). Despite his flirtation with artifice, the poet keeps a check on fantasy by maintaining his perceptual alertness: the non-literal allusions to pinpricks, stars, pearly curtains and the crystal abacus conjure up a fairytale realm of derealised forms, yet are at the same time accurate signs of

the objective aspects of falling rain. The text thus hovers on the borderline between the fantastic and the realistic, and the sparkling freshness
of its poetic inventions becomes itself an analogue for the freshness of
perceptions.

My choice of Saint-John Perse as the poet of snow is an obvious
one, for Perse is a specialist in the elements, having written long poems
with such titles as *Pluies* and *Vents*. The sequence called *Neiges* is a
poignant meditation which arose in a wartime context on the occasion
of the poet's sitting in a New York hotel during the winter of 1944
and looking out at a snowfall. The poem is a complex of themes and
suggestions, and is far more than simply a description of a time and
place. It deals with the poet's feelings about living in exile, about his
longing to communicate with his mother in France, his hopes for an
end to the war and his general yearning for purification and peace. But
these abstract themes are elaborated within a highly charged metaphoric
field in which snow acts as the one constant referent.

Et puis vinrent les neiges, les premières neiges de l'absence, sur les
grands lés tissés du songe et du réel . . .

(Perse, 1972, 157)

(And then came the snows, the first snows of absence, on the great
woven cloths of dream and reality . . .)

As the snowflakes cover the separate features of the city, its streets
and skyscrapers, its gardens and river, they create a poetic setting in
which the world perceived and the world imagined are interwoven. The
soft falling is a subtle invasion of the poet's sensibility: in no sense does
he have to force himself to achieve the vision of a transformed reality.
Subtle and fragile, the snow has the marvellous capacity to cover the
whole city, and even the whole continent. The poet watching from his
hotel window derives from it a sense of participating in a ceremonial
of universal reconciliation and unity. The snow speaks of peace for it is
an element which erases boundaries and renders all things as one: white,
serene and perfect. Not that this vision of whiteness and harmony
becomes monotonous: the poet's imagination is not lulled into an
abstract vacancy. Rather, the snow becomes a white screen onto which
he can project a succession of images: the snow is likened to the dawn,
to a feathery white owl, to a white dahlia. The drifting flakes are associated with swarms of moths; there are references to milk, to shot-silk,
to the ocean — images which illuminate the falling snow for the reader

and make him witness it along with the poet, as the source of multiple meanings which arise spontaneously from its several aspects, whiteness, softness, silence and so forth. Indeed the snow becomes a perfect medium for the poet through which he can hint magnificently at notions like loneliness, separation, expectancy and longing, all the while confident that these abstract entities will drift into the reader's mind not as abstractions but as components of an experience of participation which is both intellectual and intuitional.

The final section of the poem reveals what it is that underlies the equations which Perse has been finding for snow: the final image in the series is *language* itself, the medium of poetic communication. Having previously spoken of the snow as an ocean, the poet now imagines a journey over water, up a river, in a search for the source of pure speech. If language is made up of vowels, labial sounds, prefixes and elisions, than Perse can imagine a journey back up the river of linguistic evolution towards the pure source whence all language flows. This dream of a language without flaw, of a pure Word whence all words have sprung, is projected through the continuing presence of the snows around him:

> . . . Et ce fut au matin, sous le plus pur vocable, un beau pays sans haine ni lésine, un lieu de grâce et de merci pour la montée des sûrs présages de l'esprit; et comme un grand *Ave* de grâce sur nos pas, la grande roseraie blanche de toutes neiges à la ronde . . .

> (Perse, 1972, 163)

(. . . And there was at dawn, beneath the purest utterance, a beautiful land without hate or stinginess, a place of grace and mercy for the emergence of the mind's sure prophecies; and like a great *Ave* of grace at our feet, the great white rose-garden of all the snows all around . . .)

The poem closes on this ultimate image of the snows incarnating that which is most pure: a language which says everything, a language expressive of the deepest experience of Being. Then the poet takes his leave with an invitation to the reader to imagine something even purer than the poem he has just been reading:

> Désormais cette page où plus rien ne s'inscrit.

> (Perse, 1972, 163)

(Henceforth this page whereon nothing more is inscribed.)

A page without inscription is not merely a blank sheet, but a space pregnant with potential meanings. Perse seems finally to equate snow with the purest mode of utterance, a medium in which the reality of life becomes manifest even without passing through the mechanisms of verbal communication. The snow or the blank page: these are Perse's quintessential images, one sensory and the other 'intellectual'; together they shape a perspective of quiet recognition of reality, of reverent acceptance of the world's silent surety. The ultimate revelation of snow is wordless Being. Perse's *Neiges* has thus transported us from the substantial reality of a New York snowfall in 1944 and into a dimension which is timeless and absolute though no less real.

In each of these evocations of elemental experience, the focal element seems to take on the function of a generating source of poetic vision, sponsoring analogies of itself. The fog seems to erase all distinction between physical objects and verbal images; the tumbling raindrops fall in an instantaneous shower of metaphors; and the snow conjures up the irresistible message that all disparates are one, that both our language and our perception of the world derive from common sources of pure understanding.

Some of the so-called 'critics of consciousness' (the phrase is used by Georges Poulet) have found it meaningful to approach different poets by way of an enquiry into their elective sensations. An inventory of the objects, places, textures and so forth to which a poet can be shown constantly to return in his writings, can represent a reliable guide to his profound intentions, in the light of what Novalis calls 'this marvellous joy in things which have an intimate relationship with our secret being' (Novalis, 1962, 195). Of course, poets are drawn to a myriad things — birds and butterflies, stones and leaves, scents and shadows, and so forth — and I propose therefore simply to examine a small sample of this material.

In that euphoric poem 'The Windhover', Gerard Manley Hopkins records the experience of seeing a falcon in flight.

> I caught this morning morning's minion, king-
>> dom of daylight's dauphin, dapple-dawn-drawn Falcon, in his ridin
>> Of the rolling level underneath him steady air, and striding
> In his ecstasy! then off, off forth on swing,
>> As a skate's heel sweeps smooth on a bow-bend: the hurl and
>> gliding
>> Rebuffed the big wind. My heart in hiding
> Stirred for a bird, — the achieve of, the mastery of the thing!

(Hopkins, 1953, 30)

Dense with adjectives pressed together in breathless compacts, these lines are a celebration of the singular creature in its spontaneous mastery of its medium. Like J.A. Baker, Hopkins witnesses the falcon's flight as something incredible and alien and finds himself obliged to describe it by recourse to ardent figures of speech. Thus the falcon flies through the air like a dolphin in the rolling ocean, like a horse cantering, like an ice-skater cornering at speed. This is a sequence of tangential images, a rapid flurry of associations, none absolute, each in turn touching momentarily on the object of attention and then being discarded as the bird sweeps in new directions in space and prompts fresh associations in the mind. The poet's eagerness to bear witness to changing detail and to praise the brilliance of the whole is communicated through the stammering alliteration and stresses typical of Hopkins's diction. The writing has a baroque urgency, at once ornate and agitated, as it carries us away by its intoxicating insistence on 'the mastery of the thing'. The glittering skills of the bird are scarcely more admirable than those of the writer, whose poem achieves a perfect synthesis of perception, response and expression.

Inanimate objects can also be the receptacles of meaning for the poetic sensibility. Joë Bousquet speaks of the smell of a sea-shell picked up on a day of sunlight, and hints at the emotions it arouses (Bousquet, 1973, 31). Marcel Proust, of course, elaborated his whole theory of involuntary memory on the premiss of the necessary relation between a sense datum and a memory. Hans Bellmer writes of the way in which the external world tends to intervene in one's reveries as one walks, thus providing the subjectivity with tangible proofs of the reality of inner meanings.

> To find along one's way a stone, precious because of the relationship, hermetic only at first sight, which it seems to maintain with my existence, this is to understand that it corresponds precisely, in the morphological order which is its own idiom, to an emotion within myself which has thus far remained unexpressed.
>
> (Bellmer, 1957, 51)

The found object which corresponds to an unexpressed desire is a discovery of Surrealism, and in his essay 'Langue des pierres' André Breton theorises at length on the personal meanings that various kinds of stones can have for their finder. His own searches along the dry bed of the river Lot lead him to the discovery of several remarkable agates which are, so to speak, external embodiments of unconscious feelings

(Breton, 1970c, 151). Through these otherwise negligible objects, the concrete world can thus be said to communicate with the poet's secret being.

One of Jean Follain's poems reflects a similar activity as, walking through the countryside, the poet absorbs a whole sequence of stimuli.

> Que distraitement le promeneur pousse du pied un caillou violâtre, il rumine d'incertaines pensées. Les bruits sont bien ceux de son adolescence. Il passe devant une bâtisse où les cris des bêtes, à cause du temps couvert, semblent des appels sans recours. Il va sans but, pas comme ce cultivateur qui s'avance, qu'il va devoir saluer. Aussi, pour l'éviter, s'engage-t-il dans un chemin de traverse. Les pierres y apparaissent d'une autre couleur, les haies moins élaguées, plus accueillantes; le ciel bientôt s'y éclaircit, ouvert à l'événement.
> (Follain, 1957, 89)

(As the walker distractedly stumbles on a purplish pebble, he is ruminating vague thoughts. The sounds he hears are certainly those of his youth. He passes in front of a building where the calls of the beasts, because the weather is so dull, seem like hopeless appeals. He goes on aimlessly, not like this farmer coming towards him, to whom he'll have to say hello. So to avoid him, he turns onto a cross track. Here the stones seem to be of another colour, the hedgerows less clipped and more welcoming; soon the sky clears, open to the event.)

This is a poem about being receptive to poetic signs: and yet Follain seems to insist on the need to remain in a passive state. He thinks vague thoughts and walks aimlessly: there is no intellectual impetus to his search. None the less, there *is* a search, one carried out at the level of semi-conscious perception as the poet registers the colour of a stone, the familiar sounds of the countryside. It is as though these perceptions were signposts of a secret direction which can best be followed when the mind is not on the alert. Other people cannot possibly understand this activity of absorbing subliminal signs from the outer world: the bluff countryman coming up the track will only break in on the reverie, and has to be avoided. The poet steps away on a new path where there is more space, and the sky brightens, heralding an impending discovery. An 'event' or poetic occasion is imminent. We are not told what it will be, and in this sense the poem is but the announcement of the poetic rather than its embodiment. The ambition of these modest lines is to lead the reader to the edge of discovery, and let him imagine an epi-

phany for himself. The event which the words make real is this emotion
of expectancy, the intimation of an imminent meaning. The poetic
quest, then, is directed towards a marvellous encounter which equates
to an intuitive sense of being suddenly related to external reality.

No more powerful attachment to the world outside has been described by poets than that invoked through erotic love, for as Breton
once remarked, 'the unforeseen encounter always tends to take on the
features of a woman' (Breton, 1952, 135). Baudelaire's poem 'A Une
Passante' describes an encounter which takes place on a Paris street
when the poet exchanges a glance with a passing woman. She is a
stranger, tall and slender, wearing a mourning dress which she elegantly
lifts to reveal her shapely legs. The poet drinks in the tempestuous
expression in her eyes:

> Un éclair . . . puis la nuit! — Fugitive beauté
> Dont le regard m'a fait soudainement renaître,
> Ne te verrai-je plus que dans l'éternité?
>
> > (Baudelaire, 1961, 89)

(A flash of lightning . . . then total darkness! — Elusive beauty / Whose
look has suddenly given me new birth / Shall I only see you again in
eternity?)

The flash of an erotic invitation, a moment charged with a desire all the
more intense in that it knows its fulfilment to be infinitely deferred,
this is the poetic moment as experienced by Baudelaire. Undeniably,
the attraction of the woman is sexual: that is, the poet is physically
aroused by the encounter. Undeniably, too, the moment is a poetic
one, for the woman's glance triggers off images in his mind, and is as
much a stimulus to the imagination as to the senses. Indeed throughout
Baudelaire's work imagination and sensation lead one another into
deepening intensities of involvement, creating a world of tremulous yet
indissociable complexes of perceptions and conceptions, bathed in the
glow of emotion.

The encounter with a beautiful woman is a theme which, as the
climax of the series of privileged sensations I have examined in this
chapter, may be seen as intimately related to the poetic quest at large.
This is not to say that all poetry is amorous or sexual, but, simply, that
those poems which do celebrate the erotic attraction of a woman can
often be read as absorbing demonstrations of the poetic process in its
work of fusing imagination and sensation.

A final example will round off this survey of engagements with the poetic. René Char's poem 'Congé au vent' speaks of a privileged encounter at dusk with a lovely girl, an encounter which leads not to physical contact, but to a fascinating reverie in which the girl passes on to a transcendent plane.

CONGÉ AU VENT

A flancs de coteau du village bivouaquent des champs fournis de mimosas. A l'époque de la cueillette, il arrive que, loin de leur endroit, on fasse la rencontre extrêmement odorante d'une fille dont les bras se sont occupés durant la journée aux fragiles branches. Pareille à une lampe dont l'auréole de clarté serait de parfum, elle s'en va le dos tourné au soleil couchant.

Il serait sacrilège de lui adresser la parole.

L'espadrille foulant l'herbe, cédez-lui le pas du chemin. Peut-être aurez-vous la chance de distinguer sur ses lèvres la chimère de l'humidité de la Nuit?   (Char, 1967, 20)

(FAREWELL TO THE WIND / Along the slopes below the village there are fields encamped, full of mimosa. At harvesting time, it can happen that, far from the place itself, one has a sweet-smelling encounter with a girl whose arms have been occupied all day long with the fragile branches. Like a lamp with a halo of brightness composed of perfume, she goes on her way, her back turned to the setting sun. / It would be sacrilege to speak to her. / Your sandal crushing the grass, give way to her on the path. Perhaps you may have the chance to make out on her lips the fabulous dampness of Night?)

The encounter is with a girl who transmits her sensuality through the heady mimosa scent that radiates from her body. She passes by, unchallenged, silhouetted against the sunset, like some goddess that no ordinary mortal dares address. If her physical presence counts less than the imaginative associations released by the mimosa scents and the visual impression of her silhouette, we will see her as a symbolic figure rather than a real person. She is Beauty, Purity, Love, Poetry; she is an allegory of grace and freshness, like a figure out of Botticelli's *Primavera* (cf. Mounin, 1969, 61). Yet though her presence is sacred, and the poet must let her pass untouched, there remains a possibility that he might snatch some small proof of her physical reality. As she sways past, he hopes he may be able to discern on her lips that slight dampness which announces Night. Now on one level this may be read as a graceful peri-phrase referring to dew, the moistness which arises on the body of Nature — which the girl may be taken to represent allegorically. But on another level, the image is strongly suggestive of sexual desire. The moist lips are those of a woman ready to be embraced. The girl passes by, like a breath of wind ('congé au vent'), and at the end of the poem the reader is left undecided as to whether she has been a chimera or a true presence. Yet her scent is real, and while the poet neither caresses nor kisses her, he gains possession of a special sort of certainty, a kind of poetic contact which is more meaningful for being virtual rather than actual. The girl becomes one of those 'transcendent presences' to which Char refers elsewhere (Char, 1967, 75). This is a notion which I shall examine more closely in Chapter 11; for the moment it may be ex-plained as having to do with an experience of contact with something really *there* in the outer world which is at the same time a source of poetic meanings that cannot be physically arrested or appraised. Poetic tremors of the kind I have been describing are, after all, not humdrum events in the domain of weights and measures, but poignant intimations of a reality which, for all its attested presence in the space we share, has something almost unearthly about it.

8 NOTICING THE SIGNS

The poetic need not arise from something so dramatic or exotic as a snowfall amid the skyscrapers of New York or an encounter with a beautiful girl in a field in Provence. The poet sometimes achieves a sense of contact with the world in which he moves by virtue of experiences or sensations which might seem negligible under other circumstances. Many of Follain's poems concentrate specifically on mundane artefacts, like a cracked plate or an old photograph, allowing the object to take on extended meaning in the space of the poem in a way which seems utterly disproportionate to its 'real' significance. One poem, 'L'Épingle', draws attention to the sound of a pin falling from a mantelpiece onto a wooden floor, as if to hint that even a minimal percept like this may be a point of departure for reverie and poetic enlightenment (Follain, 1971, 57). Apollinaire once remarked that 'a handkerchief falling to the ground may be for the poet the lever with which he will lift up a whole universe' (quoted in Gibson, 1961, 46). And Conrad Aiken claims that

> Assurance can come from nothing, or almost nothing;
> the imperceptible accretion of trifles;
> the mistaken speech, acknowledged or unacknowledged,
> the penetration of a deception; it can come
> from observation of what has been unobserved:
> new knowledge of an old history, new sight
> of a known face, a known field; the path
> familiar to the foot, but with surprises,
> a raw pebble, dislodged by rain, a scarlet leaf
> drowned in a puddle, a branch of maple to brush
> the sleeve, or such other casuals.

> (Aiken, 1966, 156-7)

The poetic tremor may thus spring from unexceptional events as well as rare ones. Aiken will locate the poetic in external objects like pebbles or leaves; but he also points out what we found in Bonnefoy's reflections on places, namely that what counts in the poetic encounter is the relation between subject and object. Strange things naturally force this relation: but the poet must also heed 'casuals', commonplace things which have simply never been properly perceived, the known face or field: these may suddenly pivot round one day and vibrate within his awareness, startling him into a fresh vision of things. The world only lacks in poetry for those who are poor witnesses: 'The mediocrity of the world stems from the imperfection of our ways of seeing, from our *incapacity to pay attention*', declares Bousquet (Bousquet, 1946, 151).

Many poets have accordingly made efforts to be receptive to small signals. Thomas Hardy prided himself on being 'a man who used to notice such things'. Poetic perception may mean nothing other than paying attention to what is there before us, if it is true that 'the eye's plain version', in Wallace Stevens's phrase, is poetry enough. Stevens it is who voices the notion that there might be a poetry in the act of un-trammelled looking through

> The eye made clear of uncertainty, with the sight
> Of simply seeing, without reflection. We seek
> Nothing beyond reality.
>
>> (Stevens, 1955, 471)

This view implies that the poet should transfix an object with a seeing so intense that it will allow no room for fancy to doodle extravagant metaphors around the percept. Stevens voices a call for a straight focus upon the thing itself, stripped of all evasions and deviations:

> Let's see the very thing and nothing else.
> Let's see it with the hottest fire of sight.
> Burn everything not part of it to ash.
>
>> (Stevens, 1955, 373)

Similarly Aiken claims that he will 'dream with intolerable brightness of a single thing' (Aiken, 1966, 153).

The result of such perception should be a written poetry of singular clarity and immediacy. If what moves the poet is the intensity of his perception of the poetic, then his poem will be the enactment of an equivalent urgency. Stevens again: 'The poet speaks the poem as it is, / Not as it was' (Stevens, 1955, 473) — the poetic transcript is a render-ing so hot on the heels of the percept that it assumes all its urgency and itself becomes the 'here and now' of the poetic experience. The success-ful record of an intensely experienced poetic fact, will be the text which captures the perception in words which do not lean nostalgically towards the past tense, but speak in the present, suppressing the interval between word and experience.

An example of a poem which carries off this feat of articulating an experience which takes place in the time and the space of the poem's being read – this is not something easy to find. The tang of immediacy is something which each reader has to taste for himself. Let me hazard a personal example, though, even if its effect is lessened for another reader and even if I have myself to concede that the poem has lost some of that crispness which I found when I first read it.

The poem, by the Chinese Sung poet Liu Tsung-yuan, is the simplest notation of a thing seen:

A thousand mountains without a bird.
Ten thousand miles with no trace of man.
A boat. An old man in a straw raincoat,
Alone in the snow, fishing in the freezing river.

(Rexroth, 1966, 24)

Of course, there is some artifice here, and distance from the literal event. This is inevitable, for we are centuries distant in time from the poem's original perceived or imagined occasion, and it has been mediated for us by way of Kenneth Rexroth's translation (which may or may not be responsible for the particular effect I am responding to). What moves me in the text is the moment of astonishment as a traveller down-river suddenly comes upon a human being after going so long without seeing any trace of life. The effect of saying 'a thousand mountains' or 'ten thousand miles' is to suggest vague and immense distances, against which the apparition of a man on a boat stands out in stark silhouette on the reading mind. The moment has extraordinary sharpness. The reader will respond more intensely to this unexpected presence if, as he reads, he doesn't simply register the event impartially, but tries to imagine what it might be like to fish in such a cold and lonely place. I have never worn a straw raincoat, still less in the snow on a freezing river: but the mention of this detail of the old man's garments is sufficient to marshal unfocused associations within my memory drawn from my own store of experiences of coldness. As we have seen, it is really the reader's fund of remembered sensory experiences that acts as the connotative field within which the words on the page fertilise a felt meaning. Yet the sense of an immediate 'here and now' is real. The poem acts upon me: it is not a future or a past experience, but a sensational impulse in the moment of reading.

Such an account of literary immediacy could be a stretching of the

facts. I must admit that it is not possible for me to re-read this poem
with quite the same sense of shivering surprise I first had. My account
of this shivering is necessarily reasoned *a posteriori* and shaped by the
demands of critical clarity. A commentary is never as crisp as a spontaneous initial response. It looks as though the strict experience of the
poetic tremor can therefore only be discussed in a context of wistfulness after the event. And this applies equally to the tremor in the mind
of the participating reader and to the tremor in the sensibility of the
poet as he confronts some external poetic fact.

Now, this kind of wistfulness has become associated in the minds of
certain poets with the poetic sensation at large. It is as though they find
poetic encounters to be all too rare exceptions to commonplace existence, in which straightforward sightings and graspings of experience
are enacted without hesitation. This rarity and the lack of insistence of
the poetic signal have encouraged these poets to cultivate a perverse
taste precisely for that which is uncertain and ephemeral. There is a
couplet of Reverdy which concentrates a sense of the elusiveness of
poetic certainty:

> Un poing sur la réalité bien pleine
> Hélas que tout est loin

> (Reverdy, 1969, II, 31)

(One's fist around fullest reality / Alas how far away everything is)

No sooner does the poet begin to get a solid grasp on the real, than he
becomes conscious of its distance from him. The angle of regret is
reflected in the alternative title of Giacometti's *Invisible Object –
Hands Holding the Void*. Whereas I suggested in Chapter 2 that the
figure's hands enclose a virtual presence, something seductive, the
latter title veers the other way and suggests that the hands enclose
emptiness, sheer hopelessness.

But Reverdy is a poet who has managed to turn his perceptual
failures into literary success by articulating, with the utmost poignancy, his efforts to project consciousness into a sense of contact with
the world, to establish a firm outlook on poetic signs so that they
cohere into patterns of meaning. What is poetic about such poems?

La porte qui ne s'ouvre pas
La main qui passe
                    Au loin un verre qui se casse
   La lampe fume
Les étincelles qui s'allument
                    Le ciel est plus noir
                    Sur les toits

(Reverdy, 1969, I, 195)

(The door which does not open / The hand passing / Far off a glass which breaks / The lamp smokes / The sparks lighting up / The sky is more black / Over the rooftops)

In these lines, consciousness registers a series of details whose significance is that they do not create certainty of contact: a door remains shut, a hand passes without making any gesture, a glass shatters, a lamp begins to gutter out. There are some unexplained sparks, but their effect is cancelled by the blackness of the sky, whose oppressive weight is underlined by the only main verb in the text. These sparse details signal an almost agonising sense of discontinuity and frustration. The poetic project has been abortive, and all that remains is a feeling of strain and anguish as the universe is evacuated of meaning. Yet in this very struggle of the language — to which the reader contributes sympathetic vibrations by his own natural desire that signs should mesh together, that phrases should start making coherent sentences — there arises a tremor which, for all its slightness, has noticeable poetic impact.

Poets have probably always felt that what is most valuable in poetic experience is what is most resistant to permanent definition. Things which stay put are less likely to be productive of poetic emotion, which thrives instead on conditions of unsettlement and giddiness. As Bonnefoy puts it, 'le fugace, l'irrémédiablement emporté est le degré poétique de l'univers' (Bonnefoy, 1959, 120) — 'the fugitive, that which is borne away without possibility of remedy, represents the index of the poetic in the universe'. Isn't this just another way of saying that things are more beautiful if they are doomed to extinction at any moment? I am not satisfied with a definition of the poetic which defines it as something necessarily so vulnerable. It smacks too much of an escapist preference for aesthetic shadows as opposed to real substances. Granted, Reverdy does deal in empty echoes and failures of contact, yet he cannot be said to luxuriate in them, and in general, they are not the basis for a poetry which is truly aligned with the real. André

Breton, confronting the problematic distinction between preferring the trace on the mind ('the shadow') and preferring the perception proper ('the substance') maintains that the true poet should aspire to lay hold of 'the shadow and the substance fused in a single lightning flash' (Breton, 1966b, 32), i.e. a dialectical fusion of the two engineered, presumably, by the cogency of the expressive act. All of this means that the poet must expect to operate under conditions of stress. He must be a 'magician of insecurity' in Char's phrase (Char, 1967, 66) and be prepared to accept that engagement with the poetic may involve a vertiginous struggle, the imagination stretched to the limit so as to hold on to the elusive sensation long enough to shape a form in which it can attain permanence.

Memory is of course the faculty thanks to which an experience can survive until the right words are marshalled. John Ashbery writes of a delicate perception which at first seems incomprehensible, not to be expressed, yet which later makes itself available as meaning:

There is that sound like the wind
Forgetting in the branches that means something
Nobody can translate. And there is the sobering 'later on',
When you consider what a thing meant, and put it down.

> (Ashbery, 1976, 20)

The trace on the mind persists in memory to become the focus of reflection and an eventual 'sober' act of verbal articulation. It is notable that the poet might proceed so hesitantly, especially since I have argued that the poetic sign is something to which the poetic sensibility ought to be spontaneously attuned. Philippe Jaccottet speaks of the 'lesson' which he divined to exist embodied in the natural world, and says that it 'could only be enunciated obscurely, in the same way that it was first apprehended' (Jaccottet, 1970, 29). Poetic reality itself has an enigmatic side which poets respond to with troubled wonder, and which can slow down the action. I should therefore refine my model of the poetic process and say that it does not tend to proceed by way of the sensibility gorging itself on indiscriminate sensations, but is a process of maturation whereby meaning arises only in the course of time. In this sense one should speak of it as a process of distillation, the materials of perception being refined and blended like rare liquors, with the corollary that the finished product, the poem, might convey a taste more intense than the original raw sensation. It is in this light that we may best appreciate Mallarmé's poetry as the quintessence of experiences which are themselves superseded by the time the poem is complete. What he extracts from each item of sensory experience is an essence, which he distils into the quintessence which is the aesthetic whole. Bonnefoy speaks in parallel terms of the pursuit of essence rather than aspect (Bonnefoy, 1967, 105), while Reverdy insists that what he terms *le réel* (elusive, profound reality) is a permanent essence accessible only to the mind: 'It is the mind which, moving beyond the appearances which bring the senses to a halt, freely penetrates the essence of things until it arrives at the real' (Reverdy, 1968, 40).

Once again we are verging on the question of 'transcendence', which I intend to discuss in a later chapter. For the moment, let us consider why it is that such seemingly abstract concepts as 'essence' or 'underlying meaning' press forward when the poet is addressing himself, as I have argued that he does, to something apparently so down to earth as sensation. The explanation, as perhaps I have hinted, lies in the poet's capacity to be carried away by his experience. When a percept enters into the sphere of his awareness, it activates his psychophysical system in a profound way. He experiences something like a startled sense of movement, as his mind is impelled by the sensation in a certain direction. This direction could equally be called a movement of penetration into the essence of the thing. The overwhelming thrust of this movement is a function of the intensity of the attention that the poet has been maintaining – not necessarily an intellectual alertness, as we saw above, but an unusual availability of the sensibility. Rilke speaks of the poetic practice of *Einsehen*, or inseeing – a profound gazing into the inner life of material realities, and a consequent apprehension of what is most specific within them. Another approach to much the same point is given in Hopkins's notion of 'inscape', by which he means the perceived individual form constituted by the shape and texture of a given object. The term extends to embrace the poetic virtue adhering to such form, so that the total 'inscape' of a given phenomenon – a tree whose branches are dancing in the wind, for instance – is a cluster of qualities and perceptions: the organic beauty of the tree's natural form, plus the witnessing of that form by the suitably attuned sensibility, plus a poetic attestation of the singularity of the total phenomenon. Given this, the idea I developed a little earlier that poetic insight means recognising the potency of irreplaceable moments of poetic feeling, associated with the apprehension of single objects in all their radiant particularity, can now be reconciled with the idea of essence. For in responding fully to the 'suchness' of a given thing, the poet gains insight into its central meaning, its essence. For Hopkins at least, it seems that this essence cannot be grasped other than through an act of understanding which remains sensitive to the crisp and complex specificity of the perceptual phenomenon.

In a review of Joë Bousquet's writings, Alain Robbe-Grillet once wrote that

> The universe of Bousquet — our own universe — is a universe of signs. Everything therein is a sign; and not a sign of something other, of something more perfect which is situated out of reach for us, but a sign of itself, of that essence which asks only to be revealed.
>
> (Robbe-Grillet, 1953, 828)

The perspective which this opens up is that the world perceived by the poet is a vast space of signs, an infinite array of phenomena to which he can attend and each one of which is a signal — not of something which lies beyond itself, but a signal *of* itself. Admittedly this notion of a self-designating sign is puzzling, inasmuch as signs are traditionally pointers to something other than themselves. But we must face the paradox, since it is at the heart of so much modern poetry, and try to grasp that the poet's reaction to the thing which signifies and which encourages him to concentrate on a central meaning or essence, is to locate that meaning or essence not behind or beyond the thing, but in the total nexus of its revealed aspects.

All of this may conjure up the giddy vision of a universe of bristling meanings which all but swamp the sensibility. Louis MacNeice has a moment of vertigo when he reflects on the universe in all its signifying diversity.

> World is crazier and more of it than we think,
> Incorrigibly plural. I peel and portion
> A tangerine and spit the pips and feel
> The drunkenness of things being various.
>
> (MacNeice, 1949, 86)

Just as a tangerine contains many pips, each a separate and distinctive entity, and each capable of seeding further tangerines, so the world is seen to be full of subtleties and potencies so manifold that the mind cannot keep up with them all. The poet who attends to the signs of the poetic will eventually realise that there is too much material for him to get to grips with. There needs to be selection, especially to ensure the calmness requisite to inseeing. While younger poets may tend to delight in 'the drunkenness of things being various' and to produce poems which seethe with whirling fragments, mature poets will want to concentrate on a few selected data, and subject them to patient inseeing in order to formulate meanings with a gradually informed certainty.

Thus a poet may choose to deal with wider themes, as does Perse in his lofty contemplation of elements across the world; or he may prefer to stoop to humble objects as does Follain with his pebbles and falling needles. Either way, the validity of his meditation will rest on its power to elevate into meaningful focus whichever entity he selects and to make it into a genuine poetic 'presence'. Bonnefoy writes: 'The object of our senses is a *presence*. It is distinct from a conceptual entity by virtue of an act, the act of presence' (Bonnefoy, 1970, 35). To introduce the concept of an 'act of presence' is simply to confirm a point made earlier, namely that true poetic contemplation of an object leads not to a behaviouristic imprinting of neutral sign upon neutral mind, but to an intense engagement such that the object enters into a special relation with the percipient consciousness. In this sense, the poet's attentiveness establishes a context of receptivity within which the object can pass from being merely 'there' to being *meaningfully there*, to having poetic presence. This encounter of consciousness and its object represents the completion of the 'act of presence', and guarantees the fulfilment of poetic inseeing. In this act, the subject is no longer domineering, the object no longer passive. Poetic meaning is the fruit of a mutual accommodation.

9 THE PATTERN OF ANALOGIES

This morning I draw the curtain upon a landscape transformed by frost. It is late November, and winter begins to seem more real to the mind. There are a couple of forgotten apples dangling on the branches of the old tree at the bottom of the garden: they are spots of dull but distinct scarlet against the background of leafless woodland beyond. The low sun has appeared over the hill and spotlights the lingering leaves of the orchard; these trees gleam with dabs of yellow and russet, strangely alive. From time to time as I gaze out, birds dart across the silent space, a sparrow, a blue tit, a blackbird. Their abrupt crossing of the field of vision is all the more noticeable in this world without foliage. I think I glimpse a redwing in the shadow of a bush; there is certainly a robin darting and perching on the greened stakes piled against the dead tree. On the lawn just before the window, the grass is an untouched whiteness. Soon the sun will send thin fingers of light across this expanse as it shines through the bare branches of the elder bush; I shall watch the frost being erased in thin bands, revealing the green underneath, with alternate bands of untouched whiteness exactly corresponding to the shadow. Divided into a few basic colours – the white of frost, the green of grass and hedgerows, the ochre hues of clustered bare twigs under sunlight – the landscape has a simple unity, and accedes readily to the eye's interrogation.

Looking at the view outside, I can read off the signs of imminent winter without hesitation: bare branches, the robin, frost. It is all so legible. Indeed, now that I reflect, it would have been improbable that I should have found difficulty in reading these signs, since I knew perfectly well what the date was before I drew the curtain. My reading of the message 'winter is approaching' was in this sense almost a projection of my expectations – a reading-into rather than a reading-off. But is this all there is to read? Lingering over the view, I find myself engaged in reverie, inarticulate yet already insistent. The solitary apples, stuck on the decrepit tree like droll lanterns from a forgotten garden party; the secret flicker of motion in and out of the ribbons of sunlight as a bird darts and vanishes behind the hedge; the distinct beads of moisture on the lawn, twinkling stars to catch at the eye which might otherwise register an undifferentiated grassiness. Is there something to be fathomed in such intricate auguries as these? I am drawn to observe and to ponder, straining to see more deeply — or perhaps to hear some word wafting into consciousness out of the shadows. I linger over the decipherment of perception, of feeling.

The sensations of puzzled contemplation and frustrated under-standing are marvellously captured in those early passages in *A la Recherche du Temps perdu* in which Proust speaks of ecstatic walks through the countryside. One autumn day, the young Marcel finds himself, after an hour's struggle against rain and wind, standing by a pond in which is reflected a tiled hut on the other bank. The rain stops and the sun comes out to brighten the freshly rinsed tiles: a pink reflection smiles on the surface of the water. Unable to express his enthusiasm at this epiphany, the future artist can only shake his umbrella and cry 'Zut, zut, zut, zut'. The interpretation and articula-tion of the signs remains blocked. 'Yet at the same time I felt that my duty should have been to avoid falling back on these opaque words and to endeavour to see more clearly into my rapture' (Proust, 1954, I, 155).

The conception of the world as a hieroglyphic script, a vast and obscure cryptogram, is an ancient one. (It dates back to Boehme and his mystic treatise *De Signatura Rerum*, and beyond him to Plato and Plotinus on the one hand, and to Islamic traditions on the other.) For our present purposes, let me quote a classic statement of the Romantic doctrine of the *Chiffernschrift* or 'runic script' of Nature, the view that outer reality represents a vast text in coded form. It is a passage located on the opening page of *Die Lehrlinge zu Sais*, where Novalis speaks powerfully of

> that marvellous secret writing that one finds everywhere, upon wings, egg-shells, in clouds, in snow, crystals and the structure of stones, on water when it freezes, on the inside and the outside of mountains, of plants, of animals, of human beings, in the constella-tions of the sky, on pieces of pitch or glass when touched or rubbed, in iron filings grouped about a magnet, and in the strange conjunc-tures of chance.   (Novalis, 1962, 105)

For the Romantic sensibility, it was possible to declare that this langu-age exists and is available for scrutiny. Most Romantic poets were willing to accept that the great text of Nature is mysterious yet not impenetrable to those who approach it in the correct spirit. Poetry was the art of developing intuitions which allow the poet to pursue the work of revealing Nature to others. Novalis for one declared his faith in what he called the 'primary art of hieroglyphistics'.

Have poets since the time of Novalis changed their view on the legibility of the world? Octavio Paz is one at least who is confident in his reading skills when he turns to the decipherment of

> nieve en agosto, luna del patíbulo,
> escritura del mar sobre el basalto,
> escritura del viento en el desierto,
> testamento del sol, granada, espiga

> (Paz, 1971a, 10)

(snowfall in August, moon by the gallows, / handwriting of the sea upon basalt, / handwriting of the wind in the desert, / testament penned by sun, pomegranate, ear of corn)

Conversely, Jean Tardieu makes the wistful admission of being unable to read the natural signs:

> I have often thought that the universe was a forgotten language, a 'code' whose key we have lost. At which point this enormous structure of surfaces, this fragile edifice of colours and forms, erected in the four corners of space, crossed by beams of light, punctuated by zones of shadow, tremulous and quivering, appeared to me to be deprived of any depth and composed of mere allusions to some unfathomable reality situated in the shadows, at an infinite distance. Each of these appearances had been projected into our sight in order to mean something – but this meaning was unknown to us . . .
> (Tardieu, 1969, 58)

The poet complains of feeling that there is no profundity to which he has access: the world is an assemblage of opaque surfaces, or of blank signs. Material reality is thus depleted, and true reality displaced, now lying at an uncrossable distance from his perceptions. Tardieu claims to be perplexed, at a loss to know how to respond. Yet I cannot but feel that the tone of his complaint, its verve and clarity of expression, tends to undercut the message of frustrated renunciation. There remains something that quivers here in Tardieu's prose as well as in the 'fragile edifice' of the tangible world he describes. The aspects he mentions seem too alive, too subtly focused for the reader to believe that he can have no response to them. True, Tardieu insists that things are unfathomable, yet his implied abandonment of the unsolved riddle does not convince me that he was never anywhere near a solution. His frustration is so much more articulate than that of Marcel brandishing his brolly and swearing. It is full of echoes of Romantic expectations, and I am led to conclude that, as I have suggested before, some poets seem never to be more closely attuned to the poetic as when they write of being unable to pin it down. Just as for some readers, there is pleasure in enigmatic texts, so for Tardieu the lack of a key to reality's cryptogram is itself an incitement to strange and even pleasurable emotions. His eloquently stated frustration thus conveys to us a variant perspective on the poetic.

In Chapter 8 I described Pierre Reverdy as just such a poet, one who prospects that zone of frustration where the poetic is manifested as the 'not quite', or, more rarely, the 'only just'. It is characteristic of him that his elective landscapes should be wintry ones, for the sensations of summer are too rich and confusing for him to read their meanings.

> There is never so much sweetness in the air and in the aspects of things as in autumn or even in winter. It is not during the summer that the countryside delivers up its secret. But at the moment when its life is muffled and hidden, slowed-down and mysterious. Yet how all this seems transient, ephemeral, furtive and deliciously bitter.
>
> (Reverdy, 1948, 17)

The landscape offers a message reduced to its barest essentials. It is a plain text, very different from the many-layered scribblings of summertime. But plain though it is, it still is difficult. It is written in an idiom of hints and implications, which the poet must strain to pick up. Its fugitive meanings carry a bitter-sweet taste which is all the more delicious for being savoured only rarely and with great difficulty.

Precisely because revelation is so uncommon, poets will tend to insist on the radiance of its occurrence. They often experience it as an illumination so bright that everything else seems to fade. But however bright the illumination, the text of reality does not necessarily relinquish all its mystery. The revelation is just a beginning. It initiates a sense of coherence, opening up the poet's mind to the sense of a possible continuity where hitherto all had seemed disparate and chaotic. This poetic apprehension of reality may be epitomised in the experience of the amateur archeologist Alfred Watkins who, one day in 1920, while riding across the hills of his native Herefordshire, was all at once seized by a flash of revelation, becoming aware of a network of imaginary lines criss-crossing the entire landscape. This pattern of lines marked out what Watkins calls the system of 'leys', straight tracks across the landscape made when prehistoric men travelled across the country, orienting themselves through landmarks such as mountain tops, cairns or standing stones (see Watkins, 1925). Now I don't wish to enter into a discussion of Watkins' ley theory in terms of its scientific plausibility. What matters here is that he should have arrived at an intuition which is quintessentially poetic. At the moment of his revelation, he was graced with the rare sense of a continuity between his mind and the world outside: the countryside before him emerged as a meaningful presence, a pattern of relations which he could see in his mind's eye. The example illustrates the idea of the instantaneous poetic intuition of a vast pattern which informs the real world. It is precisely this intuition which poets are seeking to validate when they confront the outer world.

Poets may look in another direction too and find a similar coherence in outer reality. In the text I quoted, Novalis alludes to 'the constellations of the sky', and Victor Hugo suggests that the poet might turn to reading that

> sombre alphabet qui luit
> Et tremble sur la page immense de la nuit.
>
>   (Hugo, 1971, 382)

(sombre alphabet which gleams / And trembles on the vast page of night.)

Mallarmé's *Un Coup de dés jamais n'abolira le hasard* is a poetic meditation on the forces which resist the structures of human thought and clog the mind with an unmanageable sense of randomness and contingency. The climax of the poem, however, rises above the vision of chaos to offer a triumphant confirmation of the possibility of form and meaning, envisaged in terms of the coherent patterns of stars:

       ce doit être
    le Septentrion aussi Nord
          UNE CONSTELLATION
    froide d'oubli et de désuétude
                      pas tant
             qu'elle n'énumère
    sur quelque surface vacante et supérieure
             le heurt successif
                      sidéralement
    d'un compte total en formation
veillant
    doutant
       roulant
          brillant et méditant
          avant de s'arrêter
          à quelque point dernier qui le sacre
             (Mallarmé, 1961, 477)

(it must be / the Pole also North / A CONSTELLATION / cold from
neglect and disuse / but not so much / that it may not enumerate / on
some vacant and superior surface / the successive clash / sidereally / of
a total amount in formation / watching / doubting / rotating / shining
and meditating / before ending up / at some sacral climax)

At the end of a chaotic struggle, reflected in the motions of a dice-
throw which is also a mind, 'watching / doubting / rotating / shining
and meditating', the clashing motions of sidereal space throw up a
final, brilliant formation of stars upon the empty space of the sky. The
constellation flashes before consciousness as a miraculous image of
order; it is legible configuration which at last rises out of amorphous-
ness and confusion.

   The image of the constellation is particularly apt to the point I am
making. For in objective terms, constellations are not true material
units: the stars we know in their familiar groupings in the night sky are
often situated many thousands of light years apart, so that the relationship between them, which we identify as somehow 'necessary' and self-
evident, is in fact an accident of point of view. A constellation makes
sense only to a percipient looking out at it from a particular point in
space. Hence the patterns which the human mind perceives in the outer
world may, in this context at least, be said to be dependent on that
mind: or rather, they are a function of the relationship across space

established in the act of consciousness. The constellation, like the legible landscape, is nothing less than the realisation of the poetic encounter of mind and materiality.

What these examples show us is that poetic perception consists not merely in the noticing of isolated signs but in responding to the coherence they manifest as constituents of a constellation of signs. As Reverdy puts it:

> One no longer perceives a thing in isolation, but its relations with other things, and these relations between things, amongst themselves as well as with us, form the web, at once highly tenuous and solid, of an immense, profound and fragrant reality.   (Reverdy, 1968, 52)

What the poet seeks is ways to establish links between objects of perception and objects of reflection, eliciting connections that will constitute the immanent network of correspondences on which poetic reality must rest.

Perhaps the most celebrated statement of the poetic doctrine of universal analogy is Baudelaire's sonnet 'Correspondances'. In it, Nature is evoked as a realm where the distinctions between different orders of perception are annulled, allowing each sensation to be synesthetically allied to its complement in a sphere normally kept distinct, so that the acts of smelling a perfume, touching a child's soft skin, hearing a note from an oboe or looking out across a grassy meadow become equivalent acts.[16] Furthermore, these sensations are in turn linked in Baudelaire's vision to a spiritual or ideal register, in that each of these sense perceptions corresponds to a quality or essence which, so to speak, hovers above it on the spiritual plane. At this point, all the things are seen to reciprocate all other things, forming

> une ténébreuse et profonde unité
> Vaste comme la nuit et comme la clarté
>
>   (Baudelaire, 1961, 11)

(a dark and profound unity, / As vast as night and as daylight)

— a unity which transcends all rational discriminations.

To conceive of a vision of the world as a realm of interlinkings in which all objects, all ideas, all emotions are harmoniously implicated, this is an intoxicating and even mystical proposition. And when Gérard de Nerval reaches just such a realisation, we can only marvel at the splendid confidence he exhibits.

> How, I wondered, have I been able to exist for so long outside of
> Nature, without identifying with her? All things live, all things act,
> all things correspond; the magnetic rays which emanate from me or
> others travel without hindrance across the infinite chain of created
> things; the world is embraced by a transparent network.
>
> (Nerval, 1960, 403)

Whether the system of correspondences is pictured in terms of a text
in which all constituent parts reflect an overall theme, or a constellation
in which separate stars cohere into a radiant unit, or, as here (in echo of
an allusion in Novalis's text about Nature's secret writing), in terms of
a magnetic field embracing the totality of the world, the underlying
principle of *necessary interconnectedness* has now become sufficiently
clear. What is more, this system of relations which the poet perceives in
the world of phenomena is at the same time revealed to be equivalent
to the system of relations which makes up his mental world. For the
premiss that all reality is sustained by a 'transparent network' of
correspondences leads inevitably to the notion of a correspondence
between that network and the mind of the one who perceives it.

Certain anthropologists, drawing on concepts derived from psycho-
logy and linguistics, have arrived at a view of the mental processes of
so-called primitive peoples which sees them as being structured on
principles of analogy-making not dissimilar to the processes I have been
describing here. How does one cope with an external world when one
lacks technology and scientific method and has only one's perceptions
and one's imagination to draw upon? The primitive mind hunts for
analogies, elicits patterns of resemblance in the natural world and trans-
lates these into that language we call myth and which is, in effect, a
form of applied poetry. The process is described by Claude Lévi-Strauss
in *La Pensée sauvage* as one of *bricolage*. By this is meant a process of
fitting bits together, a making-sense of the teeming impressions from
life by identifying them as sets and forming these into mythical systems.
The world picture elaborated by the primitive is thus a kind of metaphorical jigsaw puzzle whose pieces are provided by the minutiae of perceptual experience and whose interlocking shapes are fashioned by acts
of imaginative interpretation. Lévi-Strauss writes:

> The savage mind deepens its knowledge with the help of *imagines
> mundi*. It builds mental structures which facilitate understanding of

the world in as much as they resemble it. In this sense savage thought can be described as analogical thought. (Lévi-Strauss, 1966, 263)

The ultimate correspondence dreamed by the Romantics was that between the structure of the individual mind and that of the total cosmos. This giddy thesis was condensed into a striking formula by the idealist philosopher Friedrich Wilhelm Joseph von Schelling: 'The system of Nature is at the same time the system of our mind' (quoted in Hayner, 1971, 48). Given such a premiss, it follows that the poet who desires to make discoveries about the world need only look inside himself. It is all there, analogically speaking, within himself. Novalis dramatises the point: 'We dream of travelling through the cosmos: but does not the cosmos lie within ourselves? The depths of our spirit are still unknown to us' (Novalis, 1962, 342).

To prospect the depths of one's own being is an enterprise quite as ambitious as exploring the universe, and it leads to the same result, intuitive insights into the analogies which implicate both mind and cosmos. A pure, self-engrossed mode of poetry could thus aim at this illumination of the coincidence of inner and outer reality. Mallarmé's least externally oriented poems may be our best examples of an abstractive project which finally crystallises verbal or formal patterns which turn out to be perfectly attuned to the cosmos at large. This is surely what Mallarmé meant when he spoke of the poet's duty as being to achieve 'the Orphic explanation of the earth' (Mallarmé, 1961, 663). Explorations of inner space will achieve conviction only if, in Albert Béguin's words, 'the profound structure of the mind or of the total being, and its spontaneous rhythms, are identical with the structure and global rhythms of the universe' (Béguin, 1946, 401). Under these conditions, the microcosm and the macrocosm will then be revealed in their reciprocal patterning.

Given the conviction of their pronouncements on universal harmony, it seems a curious feature of the German Romantic aesthetic that it should have recommended the composition of fragments. Friedrich Schlegel delighted in an aphoristic style and saw nothing wrong in stating that 'a fragment must be, like a miniature work of art, completely isolated from its surroundings and complete in itself, like a hedgehog' (Schlegel, 1956, 95). How might such a literary policy square with the view that poets ought to open up their imaginations to the totality of Being? The answer is disarmingly simple. Once it is accepted that all things in the universe, physical and spiritual, are sustained within a network of correspondences, it follows that any single item of perception, any observation or any thought, is automatically linked to the totality. And so integral is that isolated fragment to the economy of the whole, that it can be said to concentrate within itself the implicit pattern of all things. Thus in the Romantic world it is sufficient to pick up any single object at random in order to be attuned to the global network. That this world-picture is not so distant from our present sensibilities may be shown by reference to the work of the twentieth-century writer Ernst Jünger, who reveals his solidarity with the Romantic world-picture when he says that 'the first object we happen to look at becomes the universal key' and that 'if one starts to observe at any one given point, one enters into a special relationship with the world at large' (Jünger, 1941, 92 and 103).

This last variant on the general notion of the system of universal analogy may be seen to offer a fascinating invitation to poetic reverie. In practice, not just any and every object is likely to be chosen by the poet as the starting point of his contemplation: I suggested above that the individual poetic sensibility tends to be drawn to a limited range of elective objects and sensations. None the less, it still holds good to say that the poet's concentration upon one isolated phenomenon leads him not to a fragmented vision – the poem turned in on itself like the hedgehog – but to an opening-up of the single experience on to a series of expanding perceptions of what lies beyond – the hedgehog, as it were, on the prowl. In saying this, I am not quite faithful to the Romantic notion that an individual object can *contain* the whole cosmos; none the less, I am following in the spirit of the Romantic precept that the single component is indissociable from the all-encompassing system.

Let us consider some examples of singular scrutiny. In one poem by Paul Celan, there is this reference to an isolated tree:

Immer die eine, die Pappel
am Saum des Gedankens.
Immer der Finger, der aufragt
am Rain.

(Celan, 1955, 44)

(Always the one poplar / At the fringe of thought. / Always the finger, looming up / On the slope.)

The poet submits to the sight of the tree as to some insistent presence which presses at the edge of his thoughts incessantly. It is a nagging signal which the poet's consciousness can neither explain nor ignore. Like a pointing finger, it signals, yet it does not explain itself. It is interesting to compare this obsessional quality with that embodied in a poem of Robert Bly which refers to another isolated tree:

> What is so strange about a tree alone in an open field?
> It is a willow tree. I walk around and around it,
> The body is strangely torn, and cannot leave it.
> At last I sit down beneath it.

> (Bly, 1962, 14)

Here the single object is isolated in a field which can be taken as equivalent to the poet's mind. The fact of the empty space around the tree poses a problem of understanding and articulation. The tree rises up like a question mark. To walk around it is a means of confirming its location, but also its irreducible singularity. The poet feels the magnetic attraction of the dark enclosing foliage of the willow, and cannot draw away. He has become involved both mentally and physically with an enigma upon which he needs to ponder at length.

In these examples, the movement from single object to global intuition of unity is left incomplete: Celan and Bly stand as witnesses to the 'not-quite' of wistful yearning rather than accede to the final plenitude of contact with the universal harmony. Philippe Jaccottet it is who, through observing and concentrating on a single thing, a small pool which has appeared overnight on a low stretch of grass, realises the poetic potential of the isolated act of inseeing. Musing on the ways to render the pool poetically, he comes to the conclusion that mere flurries of tangential metaphors cannot illuminate its central essence. What is needed is a mode of writing that will constitute 'a prolongation, a deepening of the visible object according to its meaning which is obscure and in a way imminent, a kind of orientation, or the opening up of a *perspective*' (Jaccottet, 1970, 60). The signal he receives from the observed object leads him to enter imaginatively *into* it: and this concentration on the single thing leads not to a numbing of his consciousness of the rest of the world, but to a deepening of insight which will in due course lead him to envisage reality at large more sharply and more comprehensively.

We saw in the last chapter that the specificity of the singular object can, in the act of presence, be revealed as its underlying meaning. Now we can see that the poet who invests his attention in 'the very thing and nothing else' may find that it begins to radiate a plurality of meanings, disclosing itself as the narrow gateway that opens on to the infinite. Bousquet writes that 'any event is the mirror of the universe' (Bousquet, 1973, 196), to which I might add: any sensation holds the key to all other sensations, just as any poem can be said to engage with all other poems. Those who can accept this notion of the extension of the particular into the universal and who can understand what Blake meant when he spoke so lyrically of holding 'A World in a Grain of Sand' (Blake, 1927, 333) will appreciate the perspective in which my exposition of the poetic is now advancing.

It is in this perspective that we can best appreciate the Japanese practice of writing haikus, brief poetic notations (a mere seventeen syllables long) which strip a given perception of all extraneous material so that it floats as a completely decontextualised statement, the merest shred of discourse. The poet Bashō was a celebrated exponent of this form of poetry, and produced hundreds of these infinitesimal tokens of poetic feeling. He made several long journeys to the remote provinces of Japan whose sole justification seems to have lain in their providing the stimulus for poetic responses. His travel sketches consist of diary entries in prose interspersed with verse haikus. Each of these records a separate moment of poetic feeling, while it is evidently the writer's intention that they should be read in sequence as a chain of responses that reflect the overall mood and meaning of the poetic journey.

A given haiku can be very simple: the poet spends an afternoon on a beach in the snow and condenses this period of time into a single concise notation:

Over the darkened sea,
Only the voice of a flying duck
Is visible —
In soft white.

(Bashō, 1966, 60; tr. Nobuyuki Yuasa)

In one sense, this is a poem of reduction, for its structure is too spare to sustain any development or ornament. The poet looks out to sea and perceives only the soft whiteness of the falling snow. All that is 'visible' in the white space before him is the sound of a duck calling in flight. It is a minimal sign of presence, suggesting that Bashō is situated at the edge of a space depleted of sensation and contact. There is the thrill of feeling oneself absorbed into a white void. And yet the fact that the bird's call does get through to him on that empty beach may be taken as a positive sign. There is an 'invisible object' stirring out there: the mind has a virtuality to confront and to relate to, and may legitimately dream of the 'soft white' in terms not of snow but of the warm feathers of a living creature. The magic of the poem lies in Bashō's capacity to reduce the focus of reverie to the minimum and yet still to suggest its potential for expansion. The cry of the duck can, for a moment, concentrate within itself all the sounds of the rest of the world, becoming a miraculous synecdoche for all that is unheard and unseen.

The rationale of poetic concentration on the singular particular is, then, that it leads the poet to an acute sense of reality at large. Bashō himself explains what happens to the poet who relinquishes his vanity and absorbs himself in contemplation of the physical object. 'Your poetry issues of its own accord when you and the object have become one — when you have plunged deep enough into the object to see something like a hidden glimmering there' (Bashō, 1966, 33). The 'hidden glimmering' of which he speaks is both the aura of meaning attaching to the single fact and the relation of that fact, and its perceiving subject, to the world at large. In this perspective, the call of the duck is not only an experience in outer, phenomenal space, but a moment which confirms human and cosmic harmony. At this point, we touch upon a profound affinity between the world-pictures of German Romanticism and of Zen Buddhism.

Now the relevance of these mystic-seeming ideas to my exploration of the poetic in modern times cannot be proven outside of a context in which the reader is prepared to countenance their validity, if only in terms of a useful hypothesis that allows access to the workings of the poetic imagination. It is my view that the Romantic picture of a system of analogies that informs our conception of reality is one which is far from being a dead letter to European poets of the twentieth century. Let me close this chapter with an examination of the poetic attitudes of Paul Éluard in whose work 'necessary interconnectedness' is a constant preoccupation.

Éluard writes of the analogical principle in these terms:

This is no verbal joke. Everything is comparable to everything else; each thing finds its echo, its justification, its resemblance, its opposition, its potential everywhere. And this potential is infinite.

(Éluard, 1968, I, 971)

Everything is consistent in the analogical vision: each thing connects with each other thing, and all things cohere in a global motion which is creativity. For, Éluard insists, the network of relations is not static, but an active force which sustains the world as a living organism. The poet's task is seen as being to affirm these relationships as dynamically as possible and thereby transmit the vision of harmony to other people.

> J'établis des rapports entre l'homme et la femme
> Entre les fontes du soleil et le sac à bourdons
> Entre les grottes enchantées et l'avalanche
> Entre les yeux cernés et le rire aux abois
> Entre la merlette héraldique et l'étoile de l'ail
> Entre le fil à plomb et le bruit du vent (. . .)
> Entre les rails aux embranchements et la colombe rousse
> Entre l'homme et la femme
> Entre ma solitude et toi
>
>   (Éluard, 1968, I, 369)

(I establish relations between man and woman / Between the sun's meltings and the bumble-bee sack / Between the enchanted grottoes and the avalanche / Between the ringed eyes and the laughter at bay / Between the heraldic blackbird and the star of garlic / Between the plumb line and the sound of the wind / (. . .) / Between the forking rails and the russet dove / Between man and woman / Between my solitude and you)

The poet has drawn up a list of random associations as a sample of the work of one who 'establishes relations'. The technique is fairly typical of Surrealist writing, in which, as we saw in the discussion of Péret's poem in Chapter 2, the practice of automatism or semi-automatism tends to generate linked nouns or metaphoric chains in ways which startle the reader out of a purely intellectual stance and force him to refer to his non-rational resources. Here Éluard comes up with some delightfully improbable duos, positing compacts between such unlikely partners as the 'heraldic blackbird' and the 'star of garlic'. What connection can one perceive here? What does a plumb line have that relates it to the sound of the wind? Why should railway lines be associated with a dove? We are back again with Lewis Carroll's postage stamp that resembles an albatross. As I argued in Chapter 2, such irrational associations tend to ask to be read as declarations of verbal unreality. But Éluard certainly wants more than this: this is no 'verbal joke'. He is quite serious in his defence of the view that 'everything is comparable to everything else'. In their own time, the Romantics were relatively cautious in their exploration of analogy: the Surrealists however set about the matter with total lack of inhibition, invoking Novalis's 'strange conjunctures of chance' in creating situations where all possible linguistic signs are invited to align themselves however they choose. What Éluard is doing here is to press the argument about correspondences *ad absurdum* by presenting us with the most outlandish pairings prompted by unconscious association. In this he may be said not only to be fulfilling the Romantic programme on correspondences in a Surrealist spirit, but also making a Surrealist application of Novalis's injunction that the poet turn to the cosmos within himself. In Surrealist terms, this inner cosmos is the unconscious, the space of irrational conjunctures and unlimited analogies, and the secret counterpart of the perceptual world outside.

In the quotation the sequence of irrational relations is preceded and followed by references to the relationship between man and woman, which is for Éluard the paradigm of all relationships. To the extent that the poet finds a reader who is willing to respond to his words at the level of his own sexuality, these references will act as a guarantee that he, the poet, can rely on the reader's being likely to commit himself to the analogical scheme at large, responding to the invitation to countenance odd pairings as to an invitation to deep pleasures. It finally emerges that the source of the energy which illuminates all aspects of the analogical universe is erotic energy. In Surrealist terms, this means not simply sexual energy in the limited sense, but an energy, defined broadly as 'desire', which is integral to the general make-up of an ideal sensibility. For Éluard, imagination is the powerful amalgamating force which subsumes erotic instinct, sensory acuity and poetic fantasy.

> Les cinq sens confondus c'est l'imagination
> Qui voit qui sent qui touche qui entend qui goûte
> Qui prolonge l'instinct qui précise les routes
> Du désir ambitieux
>
> (Éluard, 1968, II, 678)

(The fusion of the five senses that is imagination / Which sees smells touches hears tastes / Which extends instinct which maps out the directions / Of ambitious desire)

In this vision of miraculous fusions, the poet becomes the synesthetic embracer of the world's multiple sensations and the ambitious desirer of a beloved who, in Éluard's poems, emerges as the incarnation of the poetic principle underlying creation at large. Éluard sees Woman as the source and goal of all imagining. Her presence creates the conditions for poetic vision, her mediation ensures the poet's contact with the forces of natural life. Her body is analogically implicated in all aspects of the world. She is the incarnation of poetry itself.

> Femme tu mets au monde un corps toujours pareil
> Le tien
> Tu es la ressemblance
>
> (Éluard, 1968, I, 459)

(Woman you bring into the world a body which is always similar / Your own / You are resemblance itself)

For Éluard, the mystery of the universe becomes explicable in the light of analogy which radiates from this woman whose body, ever changing, remains constantly the same. It is in love that the poet can find the ultimate key to Nature's cryptogram. It is desire which magnetises the universe and confirms the unity of all created things. It is imagination fired by passion which brings consciousness into creative contact with reality.

Such speculations and visions are not cursory responses to a quick scanning of the signs, but emerge from the core of the poet's being. This is why the proposition that the universe rests on a system of correspondences is emotionally so deeply rooted at the same time as it seems so intellectually indefensible. Like love, it demands to be apprehended at levels of the sensibility which empirical thought tends to exorcise. Poetic rapture is not a state recognised as of public utility, so that poets who feel that the system of their mind and that of Nature are intimately related are in an awkward position as regards objective criticism. Nevertheless, I would argue that positions such as these are not necessarily ludicrous, but can be highly enriching ways of approaching experience. I would even say that the notion of a network of correspondences is *not* an outmoded Romantic illusion: it represents a crucial intuition that can still illuminate the shapes and motives of man's relation to the world of existence.

Part Four

FIGURE AND REALITY

10 THE WORLD AS METAPHOR

Novalis's *Die Lehrlinge zu Sais* is a treatise on the proposition that reality is a vast poem, a panoply of signs which the poetic sensibility can train itself to notice and to construe. In the loose narrative, Novalis paints a portrait of the Master as a guru who patiently communicates his poetic Nature Philosophy to the young students. He teaches by way of parable and example rather than abstract intellectual exposition, and encourages his students to exploit analogy as a technique of discovery. His natural history lessons, for instance, take the form of his laying out stones or plant specimens in rows upon the ground and shifting them around until they cohere into patterns corresponding to natural laws of affinity. What the Master seeks is to arouse intuitive responses, for he knows that rational conceptualisation can never awaken his pupils to the truth. One of the students observes that

> a singular light burns in his glances when the great runic text lies before us and he stares into our eyes to see whether within us also has risen the constellation which will make the figure visible and comprehensible. (Novalis, 1962, 105)

In order to recognise the constellations of signs in which are formulated the meanings of the universal poem, one should approach the text of reality in exactly the same spirit as one should approach a difficult poem, scanning the words in all directions until cross-connections begin to impose themselves and a purposeful pattern of allusions begins to emerge and shape a sense. Suzanne Lilar defines poetic activity at large as precisely this, 'a way of approaching the real which is exercised by analogical reflection', and adds that 'to create poetry means, quite precisely, to put oneself in a state where one will glimpse many forms, and then to discern and grasp those which are revealing of profound analogy' (Lilar, 1954, 153 and 93). I mentioned earlier that Novalis recommended that the poet learn the 'primary art of hieroglyphistics' so as to decode the runic script of the real. Now the definition of the poetic process can be taken a step further by reference to what Novalis termed 'analogistics' – the practice of eliciting analogies which establish a network of illuminating relations.

I suggested in the previous chapter that the primitive mind may be taken as a useful model in this connection, inasmuch as it too relies upon analogical mechanisms to give shape to the manifold perceptions it gathers in from the world. The primitive is something of a poet, then, for he is prepared to put his trust in intuitions which are never confirmed by scientific testing but are simply taken *as* facts because they enter consciousness under circumstances of general psychological effervescence: the highly-charged affective climate in which a discovery is made seems to act as sufficient guarantee of its validity. Some fine examples of the way primitives cope with the physical problems of their environment are provided in an account by the anthropologist Kilton Stewart of the Negrito people of the mountain jungles in Northern Luzon. He describes a group of hunters who are obliged to cultivate a reliable store of knowledge about the wilderness in order to survive. They go about this task by way of a dual process of analogistics. First, they attribute human characteristics to the inert world of matter and so become acquainted with Nature by 'reading' its anthropomorphic features. Secondly, they apply their nocturnal dreams to the solution of problems in waking life by treating the dream in the way I suggested one might treat a poetic image — as a figure quite capable of literal relevance to our existence.

Two examples of Negrito 'analogistics' should suffice to show how it works. Before the Negritos embark on an excursion to collect honey, the shaman falls into a trance and speaks to the gathered group in a song which is supposedly dictated by the grandfather of all the bees. Part of the song consists of the bee explaining how he was able to cure the shaman's wounds with his honey. The reptition of this song before each expedition fixes this useful knowledge in the collective memory and also reminds the Negritos that their honey-collecting should proceed in a reverent spirit: the bees are their benefactors, not their prey (cf. Stewart, 1975, 63-4). The analysis of these associations may be pursued as follows. It seems likely that the concept of honey as having curative power came to the shaman by way of an intuited analogy. Sensory memories of the pleasant sweetness of honey on the tongue (possibly heightened by negative associations of the painful stinging of which bees are also capable) activated an association of honey with soothing and therefore healing properties. This is essentially an irrational analogy, for it leaps from a taste sensation on the tongue to a tactile sensation on the wounded skin. What makes it 'work' is that the two sensations are soothing. In this way, the primitive learns to make use of an actual property of honey. Analogistics have helped him make an important adjustment to the material world.

Civilised man may want to disparage such intuitive approaches to the problems of physical life. It would be considered an eccentricity in our society to put honey on an open wound. None the less, there is scientific evidence to show that honey does have antibacterial properties, and even the sceptic would have to admit that, all other things being equal, it would be emotionally more soothing to apply soft honey to a wound rather than antiseptic fluids out of a labelled medicine bottle.[17] (In passing we may speculate that folk medicine and popular remedies are profoundly rooted in such non-rational associationism.)

Let us return to the Negritos. The second example concerns a native who, despite the elegant high-stepping gait typical of the Negrito people, manages to stumble over a protruding root on the jungle trail and sprain his ankle badly. In his subsequent dream, the man encounters the root spirit in the shape of a gnarled old man who demands that a tobacco leaf be placed over his back. Next day the native therefore retraces his steps along the trail, finds the root and puts some tobacco upon it, adding an oral apology for his clumsiness. All this is the birth of a ritual which will be repeated at each new passing along that trail, and will even be inherited by the man's descendants. Later on the man also makes up a song to the root spirit, which he says is taught to him by the spirit as he walks: the song takes his pain completely away, and he is now confident that the spirit will henceforth help him walk with skill through the jungle (Stewart, 1975, 109). What has happened here is another piece of analogical reasoning which has marshalled faculties beyond the range of the rational intellect. The ability to see the analogy between the root and a human being establishes a fiction from which the man is able to benefit. The root becomes a stimulating point of reference in his physical environment and a source of insight into his inner life in that he now learns control over his unconscious actions: specifically, his instincts will henceforth be more keenly alerted to snags along the jungle paths. The song he learns is of course the invention of his unconscious faculties, so that we have here an example of a creative work emerging from the subliminal self at the instigation of a physical accident. The creative imagination has not only made a communicable and convivial work of art, for the song is shared with the rest of the group round the campfire, enlivening the monotony of the eternal food quest, but has proceeded with its own surety of step towards confirming the continuity between the individual being and the outer world. Myth or not, this last confirmation is absolutely vital to the Negrito's confidence and thus his ability to survive. To put the point bluntly: he wouldn't last a week in the jungle if he didn't respond to its poetic signs.

The ability felicitously to combine things which reason keeps apart is central to poetic thinking. Ernst Jünger refers to the higher insights which derive from 'a mode of thinking which does not deal in distinct, compartmentalized truths, but in their meaningful interconnectedness, and whose power to elicit order rests on the combinatory capacity' (Jünger, 1941, 26). André Breton devotes the text *Signe ascendant* to the subject of analogical thought, announcing his passionate attachment to 'anything which happens to break with the thread of discursive thought and takes off suddenly like a rocket, thereby illuminating a novel and fertile system of living relations which we may confidently assume was a secret known to primordial man' (Breton, 1968, 7). Where logical thought likes to divide, to keep its objects rigorously distinct, analogical thought tends to synthesise, to draw connections between different orders of perception and speculation and so maximise the potential meaningfulness of all things. The task of poets, Breton argues, is to establish anew this method of investigating reality. August Wilhelm Schlegel had already drawn the very same distinction between pragmatic reductivism and poetic inventiveness when he wrote that 'the non-poetic view is the one which considers that once the senses have perceived things and intellect has determined what they are, everything about them is settled once and for all; the poetic view is the one which continues to interpret them and never assigns any limit to their plenitude as sources of figures' (quoted in Le Sage, 1952, 20).

The poetic approach to reality is, then, one which assumes that the text of nature is to be construed not just as a cryptogram concealing a single meaning, but as a multiplicity of figures each of which nourishes a multiplicity of meanings. Michel Deguy puts it that 'the symbolic text of the world presents things together in the mode of *likeness* – things are figurative' (Deguy, 1966, 199). There is no single thing, a poet will argue, that is so cut and dried that one cannot attend to its secret whisper which says, 'I am more than just my appearance'. The world outside seethes with figures and associations. 'The earth moans with metaphors', writes Osip Mandelstam (Mandelstam, 1977, 71). If each object quivers with readiness to imply something other than itself, if each perception is a word in a poem dense with connotations, then the poet's selection of any given subject of speculation will become, as we saw above, a means of attuning himself to the rhythms and harmonies of reality at large. Just as an artist like Monet will spend years painting the same lily pond, or like Javlensky the same face, so the poet who restricts himself to the most limited topic can, by implementing his 'combinatory capacity', draw forth endless series of figures and meanings. When Francis Ponge comes up with a 128-page book about soap — *Le Savon* — we may be sure that this is not a *tour de force* of detailed external description, but a thorough exploration of the poetic potentialities of that substance. Ponge writes in his conclusion that his investigations have thrown up a whole whirl of bubbles, but that these are not simply more or less futile metaphors, but a series of meaningful (though unexpected) qualities. The bar of soap is no longer just a serviceable domestic object, but a creative entity in its own right (Ponge, 1967, 105).

Now Ponge is known to be a rather voluble writer, and we may be tempted to suspect that what he has done is to generate more and more 'bubbles' from the ductile substance of language rather than from the bar of soap itself. This is of course a standard objection which can be made whenever we decide that a writer has transgressed the limits of objective description. But I would argue that it is an irrelevant objection, in that poetry is a mode of writing which *by definition* goes beyond those limits. Poets will necessarily assert the figurative potential of each object they describe, the flexibility of their own associative resources seeking to match the richness of the object's figurativity. Indeed, at a certain point, it becomes impossible to lay down any hard-and-fast distinction between the figurative language which is reality and the figurative language of the poem on the page. The world speaks, and the poet responds: the dynamics of creative participation ensure that the resulting words will activate impulses which will convincingly link the mental constellation to the external one. Jacques Dupin has no hesitation in stating as much:

> Through the never-failing power of astonishment, maintained and sharpened by metaphor, the lark and the rock, the river and the olive tree, the ray of sunlight and the ripple of water penetrate the verbal fabric and act therein as living beings. (Raillard, 1974, 157)

The poet who has faith in his medium of expression, language, will also have faith in its capacity to facilitate contact with those things it designates and, in an important sense, creates. 'To abandon oneself unrestrainedly to language is to abandon oneself unrestrainedly to the world. Those writers who underestimate the powers of language by separating it from the world, those who dig a ditch between the verbal sign and that which it signifies, only emprison themselves within the limits that they assign to language', writes Alain Jouffroy (quoted in Bailly, 1971, 56). This capacity to abandon oneself to language is central to the poetics of Surrealism, but it is not only in Surrealism that the importance of letting words bring about relations has been recognised. We saw from the passage from Novalis's *Monolog* quoted earlier (see Chapter 5), that the Romantics had already hit upon the idea of letting language take over the task of shaping its meanings. Once let language loose from the obligation to serve imposed ends, Novalis claims, and it will conjure up the most unexpected truths. Words are like algebra, a play of apparently abstract signs which in fact 'mirror the strange interplay of natural relationships' (cf. Novalis, 1962, 323-4). A creative abandonment to language, a surrender to the pleasurable timbres and supple rhythms of speech, can therefore lead to the articulation and thence the active realisation of a relationship between things and the poet.

Coleridge's dream was completely to do away with the anti-poetic distinction between language and reality, and he wrote that he would 'endeavour to destroy the old antithesis of Words and Things: elevating, as it were Words into Things and living Things too' (quoted in Hawkes, 1972, 53). There are those who will say that this dream is impossible, since the very nature of imagination is that it deals in *absent* realities. Mallarmé for one seems to be stamping firmly on the notion of words as living things when he makes the claim that to utter the words 'a flower' is to summon into consciousness the pure concept *flower*, 'idée même et suave, l'absente de tous bouquets' (Mallarmé, 1961, 857) – 'the sweet idea itself, one absent from all bouquets'. Even here though, we can say that Mallarmé is toying with an adjective, *suave*, which has strong connotations of sensory pleasure: for it is widely used to refer to the sweetness of such varied sensory stimuli as perfumes, cigars and music (all of which are in fact elective elements in Mallarmé's sensibility). It is my general hope that the evidence I have been gathering from the poets will sustain the argument that Coleridge's dream is not mere empty froth.

In extreme cases, language can actually have a concrete power so great that it takes on substantiality. Michel Leiris speaks of the sensual pleasure he derived from savouring the actual taste of words, letting them melt in his mouth like rare fruits (Leiris, 1966, 219). Ponge relates that when he first discovered the Littré dictionary, the world of words became as physically real to him as the world around him (Ponge, 1970, 46). In Chapter 6, I cited evidence to show that the Surrealist poets found that language could take on concrete form, and argued that poems can open up for the empathetic reader in ways which press towards literal physical contact.

It should be stressed that the situation I am addressing is not the simple one of language confronting reality, but the more complex one of reality and consciousness being brought into meaningful contact through the mediation of language. In the poetic perspective, the mind's perceptions of the world are channelled through linguistic configurations; elements of the world enter the verbal space which immediately becomes more than just *verbal* space.

A telling demonstration of collaboration between perception and language is given in the example quoted earlier, when Jaccottet confronts a pool in a field. The poet feels what I have termed the poetic tremor as he sees white foam along the edges of the bullrushes. This seems to embody what Bashō calls the 'hidden glimmering' of the phenomenon, its insistent but secret meaning. Musing further, Jaccottet comes to the conclusion that the solicitation he feels is simultaneously perceptual and linguistic. The foam is valid both *in its own right* – 'as a thing which should simply be called "foam" and not compared to anything else' – and as a sign of *something other than itself* – 'as a reminder of the word and the object "feather", a reminder fortified by a recent reading of Góngora' (Jaccottet, 1970, 55). Here one must remember that 'foam' and 'feather' are echo-words in French: *écume, plume*. What is happening is that a process of poetic contemplation has seized on a real entity in the world, the foam, and while sustaining a recognition of its 'thereness' as unadulterated presence to the senses, is proceeding to unfold the analogies to which it gives rise in poetic reverie. What makes this such a perfect demonstration of my point is that the association *plume* arises simultaneously as an association of a sensory kind (white foam / white feather, each ruffled by the morning wind) and a purely verbal echo, the rhyme with *écume*. The reference to the poet Luis de Góngora – a specialist in baroque metaphor – suggests that this last association is 'artificial' in the sense of being a borrowing from a literary rather than an experiential source; but my argument that a reader's responses to literature are always imbricated in his experiences in life, should, I hope, disarm even this objection.

What we witness here is a kind of poetic ritual in which the poet, much like the Negrito with his root, comes to terms with the physical object he has encountered by searching within himself for a formula which will resolve a tension and create a sense of satisfaction. Until he finds that formula and composes his poem (or invents a ceremony or a song), he will remain in a state of disarray. The external solicitation creates an imbalance which only the creative response can put right. There is a pressure on Jaccottet to write something that will do justice to the event: if he writes well, his poem will in turn exercise an equivalent pressure on the reader.

If we now concentrate for a bit on the verbal formulation which we call image or metaphor, we shall find that it represents an exemplary product of the analogical act realised through the 'combinatory capacity'. Two entities are juxtaposed to form what might be seen as the tiniest constellation of all in the galaxy of the poetic. These twinned 'stars' are placed in conjunction in order that what Dupin calls their 'poignant relations' (Raillard, 1974, 157) should spring forth as active impulses within the reader's consciousness. If, as Philip Wheelwright surmises, 'poetry quickens and guides man's associative faculty' (Wheelwright, 1954, 100), it does so by virtue of the tensions it creates in the reader's mind, tensions which are only reduced when the reader begins to make sense out of the image by consulting his sensibility and constructing a plausible correspondence that will justify his seeing the two 'stars' as a constellation. Now in Surrealist theory, as we have seen, the value of a poetic image depends on the distance the mind has to travel in order to connect the two poles in question. Using an electrical analogy to illustrate what happens when one encounters a Surrealist metaphor, Breton writes that 'the value of the image depends on the beauty of the spark produced: it is, consequently, a function of the difference in potential between the two conductors' (Breton, 1963, 51). To extend the electrical parallel, the violent disparity one finds in Surrealist images may be likened to an electrical charge which overloads the habitual circuit of associations used by rational thought. The result is that the mind is forced to divert this charge through non-rational circuits, thus involving wider sectors of the network of the sensibility. Speed is a cardinal feature of this process, which is why images are most compelling when they are succinctly formulated. The faster the reading, the sooner the overload will occur, dumbfounding rationality and forcing the intuitive faculties to take over the task of 'justifying' the image.

One of Breton's metaphors, 'mes paupières de caoutchouc' (Breton, 1968, 94) — 'my eyelids of rubber' — shocks the reader because it so swiftly conjoins — by the small yet authoritative preposition *de* — two nouns which represent entities kept far apart under normal conditions of perception. Eyelids are part of the human body; rubber is a non-human substance. Eyelids are fragile; rubber has a certain robustness.

And so on — one can count up the various differences which make the two terms incompatible: these differences are an irritant to reason. Only the fact that the words are there on the page, and therefore remain as a provocation, causes us to reflect further on how this scandalous marriage of disparates might merit eventual approval. I leave it to the reader to try scanning the associative fields on the two sides of the image in the hope of hitting upon the common denominator.

Apollinaire offers us a fascinating image in the following lines:

La fontaine coule
Robe noire comme ses ongles

> (Apollinaire, 1956, 181)

(The fountain flows / Dress black as her nails)

The lines are difficult in that they are set in an ambience of syntactical ambiguity similar to the one I examined in an earlier discussion of Apollinaire (see Chapter 3). Strictly speaking, one should not isolate an image from its context, since the surrounding text might very well carry signals as to how it should best be justified. None the less, if we do elect to look at this couplet on its own, and to accept the syntactical reading that there is a relation of apposition between *fontaine* and *robe*, we find ourselves faced with a most interesting image to try to justify. The fountain mentioned in the first line can carry associations of water, hence of fluid motion, transparency and purity. The second line brings the fountain into conjunction with the black dress. At once this invalidates the association *transparency*, while foregrounding the association *fluidity* (to the extent that a dress may be said to 'flow'). The metaphoric equation 'fountain = black dress' is followed by a simile which further complicates matters: 'dress = black as her nails'. Here I am opting for a commonsense reading in assuming that *ses* makes best sense if taken to refer to a woman, albeit otherwise unmentioned. To read *ses* as meaning 'its' would lead us into further images and further problems of justification: what sense would we find in 'the fountain's nails' or 'the nails of the black dress'? I leave the reader to wrestle with these versions if he so insists. My decision at this point leaves me with a fairly simple problem. First, the phrase 'dress black as her nails' might signify that the woman has not cleaned her fingernails. But this is not a satisfactory solution in a context where *flowing water* and *purity* remain dominant in my mind. Let me therefore turn to another association and assume that the woman's fingernails are lacquered with black varnish. This is an unusual yet not an implausible nor an unattractive proposition. If I adopt it, I end up with a nexus of connotations centred on the paradoxical mixture of attraction and strangeness in the woman. In a sense, my reading has been an exercise in creating for myself a portrait of this phantom: she is dressed in an insubstantial black gown that flows like water from a fountain; she wears black varnish on her nails; she is a desirable yet slightly disquieting creature. And yet the fountain continues to flow – her strangeness may yet modulate into transparency, her mystery wash away. She may even become real for me if I allow the words which create her to exercise prolonged influence over my mind.

There are poets who have looked on what I have called the 'language' of the natural world and have decided that it is about as arbitrary as the signs which human language uses to designate things in that world. Antonin Artaud suggests that nature, like our ordinary human language, has become a purely arbitrary sign-system: 'When nature gave a tree the form of a tree, it might just as well have given it the form of an animal or a hill, and then we would have thought *tree* when faced with the animal or the hill, and the trick would have worked' (Artaud, 1971, 61). A similar distrust of the thesis that identity is ratified in the act of designation may have motivated the startling opening to the Fourth Canto of Lautréamont's *Les Chants de Maldoror*: 'It is a man or a stone or a tree which is going to start the fourth canto' (Lautréamont, 1953, 250). The literary attitude this exhibits would appear to be one of studied carelessness: we normally expect an author to know where he is going and what he wants to say, and we will therefore tend to be flummoxed by this statement of cavalier unconcern. Of course, Lautréamont knows perfectly well where he is going. For a start, he knows that he is out to irritate his reader. More importantly, he is aiming to capitalise on the mental energy released by such ploys as the aggressive disavowal of established literary conventions, and open the reader up to experiences of mental reality he has never before contemplated. If the author asserts that it does not matter *which* thing begins the canto, it does matter that *something* is being brought into the textual space and offered to our attention. For as I have argued above, even when verbal references are made in a context of randomness, semantic relations do inevitably emerge: no collection of signs can be imagined which does not at some level sponsor a patterning of sense.

The fifth canto of *Les Chants de Maldoror* contains a particularly impressive sequence of verbal permutations when the author leads us

through a series of similes based on the recurrent formula *beau comme*.
Here is one of these:

> Le scarabée, beau comme le tremblement des mains dans l'alcool-
> isme, disparaissait à l'horizon.   (Lautréamont, 1953, 294)

(The scarab beetle, beautiful as the trembling of hands in alcoholism,
faded from sight on the horizon.)

Here again, one needs to bear in mind the wider context of the single
image quoted: there is no point in my hiding that it is one of eerie
unsettlement in as much as the putative story-line in this section of the
book has been dealing with a scarab beetle and its dung-ball, which
takes part in a kind of black charade also involving an owl, a pelican
and a vulture! In context, the scarab beetle seems to be no more than an
arbitrary *word*, its referent of no more import than any other: the
scarabée might just as well have been an *araignée* – or a tree or a hill.
Its disappearance on the horizon of the story in the line quoted would
be totally unceremonious were it not for the simile interjected at this
point. The *beau comme* formula is a nagging parenthesis which sus-
pends the action: it serves no function at the level of narrative. Yet in
terms of verbal sequence, it does function as a significant link in a
chain. In one sense, it is a reminder that the whole text has arbitrary
status: the scarab beetle and the trembling hands are on a par, each
reference as random as the other. Alternatively, the *beau comme* may
be taken as an invitation to posit relations along the lines I have sketched. However, I don't know that we can find many points of resemblance. Indeed the ornate longwindedness of the simile seems to dis-
courage us from expecting plausible points of comparison between the
two elements of the image. The formula foregrounds its own artificial-
ity. Far from reconciling 'beetle' and 'trembling hands', we tend therefore to leave the two terms to float unjustified in our mental space
and read limply on, unable to cope, submissive to the demands of a
text which, delighting in enigma and artifice, tends to numb *all* our
faculties.

The fact that a reader ends up feeling completely stunned in this
way might be an argument for the logological limitation on the image,
its lack of transitivity. But at the extreme pitch of non-functioning of
the image – assuming that I now admit that my associative faculty
has seized up (it is not of course excluded that a plausible connection
might suggest itself to other readers) – I may none the less experience

a sense of exhilaration, a feeling of adventure which derives from my being whisked away so rapidly to such a splendid distance from the security I expect of an average statement in prose. I am tempted by the perhaps perverse argument that *because* I cannot make sense of the image, it can function for me as an emblem of pure poetic feeling. In the same way that I suggested earlier that enigmas in poetry or reality can be productive of pleasure, so I am now suggesting that an unresolved comparison may actually induce an alertness in the reader — something very different from a state of superficial irritation or general numbness. My personal experience of reading Lautréamont is not that I feel cretinised, thrust into a posture of frustrated submission to an aggressive piece of nonsense. On the contrary, the structures developed in *Les Chants* are highly stimulating and, in their own way, rigorous, for the book is not so much a wallowing in the arbitrary (as perhaps are some of Tzara's earlier word-salads) as an investigation of the *shapes* of the arbitrary. The style of the book is multifarious, but one feature remains crucial throughout, namely the use of figures of speech or images (especially anthropomorphic ones). These are what sustain the characteristic ambience of uncertainty, in that the text is constantly sliding away from the literal to the figurative, never settling on the solid ground of down-to-earth univocal meaning.

The reader sympathetic to my earlier arguments can accommodate my next suggestion, that *Les Chants de Maldoror* at large constitute a vast figure of speech, a demonstration of the power of language to fertilise whole chains of images and allusions. And these, however random, must conform to certain patterns, which are, in the last resort, the ground rules of syntax which shape the figurative utterance. In our example, at the point where the two terms of the comparison fade into vagueness, the linking mechanism is foregrounded: the phrase *beau comme* is in any event repeated many times during this part of the book. What begins to engage my enthusiasm as a reader is the sense of being a witness to the invention and exploitation of a prodigious device for conjuring up wild images and thereby inducing poetic responses. I must insist that there *are* responses, for as if by magic, the more logological and blank the signs become, the more they induce in me a feeling of poetic expectancy. This expectancy (analogous to the expectancy which I suggested could be the result of reading a poem by Follain — see Chapter 7), this feeling that something poetic is about to erupt at any moment, is in a sense the literary response at its purest. That Lautréamont can call up such a response is an index of the power of his poetic extremism. Through terroristic methods, he has managed to isolate the pure figure of poetic feeling – he has sketched the shape of the mental leap in its simplest form. *Beau comme* is, then, the prototype of all analogical acts.

Reading Lautréamont is not unlike reading Mallarmé, an experience of flexing mental muscles in the void. We turn back to the real world with relief that it is still there: but we also find that it is there *for us* in an enhanced way, since our capacity to perceive things poetically has in the meantime been subtly deepened. Analogistics now comes into its own. The textual void becomes a space which sucks reality back into itself. All at once, the non-referential figures make sense to us in terms of natural process. Nature herself is just such a creator of shapes and figures as is the text energised by simile. The motions of the book mime those of the world: both shape metamorphoses, both develop chains of living things in evolutionary spirals.

Finally it dawns on me that the overt theme of metamorphosis, which is the superficial subject of much of the pseudo-narrative in Lautréamont's work, is in fact emblematic. For it corresponds to the linguistic principle on which the text is based, namely *convertibility*, the capacity of each sign to point towards something else. Then, over and above this intellectual discovery, I feel a strong pleasure. The reason for this is that I can sense that the text is attuned to other metamorphic processes, those which take place in the natural world and in my own sensibility. I turn back to Lautréamont's image and try again:

> The scarab beetle, beautiful as the trembling of hands in alcoholism, faded from sight on the horizon.

The scarab and its dung-ball can now be envisaged as an image of cyclical life, excrement being the source of nourishment for the beetle's offspring. Did not the Egyptians honour the scarab as a symbol of eternal recurrence? What then of the trembling hands? The sense is of imminent physical collapse, and yet also of rhythmical motion. The alcoholic's *delirium tremens* is paradoxically both limpness and animation, inertia and energy. Nourishment and excrement run parallel to this, and Lautréamont's image is to this extent 'justified' for me in that I find it bringing into focus certain aspects of the real world, the cycle of natural change whereby disintegration leads to regeneration.

Scanning back across the whole book again, I can apply (analogically) the shape of this realisation. Lautréamont's text is one of disintegration in its apparent refusal to focus on a logical theme or to make proper sense. Yet this refusal, this sabotaging of normal mental habits, is a prelude to regeneration. Given time, the reader can adjust himself to surprise and learn to steer a course amid shifting meanings. Such works as *Les Chants de Maldoror*, once we have learned to cope with them, impart lessons in how to read which will inform all our encounters thereafter, both literary and material.

Implicit in the notion of 'justifying' an image is the idea that the successful image is one which resists easy resolution. For it to function well, the distance between the two entities must be considerable, i.e. there must be evident differentness; at the same time, the distance must eventually be crossable, i.e. there must be potential sameness. All metaphorical procedures exploit the mutual tensions of these two. A comparison whose terms are not divergent, has no bite to it; a comparison in which there is no discernible point of likeness, has no weight to it.

It is an important element in our apprenticeship in analogistics to note that an observed resemblance carries with it an implicit observation of a difference. As Paul Éluard wrote,

Les ressemblances ne sont pas en rapport,
Elles se heurtent.

(Éluard, 1968, I, 220)

(Resemblances are not adjusted, / They clash one against the other.)

The Surrealist metaphor is, as we have seen, productive of conflict: how else could it continue to function and not lead speedily to a vision of intolerable sameness? For each image, there is a quotient of familiarity and another of unfamiliarity. The effort we expend in trying to make sense of it is proportionate to the pleasure felt when we realise it is possible to hold the two sides of the equation in our mind at once. This realisation is not however reductive: a metaphor 'grasped' is not a metaphor annihilated. Differences continue to operate even where resemblance has been identified.

The challenge of metaphoric writing, as of analogical thinking in general, is that it demands a constant alertness of mind. To achieve this flexibility is crucial to us in more than one respect. If we can handle shifts of stress and meaning, if we can cheerfully swallow images which make no immediate sense, and engage in spaces where zones of coherence clash with zones of incoherence, then we shall have adapted our minds and our sensibilities to a situation which, in the last analysis, is precisely that of our global being-in-the-world. For our perceptual knowledge of reality is derived from exactly the same reading skills as we apply to poetry. We learn about the world by scanning its signs. We collate experiences and grade them in accordance with principles of sameness and difference. We shape our appreciation of the way reality behaves by scrutinising as it were the stylistic habits of the tangible world, reading objects and their movements in space as so many tropes in a discourse of which we too form a part. Poetic language, which teaches us to notice more and more *different* things at the same time as it encourages us to keep track of them by also noticing patterns of *resemblance*, gives us practice in responding more alertly to the world itself, that space of fluidity and metamorphosis whose language of images swerves now towards alterity and confusion, now towards echo and order, in ceaselessly shifting configurations of enigma and meaning.

The poetic view of the world as a space of flux is crystallised in Ovid's *Metamorphoses*, a work to which *Les Chants de Maldoror* may be said to pay an oblique, caricatural homage. Ovid's poem is a compendium of Greek myths concerning 'bodies which have been transformed into shapes of a different kind' (Ovid, 1955, 31), and offers us a whole series of quasi-Surrealist pairings and fusions in a marvellous polyphony of free-ranging associations. Ovid tells how Apollo pursues Daphne, whom he loves madly, and how she is turned into a tree just as he embraces her. Actaeon stumbles into a cave where Diana is bathing, is punished by being turned into a stag, and dies ripped to pieces by his own hounds. Arachne engages in a weaving contest with the goddess Athene and produces a flawless portrayal of the metamorphic adventures involving deities which Ovid relates elsewhere in the book; in a fit of jealousy, Athene tears the tapestry into shreds and turns Arachne into a spider. Narcissus spurns the love of the nymph Echo, who wastes away till only her voice remains; he in turn falls in love with his own image in a pool and wastes away in contemplation of its inaccessible beauty.

At one level, these stories are moral allegories: mortals are punished for having defied the authority of the gods; Narcissus demonstrates the negative effects of selfishness; Actaeon is perhaps the bloodthirsty hunter who gets his just deserts. At a deeper level, they are allegories of creation which reflect the way the early Greeks pictured the workings of nature. And as parables of natural creativity, the myths have equally to do with the functioning of the human imagination. Ovid's account of Arachne's contest with Athene hints at the idea that mortal art can rival

the creations of the gods. Ironically, the heroine of that story, having
portrayed metamorphoses in her tapestry, is herself metamorphosed,
the artist herself becoming a convertible sign and thence a mythical
figure! Ovid's combination of the myths of Echo and Narcissus is a
poetic demonstration of a kind of negative metamorphosis. Echo's
individuality is depleted because there is no spark of love to link her
with the one she desires and so nourish a meaningful relation. Narcissus
comes across to the reader as one who is incapable of extending his
consciousness beyond its own limits: he falls victim to the solipsistic
temptation as, obsessed by his subjectivity, he vainly tries to impose it
on the external world. The self-projection is chimerical, a shadow without substance, and the attempt to place mirage above experience may
be seen as the equivalent of prefering the logological artefact to one
which opens onto reality.

Ovid's description of Actaeon after the metamorphosis is a *tour de
force* of imaginative evocation: for while his body is that of a stag,
Actaeon's human mind remains intact, and we witness his panic
thoughts as he perishes under the claws and teeth of his dogs, vainly
trying to call them off. The collision of two orders of reality in this
story makes of it perhaps one of the earliest examples of the literary
effect of the Fantastic, which derives from the parallel credibility of
two antithetical realities. The sequence as described by Ovid indicates
that he was well aware of the vital moment of transition at the heart of
change. There is a point (and sometimes even an extended period of
time) where the metamorphosis is suspended halfway between the two
forms in question. Here, the shift from man to stag is handled in a way
which dramatises what I would like to suggest is one of the poetic
implications of the episode, namely that there can be a transitional
zone of intense disquiet between the human mind and the inarticulate
otherness which it seeks to make its own in the act of consciousness.
The Daphne myth equally exemplifies Ovid's pleasure in the poetic
ambiguity of metamorphosis: though Daphne is no longer woman but
tree, Apollo continues his amorous advances, embracing the branches as
if they were limbs and placing his hand on the bark to feel Daphne's
heartbeat. There is an erotic thrill in reading this suspended metaphor
and letting mingled associations of sameness and differentness play
across the sensibility. (In much the same way, David Garnett's novella
Lady into Fox explores the troubling paradox of a man's deep and
tender attachment to a wild fox, his transformed wife.) In a pictorial
version of Ovid's story, the Pollaiuolo brothers' painting *Apollo and
Daphne*, attention is frozen on the precise moment of transformation

'to dwell at the instant of change'

Antonio and Piero del Pollaiuolo, *Apollo and Daphne*

Source: Reproduced by courtesy of the Trustees, the National Gallery, London

when, just as Apollo grasps her about the waist, Daphne sprouts leaves and twigs from her outstretched arms, one leg trailing its naked human beauty while the other is already rooting itself woodily into the earth. As Brigid Brophy says, 'a legend of metamorphosis is itself a metaphor of the very process of metaphor' (Brophy, 1966, 11-12). The thrill induced by Ovid's synthesis of contraries reminds me of the thrill I feel when reading a brilliant Surrealist image or the one I felt when I saw a flag as a falling woman. Poetic responses are aroused precisely because one yearns to dwell at the instant of change, the impossible centre of the transformation. Suzanne Lilar observes of a similar experience, 'my rapture was located at the very heart of the metamorphosis and at the precise moment of its accomplishment' (Lilar, 1954, 16).

To linger at the 'magic moment of the metamorphosis' (Galinsky, 1975, 181) is to savour the mixed pleasures of startling strangeness and reassuring sameness. It is very odd indeed that a woman should become a tree; yet *as* a tree, the shy Daphne retains her personality, and her bark shrinks timidly away from Apollo's kisses. Similarly, Arachne the spider still keeps a skill she had as Arachne the woman — she can weave marvellously well. Such metamorphoses, asserting the powerful logic of the non-rational, demonstrate how identity or specificity can actually be highlighted by the enactment of a process which, ostensibly, is aimed at suppressing that identity or specificity. In terms of the poetic metaphor, the lesson for the reader is one of reciprocal illumination: just as his sensibility is made more aware of the pattern of analogies which draws all aspects of perceptual reality into communion, so he is also being sensitised to the singularity of each given phenomenon. The 'dark and profound unity' of the network of correspondences is thus balanced off against the 'intolerable brightness' of the single thing, in a two-way sharpening of the poetic faculties.

The dramatic changes described in *Metamorphoses* are invariably tinged with sadness: each transformation is the result of an enforced renunciation or of a punishment. And yet there is a strange aura of attractiveness that touches these unfortunates: Echo as echo, Daphne as laurel tree, Arachne as spider continue to engage our sympathy, our admiration, even our erotic fantasy. Perhaps this is because they do not actually die. We know that echoes, laurel trees and spiders do still exist. The gods may have annihilated a human being, but they have also created a new entity in the physical world. Hence these metamorphoses represent myths of regeneration as much as of destruction, and may be seen as a primitive representation of that dialectical process of change which, from Heraclitus to Hegel, has been posited as the fundamental mode of operation of the cosmos. Indeed, Ovid actually discusses this cosmic theme in explicit terms, attributing to the philosopher Pythagoras what could be taken as the motto for the entire book: 'Nothing in the entire universe ever perishes, believe me, but the things vary, and adopt a new form' (Ovid, 1955, 371). In responding to Ovid's tales, the reader's imagination is being stirred both by the literary gestures which conjure up change, i.e. the style of writing which promotes the convertibility of literary signs, and by the exactly equivalent theme of the continuous process of change which is the natural idiom of all creation. Such poetry thus operates within a perspective where imaginary figures are dramatised in their transition towards becoming aspects of the real world.

11 TRANSCENDENCE AND TRANSPARENCY

The previous chapter led us to the proposition that there is a meaningful analogy to be drawn between the operations of nature, involving the evolutions of physical life, and the operations of poetic language, involving changes brought about by figurative speech. The correspondence of these two sorts of operation represents an important poetic intuition. But it remains to clarify the nature of the correspondence. Is poetic process simply a replication of natural process? I have tried to argue that poems do not simply catch forms from outside in order to exploit them as props within an hermetically sealed arena. The textual pattern *is* a pattern porous to external experience: it has a living relationship to what we know of nature. Poetry is therefore not just passive reflection of the *status quo*. As Paz observes, 'if art mirrors the world, then the mirror is magical; it changes the world' (Paz, 1974, 60). Poetry is not feeble mimesis, but active intervention. It now remains to elucidate the nature of the change which it effects upon reality.

Philip Wheelwright introduces a significant consideration when he observes that 'the intimation of a something more, a beyond the horizon, belongs to the very nature of consciousness' (Wheelwright, 1954, 8). There is a natural tendency for our acts of making sense to be conditioned by some element of expectancy such that the meaning of whatever it is we observe is coloured by our desire that it have accessible shape and direction, that it both fit into our perspective upon it and also take us further than we have hitherto come. The mind dreams of the bare facts of existence being aligned to its own concerns, thereby leading it smoothly forward beyond its immediate limitations. If I argue that poetry is a serious game with words which carries with it the possibility of an enhanced perception of the non-verbal realm of materiality, then the reader will naturally expect to be told what it is that poetry offers him which ordinary, 'prosaic' perception cannot. Does poetry present us with a seductive glimpse of what is not? I have argued that it is an incomplete view to see poetry as only the conjuring up of effects of unreality. Is then that to which poetry gives us access a reality of crystal-clear sense impressions? It is not just this either — though to be able to perceive with crystal clarity is far from being a dispassionate condition. Poetry, I will suggest, allows us access to modes of perception which disclose aspects of the world upon which we would not normally focus, and in so doing, affords us a heightened sense of the meaningful presence of things. But this still does not settle the question. In what consists that something more which poetic insight appears to offer?

At the risk of providing an excess of examples of poems which celebrate that 'moment of heightened perception' which is so often the core and *raison d'être* of a poetic text, let me cite the key passage from Kenneth Rexroth's poem 'Incarnation' (also known as 'The Webs of Being').

> And as I stood on the stones
> In the midst of whirling water,
> The whirling iris perfume
> Caught me in a vision of you
> More real than reality:
> Fire in the deep curves of your hair:
> Your hips whirled in a tango,
> Out and back in dim scented light
>
> (Rexroth, 1966, 162)

The poet is describing an epiphany which occurs after a day spent climbing in snowy mountains. His body is fatigued and his eyes weary from the glare of snow: physiologically the conditions are conducive to perceptual illusion. He comes down at sunset to a green meadow where wild iris grows. At the end of the canyon, smoke rises from a camp fire, where (we may legitimately suppose) his beloved, the 'you' of the poem, awaits him. Then a swirl of sense impressions overwhelms him. It is as though, of a sudden, the data he is asked to absorb at the end of his exertions are too abundant for his senses to handle. The moment is one of dramatic sensory fullness as his feet move from snow to stones, and the icy air at his nostrils gives way to the alluring scent of the wild flower. Erotic expectancy and desire seize him and prompt a vision which represents a kind of metaphoric substitution for the sense impressions he has just gathered in. The words *perfume* and *scented* appear in these lines as pointers to the crucial association between the scent of flowers and the scent of the woman. They help to ground the connection between an actual and an imagined sensation. The *whirling* motion of the water is an actuality: it is transferred on to the iris perfume, in a process of contiguous association which is more metonymic than metaphoric. This 'whirling iris perfume' (which, be it noted, is the active subject of the sentence, rather than the 'I' who has the vision) then gives rise to the final association, the woman, envisaged as a 'whirling' entity herself in that her hair has florid waves and her hips are 'whirled in a tango'. The connotative field is erotically alluring: sinuousness, rhythmicality, mysterious stimulation – the swirl of a torrent, the sexiness of tango steps. To this the last reference to fire adds a further dimension of surprise. It comes across as something at odds with what has gone before (snow, cold water) and in this way lends a final twist of strangeness to the sequence. Yet with its associations of erotic passion, it helps to compound the irruption in the text of a sensual, fleshly presence.

Now the gist of my earlier argument in such chapters as 'The Poem Opens Onto the World' has been that the figurative language of poetry tends to strain out of its condition of intransitivity in order to be transitive. That is to say, the verbal construct presses for an intentional relation to the perceived world such that we may, without feeling silly, say that we 'feel' the poem, i.e. we take in its meanings as gestures towards literality, hence as experiences implicit in our sensory lives. A participatory reading of Rexroth's poem will set the reader on a par with its narrator, and allow him to make what I will call 'deep sense' (rather than merely intellectual sense) out of the sudden transformation of a set of percepts into a hallucination, each time engaging the same senses (smell, hearing, touch). What makes the poem exciting is the overwhelming character of this metamorphosis, the fact that the drawing-together of the various 'webs of being' create an effect which is 'more real than reality'.

Now hallucinations are experiences which, in objective terms, are illusory. Their very attractiveness lies in part, I argued in my opening chapter, in that they contradict our knowledge of natural laws, and thus summon up the queer feeling of strangeness. This feeling could be compared to the literary effect known as the Fantastic, for the poetic emotion located at the junction of unreality and reality provokes the same kind of *frisson* as that felt by the reader of a fantastic tale, what Tzvetan Todorov terms 'the hesitation experienced by a being who knows only natural laws when faced by an event which is apparently supernatural' (Todorov, 1970, 29). However, as I argued above, the appeal of the unreal lies in its having plausibility for the percipient *none the less*. In Rexroth's text, the narrator does not feel that his vision is unreal, nor indeed that it hovers on the borderline between the unreal and the real: in other words, he does not feel that it can be defined in any way which suggests it to be a depletion of reality, and, instead, exclaims that it is more real than reality. This condition I will call that of the surreal.

We are once more probing into the exact nature of the transformation which poetry asks us to contemplate. Let me go back over the
ground I have just covered to make quite sure where we stand. When we
engage with the poetic text at the level of our deep sensibility, we
experience it in ways which posit it as being both real and unreal. This
is to say that we bring to the poem our perceptually-oriented faculties,
including our memory with its many combinations of linked sensations;
and we bring also our dream faculties, our reveries, our ability to entertain totally unlikely entities as realities. Now, the net result of our
acceding to a text in its simultaneous reality and unreality is that it
adds up to more than simply a clash of contraries or an ambiguity. The
effect of a genuinely receptive reading is exactly what Rexroth experiences in his alpine vision, namely the effect of reality marvellously
enhanced — of surreality. The moment of the 'fascinating image' introduces us, finally, to a perspective within which we can admit the dialectical fusion of the categories *real* and *unreal*, which we have hitherto
supposed to be attractive to us because of their sharp differentness.

In proposing to see these two reconciled within the category *surreal*,
I am of course opening up the perspective of sameness. And at once I
am running the risk of forgetting all that I said earlier, namely that the
proper practice of analogistics requires us to posit *sameness* but also to
preserve our receptivity to *differentness*. If I commit myself to the
'higher' category of the surreal, I might find myself suppressing the
specificity of the objects of my consciousness and embarking on an
abstractive journey which will lead me to a detached, transcendent
plane. The purpose of this chapter is to settle this issue once and for all.
How does the temptation of transcendence arise, and should we give in
to it?

The Romantic poets sought to transfigure reality by conferring an aura
of mystery or fascination upon phenomena. Novalis defines the operation as of one of 'Romanticisation'.

> The world must be romanticized. In this way we will rediscover its
> original meaning. Romanticization is nothing more than a process of
> raising to a higher power . . . When I confer a higher meaning upon
> the commonplace, a secret aspect upon the ordinary, the dignity of
> the unknown upon what is known, or an appearance of infinity
> upon what is finite, I romanticize it.   (Novalis, 1962, 424)

The practice of Romanticisation means a stretching of our apperception of the normal. But it is not simply a 'strangifying' or a 'derealising' of perceptions, not a projection of dreams into materiality, but a transfiguration of the aspects of the world which renders it other and more valuable than it now is. I will leave aside the question of the power of the poet to effect this transformation: evidently Novalis intends that his conferring of higher meaning should be understood not as an arbitrary projection of a subjective colouring on to things, but as a genuine regeneration of everyone's vision of the world, a collective renewal of perception. What I want to concentrate on at present is the actual nature of the transformation. What happens to the normal world of the commonplace, the ordinary, the known, the finite? It alters in that its signifying function is to point in the direction of the infinite; it becomes accessible to us in its role as opening onto a higher plane. It is altered by being *transcended*. Let me illustrate this by reviewing a number of examples.

Transcendence is the Romantic mode par excellence.[18] This is true not only in terms of thought process (in the sense that Romantics were able to swallow contradictions and so think their way up and above them, in a kind of intuitive dialectics), but also in terms of elective imagery. Rousseau, who may be said to have initiated the era of Romantic reverie, announces the transcendent character of dreaming when in a climactic passage of *Les Rêveries du promeneur solitaire*, he speaks of the sensation of drifting upwards: 'During these distractions, my soul wanders and glides in the universe upon the wings of the imagination, in ecstasies which surpass all other pleasure' (Rousseau, 1960, 89). The cornerstone of the Romantic poetics is the primacy of the imagination, and it is natural for them to equate any active engagement in the processes of imagination with a sense of uplift, of movement above the level of mundane existence. Baudelaire's poetry is based upon the premiss that the physical level of experience is intimately linked to the spiritual level, the natural world being a storehouse of impressions which the imagination uses as springboards for flights of the spirit. There is therefore in Baudelaire's poetry scarcely a thing, or an aspect of a thing, which does not in some way or other hold out a promise of higher meaning. 'The principle of poetry', he once wrote, 'is strictly and simply the human aspiration to a superior beauty – this principle is made manifest in an enthusiasm and an excitation of the soul' (quoted in Gibson, 1961, 63-4). And these movements of the soul are directed upwards.

Elevation and flight become typical Romantic themes, representing the physical and spatial equivalent of imaginative euphoria. The motif of *flying upwards* may be traced through its variants as a strongly meaningful constituent in the poetic experience of the later French Romantics and Symbolists, and of the German Symbolists. Many of Victor Hugo's later poems, such as the dramatic and declarative 'Ibo', evoke vast spaces through which the poet, that 'winged dreamer', speeds on a Promethean ascent towards the final transcendent point where imagination confronts the infinite. And blissful transport is the keynote of Stefan George's poem 'Entrückung', the report of an experience of mystical expansion in which the limits of finite consciousness dissolve in a metamorphic vision of cosmic proportions.

> Ich fühle luft von anderem planeten (. . .)
> Ich steige über schluchten ungeheuer,
> Ich fühle wie ich über letzter wolke
> In einem meer kristallnen glanzes schwimme –
> Ich bin ein funke nur vom heiligen feuer
> Ich bin ein dröhnen nur der heiligen stimme.

> (George, 1949, 122-3)

(I feel air from another planet / I mount over monstrous chasms, / I feel myself swimming over the last cloud / In a sea of crystal splendour – / I am but a spark of the holy fire / I am but a droning within the holy voice.)

The flight of consciousness here attains a level incommensurate with the experience of earthly phenomena. The poet is projecting himself onto a plane in which human and worldly features are submerged and all is envisaged as sameness, a vast undifferentiated oneness which is finally recognised as divine in nature. Transcendence here means departing from the world of the human condition and soaring into superhuman realms, and the poetry which sustains this vision is not really accessible to understanding in a terrestrial context.

Slightly more earthly because still more or less dependent on gravity is the poetry of the Chinese mystic Han-shan. His collection of poems called *Cold Mountain* speaks of the hermit's life on an isolated mountain peak. The descriptions of the place are often detailed enough to be evocative in a realistic way, though the tenor of the evocations is such as to ask the reader to move beyond the visual and tangible in the direction of a higher truth.

I climb the road to Cold Mountain,
The road to Cold Mountain that never ends.
The valleys are long and strewn with stones;
The streams are broad and banked with thick grass.
Moss is slippery, though no rain has fallen;
Pines sigh, but it isn't the wind.
Who can break from the snares of the world
And sit with me among the white clouds?

(Han-shan, 1970, 58; tr. Burton Watson)

The ascent of a mountain is an archetypal allegory of spiritual perfection. Han-shan describes the way up the steep road by indicating certain striking details: stones, grass, moss, pines. Gradually the detail slips away, for the higher up one climbs, the less one can physically perceive. In a literal sense, the top of the mountain is a place where the senses become superfluous, for he who sits among clouds can see nothing. And the figurative sense of this arrival at a level where the phenomenal world is removed from the   purview of consciousness is clear enough. As Arthur Waley points out, 'Cold Mountain is the name of a state of mind rather than a locality' (quoted in Han-shan, 1970, 10). The geographical peak is identified as a peak of spiritual awareness, the release of consciousness from its dependence on the objects of sensation. For in the Buddhist view, illumination occurs only at the point when one breaks free of 'the snares of the world' in order to merge with the Oneness which transcends both phenomenal diversity and the individual consciousness.

For another example of poetic transcendence, let us return to a poem which I referred to earlier as an example of the poetic treatment of a specific natural phenomenon. This is Hopkins's sonnet 'The Windhover', whose first eight lines I quoted in Chapter 7. In those lines the poet gives a report on a perceptual experience, the sighting of a kestrel in rapid flight across the sky. But already, as we saw, the accent is placed on the observer's exhilaration, his *responses* to the phenomenon, so that the reader's mind is implicitly being prepared for a modulation of meaning, from bird-flight to the flight of the poetic imagination. In the next lines, continuity of tone is maintained by a succession of staccato exclamations, but now the vocabulary shifts from the transcription of stunning sense impressions to an idiom of abstract nouns and cryptic hintings:

Brute beauty and valour and act, oh, air, pride, plume here
   Buckle! AND the fire that breaks from thee then, a billion
Times told lovelier, more dangerous, O my chevalier!

    (Hopkins, 1953, 30)

At first glance these lines seem particularly obscure. But the poet's
intentions are made manifest if one now looks back at the subtitle of
the poem, 'To Christ our Lord'. Quite clearly the poet is using the hawk
as a point of departure for analogical developments: the hawk is not so
much a real creature as a symbol of Christ. The parallelism rests on
resemblances which the poem invites us to contemplate. For example,
the downward plunge of the bird equates to the descent of Christ from
heaven to earth; its ascent equates to the Resurrection. The dual register of references is confirmed by a number of double meanings which
Hopkins has inserted into the fabric of the poem. For instance, the bird
is described as 'dauphin', on one level a 'realistic' reference to its fluent
movements (like those of a dolphin), on another, a symbolic allusion to
Christ's rank as son of God (dauphin = prince regent). The word 'plume'
denotes the bird's plumage, yet also connotes the feathered insignium
worn by a triumphant knight ('chevalier'), in turn an image of the
resurrected Christ ascending to glory.

   Much remains to be explained about 'The Windhover', including the
meaning of the notoriously ambiguous word 'buckle'. But I am content
to curtail my examination here in order to underline the relevance of
the example to my general argument. It is this: that despite the stress I
previously laid on Hopkins's interest in natural detail, the ultimate
thrust of his poem on the kestrel is symbolic and religious. We may
conclude that, following the mysterious logic of the mystic imagination,
the observation of the single thing in all its specificity has disclosed that
radiant 'inscape' which then prompts the reading of the thing as a sign
carried to a higher power.

   As one who does not share Hopkins's religious faith I find it difficult
to decide how I should best respond to this symbolism. Is it legitimate
to be sensitive to the exhilaration of the description and to ignore its
religious connotations? It seems to me that the sheer impetus and verve
of the language are good enough reasons to take pleasure in the poem:
secondary meanings may be more or less permanently deferred without
compromising initial responses. But once I have had it pointed out to
me that Hopkins is a Jesuit and that I ought to expect him to set off in
pursuit of the transcendental register, I am going to be aware that his
hawk poem is straining to reveal to me something other than its osten-

sible object. How can I adjust my reading creatively to these under-currents of implication, if it is the case that my sensibility is unwilling to be swayed by the religious grace by which the poem, theologically speaking, is oriented?

Those who can supply a context of religious response will presum-ably find that the poem functions well as the bearer of religious rather than sensory insights. But for those who cannot thrill to the religious meaning, the poem may still be exciting in a way which is not restric-ted to the evocation of bird-flight. There can be an intellectual *frisson* for me in the notion that the dense syntax of the poem is the vehicle of potential eruptions of secondary meaning. The intensity of Hopkins's diction invokes the same exhilaration which I associate with the ana-logy-making process, so that while I remain untouched by the strictly religious dimension, I can still experience a thrill in witnessing the *gesture of transcendence* which his poetic language enacts.

The poetry of Mallarmé extends the principle of extracting spiritual correspondences from earthly objects into a veritable aesthetics of absence, whereby sense-bound reality is gradually distilled into verbal statements, and thereby negated and transcended: the resultant poem stands as a splendidly vacuous structure erected around the echo or the shadow rather than the percept proper. (See the discussion of Mallarmé's poetic project in Chapter 2.) This abstractive approach to reality became so instinctive to Mallarmé that even when recording an actual event in space and time (as distinct from writing ethereal poetry to escape from such considerations), he is unable to suppress his literary habit of treating writing as an 'envol tacite d'abstraction' (Mallarmé, 1961, 385) — a 'tacit flight of abstraction'. Thus a mediocre intermezzo at the ballet earns his praise in these terms:

> L'émerveillante Mademoiselle Mauri résume le sujet par sa divination mêlée d'animalité trouble et pure à tous propos désignant les allu-sions non mises au point, ainsi qu'avant un pas elle invite, avec deux doigts, un pli frémissant de sa jupe et simule une impatience de plumes vers l'idée.   (Mallarmé, 1961, 305-6)

(The marvellous Miss Mauri summarises the subject through her intui-tion mingled with an obscure yet pure animality, again and again desig-nating allusions which are not spelt out, as when before making a step she coaxes forth, with two fingers, a shimmering fold of her skirt, thus depicting the impatience of feathers as they veer towards the idea.)

What has excited Mallarmé is a mere gesture, the dancer's fingers pluck-ing at her feathery skirt. Why is Mallarmé worked up over this? Because it represents an association to which his sensibility is peculiarly attuned, that between an attractive woman and a bird in flight (an association which in Chapter 4 we saw to be the basis of the poem 'Petit Air'). More importantly, because it suggests to him the moment of transcend-ence whereby the corporeal being of the girl is abstracted through the enactment of dance figures. Thus the physical gesture becomes indica-tive of a pure meaning; and Mallarmé sees the dancer's body as the vehicle of a poignant, because always intermittent, sequence of trans-cendental flights.

My final example of poetic transcendence is taken from the work of Rilke, which so often deals with the exemplary metamorphosis of external phenomena into inner qualities. His ninth *Duino Elegy* con-tains a meditation which describes the way mortal beings can express the transitory features of existence, and then implicitly modulates into an extreme form of transcendent imagining: things in the world, claims Rilke, actually 'need' us — they can only be 'saved' by virtue of human acts of saying, acts of poetic naming or representation.

> Und diese, von Hingang
> lebenden Dinge verstehn, dass du sie rühmst; vergänglich,
> traun sie ein Rettendes uns, den Vergänglichsten, zu.
> Wollen, wir sollen sie ganz im unsichtbaren Herzen verwandeln
> in — o unendlich! — in uns! wer wir am Ende auch seien.
>
> Erde, ist es nicht dies, was du willst: *unsichtbar*
> in uns erstehn? — Ist es dein Traum nicht,
> einmal unsichtbar zu sein? — Erde! unsichtbar!
> Was, wenn Verwandlung nicht, ist dein drängender Auftrag?
>
>   (Rilke, 1955, 719-20)

(And these things, which thrive on decease, / understand when you praise them; ephemeral themselves, / they credit us, the most ephemeral of all, with the power to save. / They desire that we should transform them utterly within the invisible heart / into — o infinity! — into our-selves! whoever we may be in the end. / Earth, is not this your desire: *invisibly* / to be resurrected within us? Is it not your dream / to be invisible one day? — Earth! invisible! / What is your insistent demand if not metamorphosis?)

If we accept that, as I suggested earlier, convertibility and metamorphosis are fundamentals which the poet attributes to natural life, it may be quite logical to suppose that the destiny of the world is to enter on a cycle of change which will result in some final apotheosis of change. Yet Rilke's vision is curious. Poetically it represents a peak of poetic transcendence in that it supposes mortal consciousness itself to be capable of achieving the ultimate conversion — of 'romanticising' nature so that it abandons all lowly ties and is subsumed within the superior poetic mind. The vision is ambitious in the extreme, all the more so since, as Rilke admits, man is himself as subject to involuntary change as the world and its objects. What is most significant in the statement is not that it posits a higher reality lying beyond our present horizons, but that it assumes that all aspects of existence are subservient to the poet's desire and imagination. Effectively the poet has placed himself in the superior position of a magus who contains and controls all things. Perhaps Rilke does not quite want this much: his lines are full of hesitation and questionings. But the implications of the poet's reverie are clearly domineering: the vision is of a consciousness which has the godlike power to make all creation dependent upon it.

These varied examples are consistent in that they all reflect the poetic tendency to see an external fact or object in relation to something other than itself: it is as if poets could not fail to see something other and higher whenever they are faced with a given item of experience. Novalis speaks of the poetic task as the conferring of a higher meaning upon the commonplace, the appearance of the infinite upon the finite. Rexroth transforms the scent of a flower into an erotic vision of a woman. Han-shan's mountain top is also a spiritual peak. Hopkins's hawk is equally a sign of the supernatural. Mallarmé's dancer veers from the material to the ideal, and Rilke suggests that the visible world may become invisible and therefore assimilable within the poet's consciousness. These are all examples of operations of poetic transcendence whereby earthbound sensations are transposed onto a spiritual plane.

The fundamental question is this: if a poet can discern a spiritual value or essence within a given object, and can, through the processes of poetic imagining and utterance, elicit a focal meaning from it, should he feel any obligation to concern himself further with the original vehicle of the intuition? Does his accession to a higher level of poetic insight mean that the things he has transcended are automatically eclipsed, made redundant? Does poetic transcendence entail a cancellation of sensations, as if material reality were something to be consumed, then discarded?

André Breton once defined the poetic function in the observation that 'what seems to me to be the secret of poetry is the faculty, granted to a rare few, to transmute a sensible reality by firstly bringing it to that pitch of incandescence which makes it liable to veer into a superior category' (in Ponge, 1961, 298). The statement would seem to bear out the tendency I have been examining. That is to say, poetry is being likened to an alchemical process whereby the base elements of perception are so transfigured that they no longer count as elements of material reality, but become the pure gold of a higher realm. This 'superior category' — whether it be an aesthetic, religious or otherwise enhanced mode — seems to be distinguished by being inaccessible to commonplace perception.

It is, I think, undeniable that the prospect of leaping high above the level of earthly reality is intrinsically exciting, and one can appreciate why poets in the Symbolist and post-Symbolist mould should have been drawn to this idea. But there is a less attractive corollary of this model of poetic process, the association of literary expression with exclusivity. The poem arising from the process of transcendence will require that the reader approach it without reference to sensations and emotions, relying only on his intellect. The poem thereby becomes a hermetic artefact, one which not only speaks *about* an exclusive realm but equally speaks *to* an exclusive circle of initiates. The principle of transcendence tends to have elitist connotations, as though only the pure can grasp the poet's meaning. But I want to argue that such exclusiveness is a mirage, and that no poem of value can so transcend our shared terrestrial reality as to maintain itself absolutely within a category completely remote from that of normal apprehension.

Proust has a good deal to say about the artistic process which concerns us here, the process whereby, in his phrase, sensations are translated into their 'spiritual equivalent'. His meditations in *Le Temps retrouvé* offer us a model of art as that which embodies the immaterial essence of experiences. 'Things, as soon as they are perceived by us, become something immaterial within ourselves' (Proust, 1954, III, 885). External objects strike us because they are figures of higher realities: art helps us to move towards an eventual intuition of the higher reality by means of a complex process of conversion. So far so good — Proust seems to be arguing for the transcendence of sensation, its eventual supersession in the aesthetic metamorphosis. However, as we read on, we discover that Proust is much too fond of details and flavours to want to exile himself from the world of sensations. Unlike the Mallarmé of the sonnets of absence, he cannot feel distaste for the allurements of contingent sensation, and even insists on the need to welcome unforeseen impressions as the stimuli of involuntary memories. In the end Proust adopts a conciliatory position, inviting chance and sensation into the centre of his vision, and insisting that the spiritual equivalent of an impression is not an ethereal transcendence. The impression remains indelibly present to him: its trace on the sensibility cannot be erased by any dream of pure flight towards the Ideal.

Proust's primary proposition that art is an austere distillation of essences, a means to transpose experience into a higher register, is thus significantly modified by the concomitant insistence that ideas which have no link to sensory experience have no durability. The implication is that sensibility alone can function as a guarantor of the validity of our ideas. 'No matter what idea is left within us by life, its material shape, the trace of the impression which is made on us, is still the guarantee of its necessary truth' (Proust, 1954, III, 880). In other words, Proust is arguing that poetic transcendence which annihilates its sources is doomed to sterility: aesthetic transformation must nourish itself on the ground of sensed discovery. What Hugo Friedrich has called the 'empty transcendentalism' of modern poetry (Friedrich, 1956, 196) is the enticing but frustrating dead-end from which Proust's argument can now help us to return.

My account of Proust's ideas is lacking in substance, and I must leave it to the reader to explore the point more closely by engaging directly with Proust in his lengthy exploration of the relevance of involuntary sensation and private impressionability to the task of opening windows onto deep reality. All the same, the gist of the declarations I have touched on is useful to my argument, and enables me to press forward to a final clarification of my position. I will preface it by a crisp interjection from Charles Tomlinson.

> The given is ground. You are bound by it
> as the eyes are bound — by a frame of nearnesses
> surrounding things half-seen: thick, bare
> calligraphy and confusion of boughs on air.

> (In Paz, 1971b, 70)

Tomlinson reminds us that poetry must concern itself with the substantial reality to which our senses bind us. We may be lured by ideas, schemas and perfect intellectual patterns, but we must recognise that the ground of our being lies in the confused richness of phenomenal experience. This is 'the given'. Occasionally we may apprehend the world as framed 'calligraphy', that is, as intellectually accessible meaning which seems to by-pass sensory channels. But as often as not, the world comes across as 'confusion of boughs on air' — a ramification without appreciable shape, sheer profusion in which there is no immediate configuration for the mind to grasp. It seems to me that poetic perception takes as its task the reconciliation of these two sorts of experience. It is neither a sleek intellectual reading-off of the signs, nor is it a surrender to shapeless multiplicity. It is a perspective which allows the external given to become incandescent, in Breton's phrase. And by this I mean a mode of perception and response which will elicit *figures*. Poetic perception is that way of viewing the world which focuses on the figures of reality.

In which direction does this take us? Let me summarise the propositions which formulate our problem. The ground of our experience is an inchoate mass of sensations and impressions. Poets are gifted in being able to identify certain sensations as privileged ones: they isolate and express these sensations in poems and instigate a process of transmutation whereby the original sensation becomes a spiritual equivalent or poetic figure which makes deep sense. Now if at this point the original sensation looks to be transcended and forgotten, we arrive at a contradiction. I am faced with two contrary propositions: first, that poetry celebrates the Real (it deals with actual events in an actual world) and secondly that poetry celebrates the Ideal (it negates or supersedes these events in the elevating operation of transcendence). How should this paradox be resolved?

The whole question of the relation of the Real to the Ideal was, of course, a major concern of the Romantic poets. Novalis it is who can provide an answer to our problem. In his earlier writings, he projects his hopes onto the transcendental plane, dreaming of a Beyond to which all terrestrial yearning is directed. Poetry at this stage is a means to decipher the text of nature and to 'take off' from it and gain glimpses of paradise. But in his later writings, and in particular his notebooks, Novalis shows himself to be concerned to reinstate the reality of the senses, dreaming now of a poetic sensitisation whereby man would be enabled 'to feel the invisible, touch the intangible' (Novalis, 1962, 415), and thus achieve within real life a complementary contact between sensation and vision, between presence and ideal. What he terms 'magic idealism' is a poetic process involving the reciprocal transformation of external reality and human thought. The ability to represent abstract concepts in concrete form, and the ability to see spiritual values in physical phenomena, are the basis of 'creative observation' (Novalis, 1962,

129). This is essentially a mode of analogical thinking in which outer and inner events are seen to be complementary, so that one is aware of external reality in its 'incandescent' mutation at the same time as one projects one's spiritual intuitions into the world as a practical fact. If, as Schelling observes, there is an invisible wall which separates the world of the Real from that of the Ideal, then the creative perception which Novalis proposes is the means to ensure that one can pass freely through it.

The Romantic account of poetic perception may seem a wanton refusal of rational examination. Yet it rests on the simple truth, ratified by contemporary physics indeed, that, in Éluard's words, 'a truly materialist interpretation of the world should not exclude from the world the one who registers it' (Éluard, 1968, I, 945). In Chapter 6 I quoted J.A. Baker's assertion that an authentic account of the peregrine falcon would encompass such associated facts as the observer's posture and his emotional part in the act of observation. Now, I am arguing in a wider perspective that it makes no sense to try to restrict a man's general perception of the phenomenal world to the purely physical dimension. Moreover, no event which takes place within the mind can in the final analysis be completely dissociated from the store of sense-impressions from which our psychophysical being draws its sustenance.

> Sans soucis sans soupçons
> Tes yeux sont livrés à ce qu'ils voient
> Vus par ce qu'ils regardent
>
> (Éluard, 1968, I, 394)

(Without cares without suspicion / Your eyes are exposed to what they see / And are seen by what they look upon)

There is, Éluard is suggesting, a reciprocity about the act of observation which allows the percipient of a poetic phenomenon to envisage himself and that phenomenon as participants in the total activity of seeing. The experience of 'inseeing' is one in which subject and object are drawn into a relation of meaning which, indeed, constitutes the poetic fact, the fact of the poetic. Both inner and outer reality are here conjoined, the Ideal and the Real brought into luminous contact. And if this applies to the poet reading the signs in the real world, it applies equally to the reader of the signs in the poetic text.

My conclusion is this. Poetic transcendence, as a process — just like metaphor — in which separate entities (subject and object) are brought together into an incandescent relation, is not an event which departs from the context of phenomenal reality. In one sense it could even be argued that immediately it did do so, it would by definition become unavailable to us, who are mortal and sense-bound. Hopkins's images of Resurrection are to this degree lost on me: for figures of speech which are cut off from their anchorage in the ground of physical life forfeit all immediacy and authenticity. Poetry which loses touch with the fact of existence becomes poetry for the angels, not for us humans. It is in a similar context that Breton underlines the difference between mystical analogy and poetic analogy. Whereas the former leaves go of this world, the latter does not. Granted, it may very well 'transcend' the habits of rational association – but however irrationally it behaves, it cannot lose contact with the circuit of sensory correspondences which link man to the world. Poetic analogy 'maintains itself without any constraint within the framework of the sensory, indeed of the sensual, without manifesting any propensity to spill over into the supernatural' (Breton, 1968, 9).

Since I have more or less discredited the notion of transcendence, it would be useful to introduce at this point the alternative term *transparency*. In Chapter 6, I spoke of the 'transparent' mode of reading which would permit the reader to envisage the poetic text as a movement between the figurative and the literal. By a transparent view of the real world, I mean one in which the subject is receptive to those appearances in actual reality which correspond to the ideal postulated within his mind. The world becomes transparent to those who view it in the light of a creative passion. The object of poetic contemplation becomes incandescent and modulates into a superior category: and yet this category remains closely allied to the perception, so that the perception is at the same time the apprehension of a deeper meaning *and* an appreciation of the specific character of the medium of that meaning.

The point is confirmed in a passage from *Paysages avec figures absentes* in which Philippe Jaccottet contemplates a landscape at sunset. The horizon is bordered by a band of gold, with a circle of powdery pink above it. Below, the world is dark and straw-coloured. Jaccottet tries to probe into the experience of witnessing these data, to articulate and so capture the set of impressions. Language at once offers itself as the means to transliterate the experience. Yet Jaccottet is hesitant, for he knows that words can flatten out one's immediate responses and destroy the halo of luminosity which is what is essential. Yet he does turn to words to express his hesitancy, and in so doing finds himself writing poetry.

Il faudrait parler d'un poudroiement de feu, d'une ouverture et aussi d'une ascension, d'une *transfiguration*, frôlant ainsi sans cesse des idées religieuses, quand les frôler seulement est déjà trop; car c'est cela, et c'est toujours autre chose encore. Car ce sont les *choses* qui sont telles, terre et ciel, nuées, sillons, broussailles, étoiles; ce sont les choses seules qui se transfigurent, n'étant absolument pas des symboles, étant le monde où l'on respire, où l'on meurt quand le souffle n'en peut plus.   (Jaccottet, 1970, 18-19)

(One ought to speak of a fiery powdering, of an opening and also an ascent, a *transfiguration*, thereby brushing up against religious ideas when merely to brush against them is to go too far. For that is what it is, and yet it is always something else again. For it is *things* which are thus, earth and sky, clouds, furrows, thickets, stars; it is things alone which are transfigured. They are absolutely not symbols: they are the world in which one breathes, in which one dies when one can no longer draw breath.)

Jaccottet insists that the objects of poetic contemplation are not the symbolic representation of a higher order which eclipses their right to existence. The transfigured appearance of the world should not prompt intimations of a religious kind. The poet remains rooted in the soil of terrestrial existence, unwilling to relinquish his grasp on the 'suchness' of things. Granted, a thing may seem like 'something else again'; it may have the power to provoke analogies or to appear radiant to perception. Yet it still remains 'what it is' − a thing. No act of poetic transcendence can prevent the world from continuing to be itself. No refined taste for incandescent analogies can stop a sunset from being a glorious feast for the senses. '*The immediate*: it is to this that I decidedly owe all my allegiance' (Jaccottet, 1970, 22).

A transparent view of the real is, then, one which sees objects not just as things, nor just as symbols, but as pulsating conjunctions of the two. It is because the poet can remind himself that he is looking at a thing which is still a thing, that his vision of that thing as something incandescent or transfigured gains its strength. The experience of uplift on which poets thrive is not mystical ecstasy, else it would cease to be truly poetic. The euphoric moment of true poetic perception is the sensation of flying without quite losing contact with the ground underfoot.[19] A transparent perspective on reality is one which sees the world as intensified and renewed, not one in which that world is superseded by superior authority. Transcendence must, so to speak, be pinned down by presence. Reality is figure, but a figure of itself. Or as Alain Jouffroy puts it, 'There isn't any poetic universe, there is just the universe, and that's enough' (Jouffroy, 1970, 37).

Conclusion
AT THE WINDOW

AT THE WINDOW

Poetry hesitates, flickering along the contours of the shapes I perceive, or seek to perceive. My senses reach out, as does my mind, aware of words as the frail net thrown after perception onto the dim forms of the real. There is a faltering, as the surfaces of material fact elude the definition which the poetic word strains to impart.

I have found that it is only rarely that I look up from a book and witness an outer world brought closer thanks to the magnetic pull of language. Not every day can I open the window after waking out of self-engrossment and look out like Su Tung P'o upon a space made miraculously accessible to the self shut inside the room. This image of the window from which I look out upon the real world is a haunting one, and I think it symbolises an abiding concern of poets ever since Romanticism first voiced the spectral suggestion that there might be a disquieting gap between self and world. Kafka once remarked that 'the tension between the subjective world of the ego and the objective world outside is the major problem of all art' (Janouch, 1968, 248), and I can imagine no better representation of this tension than the image of a person sitting quietly before a window, looking out on to a world apparently beyond reach.

Edgar Degas has a painting which epitomises this sense of vacillation between subjectivity and materiality. The picture, *Woman at a Window*, is the simple portrayal of a woman in a plain black dress seated with her back to a window, towards which she half turns. The figure is strangely unemphatic, as though she were of minimal importance and the point of the painting lay somewhere else than in being the portrait of a lady. Her face is dim, while from outside a bright light penetrates the gloomy brownness of the interior and illuminates her hands as they lie motionless on her lap. The room around the figure seems to evanesce, to become all shadow; and indeed the figure too seems to darken, to lose definition and identity. The woman is entranced, caught in a power which she may not resist, in a vision of that which lies beyond herself; and this vision is, one feels, associated with the magical white light that picks out her frozen hands and the barest hint of her profile. Gradually it becomes clear that the woman is only being sustained by the presence of what lies beyond the window: the thought of a landscape outside is what absorbs her, and this thought 'caught in a vision of that which lies beyond herself'

Edgar Degas, *Woman at a Window*
Source: Courtauld Institute Galleries, London

alone informs all her being. Without that white light reflected from the window, her consciousness would lapse into the uniform gloom of an amorphous interior and be extinguished. It is as though the woman were concentrating on a nigh impossible task, that of making the world real to herself and thus maintaining her own fragile claim to existence.

In an earlier discussion of the way poets may be preoccupied by the appeal of the fantastic and direct their language to the making of un-reality, I quoted Mallarmé's 'Sonnet en -yx' as a paradigm of the urge to banish material presence from the literary text (see Chapter 2). The quatrains of that sonnet do indeed enact a portentous ritual of extinc-tion in which all contents of a room are extinguished or filtered off, leaving the reader with the breathless sense of a space — the midnight chamber, or the space of the sonnet itself — which hovers in spell-bound suspension, kept imaginable only by virtue of a verbal incanta-tion and lacking in the slightest spark of reality. The emotional tension arising from this contemplation of sheer Nothingness is one which Mallarmé accustoms us to see as an ingredient in the experience of poetic beauty; it could be said that the *frisson* of poetic pleasure that attends our intellectual involvement in the forms of Mallarmé's langu-age is in part at least dependent on our feeling the air go out of the poem, its referentiality to any realm outside of itself being systematic-ally erased by the sheer textuality of the language object. Yet the poem moves on:

Mais proche la croisée au nord vacante, un or
Agonise selon peut-être le décor
Des licornes ruant du feu contre une nixe,

Elle, défunte nue en le miroir, encor
Que, dans l'oubli fermé par le cadre, se fixe
De scintillations sitôt le septuor.

(Mallarmé, 1961, 69)

(Yet near the window open to the North, a gilt frame / Agonises accor-ding perhaps to the decor / Of unicorns rearing from the fire against a naiad, / Herself, dead and naked in the mirror, / While, in the oblivion enclosed by the frame, are fixed, / Scintillation upon immediate scintil-lation, the seven stars.)

These tercets continue the tightening up of negatives which the qua-trains had so uncompromisingly initiated: there is mention of a naiad, and yet at once we are told she is dead; there are unicorns, yet we know them to be only part of a gilt design on a frame. In any case we already know that naiads and unicorns are creatures of mythology, and are therefore unreal anyway. We are in a room which is emptied of content, down to the mirror which stares blankly through an open window, onto the midnight sky. By now we have been conditioned to expect emptiness: the poem ought logically to end up with the perfect image of looking out upon vastness and the void, the mirror reflecting the extinction which has just taken place within the room, where all that remains is that echo of Nothingness, the obliterated *ptyx*. Outside, we expect to witness only the infinite emptiness of space.

Yet what we see is *something*, namely a group of seven stars which, given that the window faces north, are easily identifiable as the constellation of the Plough, which is aligned in relation to the Pole Star itself. The mention of this constellation, echoing the reference to a constellation at the climax of *Un Coup de dés* (see Chapter 9), appears as an unexpected and triumphant reversal of the gist of the rest of the poem.

Admittedly it can be argued that Mallarmé wants us to see these distant stars as inhuman and empty, analogues of the *nul ptyx*. The constellation could indeed be taken as symbolic of unutterable beauty, something beyond human reach, and therefore 'unreal'. For my part, I cannot resist the emotional tug I feel on reading this final orienting image of the poem, so much a relief after the desperate claustrophobia built up during the quatrains. Is there not a quickening of pace in these last lines? Do we not as readers feel ourselves being drawn to the window as by a breath of fresh air that might save us from suffocation? The poem closes on a set of sibilants which pinpoint the final word *septuor*, clearly the 'destination' of the poetic advance. The word denotes either a constellation of seven stars, hence the Plough, or else a musical septet. Now this latter meaning makes little sense in terms of a group of seven musicians, but makes excellent sense if taken as the piece of music they play. This music is like the music of the spheres, or rather it is the visual music of stars twinkling upon the black sky, an image of the ineffable music of pure poetry, the Mallarméan ideal. Its evocation, however, need not lead us towards the point of pure aesthetic contemplation, provided we remain attentive on the setting implied in the poem. We are lending our imagination to a space similar to that suggested by Degas: there is a sense of our being absorbed in something which exists beyond the window, and I feel that this sense of absorption, this entrancement caused by a brightness that lies beyond immediate apprehension and yet maintains a hypnotic hold over the senses, is suggestive of a signal or a *direction*. The window is a figure of our yearning for unknown spaces, of the compulsion which plunges our sensibility towards otherness, the non-self. And the Pole Star to which the Plough points is the answer to our gamble; it reassures us that we have not lost all points of reference.

It is thus possible to interpret Mallarmé's sonnet as a gesture towards transcendence whereby the poetic vision is focused on a transhuman ideal symbolised by the unearthly stars; or else we can read it as an anguished allegory of the need of subjectivity to look beyond the closed chambers of the mind in order to apprehend something which can be construed as objective meaning. Either way, these readings illustrate the dilemma of the poet which I have insisted on highlighting in this book. The glass of the window represents the caesura which makes the poetic perception of the world problematic. For we cannot be sure that what lies within the room will be matched by what lies outside: we cannot feel safe inside or outside, enclosed or thrust out into the night air. Uncannily, the stars might even begin to mock our stare, exhibiting themselves as an artificial pattern which we are deemed to have projected onto the arbitrary spill of bright dots in the black firmament. Configurations are, after all, constructions of the percipient. Personally, I am prepared to accept that the stars are 'meaningfully there', and this is why I take Mallarmé's poem as a dramatisation of the unsuppressed appeal of an existing outer reality even for one who has submerged his inner self in the darkness of intellectual paradoxes and the vacuum of an aesthetic system. A person sitting by a window enacts the ontological predicament, and part of that predicament consists in the temptation to believe that what lies outside might have some form of *relation* to what lies within.

In an article about the 'concrete thinking' characteristic of the schizophrenic mentality, the psychiatrist Harold F. Searles argues that it should be seen as a symptom of abnormal regression if a person registers all events, whether mental or physical, on a par with one another. Concrete thinking means the inability to differentiate between the concrete and the metaphorical, and is a concomitant of the collapse of the ego-boundary in schizophrenia, i.e. the erasure of the line demarcating the limits of the individual and the outside world (see Searles, 1962). The corollary of this mental regression is an inability to differentiate between sensation and idea, between what is literally the case and what is only figuratively the case. Now, in Chapter 1 we saw that a poet like Rimbaud might deliberately choose to concoct fantasies so vivid as to take on the character of phenomenal fact. Later, we saw that the early Surrealists found exhilaration in the hallucinations provoked by the practice of automatism. But we would probably distinguish such experimentation (however 'extra-literary' it may be claimed to be) from the experience of the psychotic whose delusion is situated in a context of psychological anguish and emotional insecurity.[20] When we read a psychiatrist's discussion of the schizophrenic view of reality, we identify this lack of differentiation between the literal and the figurative as a deficiency, since it rests upon an involuntary collapse of a normal faculty. Hence we feel troubled by Searles's story of a patient who insists that people can literally be turned into trees, rocks or sheep, and find the suggestion callous that there is something genuinely poetic here — an echo of Ovid indeed. It therefore comes as something of a shock to find that after writing at length about the schizophrenic's regrettable inability to see any difference between literality and metaphoricity, Searles ends his paper with the following wistful observation:

> Perhaps the reason why so many metaphors have a peculiarly poignant beauty is because each of them kindles in us, momentarily, a dim memory of the time when we lost the outer world — when we first realized that the outer world *is* outside, and we are unbridgeably apart from it, and alone.   (Searles, 1962, 583)

In effect, the psychiatrist finds himself voicing a rather unprofessional nostalgia for a time in infancy to which his patients may be said to regress — the time one first becomes aware of one's separateness from one's environment. This is the moment of incipient consciousness, properly speaking, the recognition by the mind that it has a being of its own and functions separately from what goes on outside. But is Searles wrong to voice his nostalgia?

As adults with minds that look out of the window of consciousness upon the world, we might think it inevitable that we should register that world as distant, separate. Consciousness witnesses the space beyond the ego-boundary as alien, a territory to which access is made difficult by distance. Like the man in Stevens's poem who rides out over Connecticut in a glass coach, we may sometimes even doubt that there *is* space out there to which we can gain access: there is hard glass between the mind which seeks to project itself and the objects towards which it strains.

This threshold experience is crucial, inasmuch as it underlies almost all the distinctions we may care to make in the domain of poetic experience, touching on sensation, mental images, concepts and words.

Lefebve writes that

> The world exists for us only to the extent that it is known to us, yet
> this very knowledge we have presupposes, as a condition of its being
> possible, that the world be placed at a distance from us, thus preven-
> ting us from reaching it and entirely merging with it. The result is
> the simultaneous existence of identity and duality – the duality
> between being and appearance, between the thing and the idea of
> the thing, between the idea and the word which expresses the idea,
> between the word and the thing.   (Lefebve, 1965, 108)

Such is the dilemma which Degas's *Woman at a Window* may be said
to epitomise. For she looks out on a world which she can only register
as distance, as space to be visualised but not touched. The situation can
be further dramatised if we imagine looking out across a valley to a
remote mountain peak. The distance we would have to travel to reach
that peak, feel its rock beneath our feet and breathe the cold air which
blows around it, is too great for it to seem at all feasible that we might
literally make the climb. Hence we witness the mountain as something
visible and yet untouchable, more an image than a provable fact. We
can be conscious of the mountain top yet not be entirely sure that it is
not a trick of light – an odd-shaped cloud perhaps. This is the nostalgic
ache of consciousness in its extreme form, and it can prompt the percipient to strange emotions, often perversely euphoric, as when
Sacheverell Sitwell flirts with the ambiguity about whether the mountains he sees are real or unreal (see Chapter 1), or when Yves Bonnefoy
decides that it is best not to actually set foot in the true place of poetry,
since the essence of the poetic emotion lies in the sense of yearning
which distance sustains (see Chapter 7). Much of the brooding tension
in the images of the Romantic painter Caspar David Friedrich, depic-
tions of silent people standing as if mesmerised by immense, mist-
bound spaces, arises from the *mise en scène* of this Idealist temptation,
the seductive thought that what our senses perceive might simply be
what Stevens calls 'reality as a thing seen by the mind'   (Stevens,
1955, 468).

Now I suggested in my opening chapters that a sense of unreality
might be a factor of poetic pleasure, and that certain poets are prepared
to induce solipsistic doubt as a means to establish a space for the
making of unreal constructions, i.e. poems. But I went on to argue that
this poetic flirtation with the unreal was but the obverse of a powerful
yearning for deep contact with the real. Poetic fantasy may be a temp-

orary stance adopted by the poet when faced with certain facts of consciousness; ultimately it can show itself to be shaped by the desire to
restore that lost sense of oneness to which Searles, very poetically,
alludes.

The major justification of poetry is that it affirms the existence of
'that bridge which links the external world and the internal world'
(Breton, 1954, 20). The moment of the poetic is characterised by the
re-discovery of this bridge, the crossing of distance, the annulment of
the glass barrier. The perfect state of poetic grace would consist in
dwelling at this point of contact, in such a way that one would stand 'at
the level of objects and of things, and have within oneself their global
form and, simultaneously, their definition', as Artaud puts it (Artaud,
1968, 176). This is the state of perfect osmosis between thinking and
its object, between the mind and the world. It is what Rilke was dreaming of when he spoke of *Weltinnenraum*, 'world-inner-space', the undifferentiated oneness of outer and inner:

> Durch alle Wesen reicht der *eine* Raum:
> Weltinnenraum. Die Vögel fliegen still
> durch uns hindurch. O, der ich wachsen will,
> ich seh hinaus, und *in* mir wächst der Baum.

> (Rilke, 1957, 93)

(Through all beings stretches the *one* space: / world-inner-space. The
birds silently fly / right through us. O, I who wish to grow, / I look outside, and the tree grows *inside* me.)

As I acknowledged earlier, it is often very difficult to accept a poetic
statement of such magnitude as being literally the case. At one level,
Rilke is claiming that the relation of mind to perceived reality has
become so intense that subject and object enact a union, the perceived
thing literally entering into the physical space occupied by the percipient. At another level, we can surmise that the act of articulating the
ecstatic feeling of union has become the act of authenticating that
intuition in an 'objective' way, so that it is really the written word (or
the fact of Rilke's having written these words) which has taken on the
task of authorising his and perhaps also our belief. The poem, that set
of inscriptions on paper, draws unto itself a force of conviction sufficient to enable Rilke to feel fulfilled and to confidently claim that
birds fly through his body without emitting an 'as if', or other marker
of figurativity.[21]

It is obvious that such a state of confidence will only come about where the poet has as much faith in words as in perceptions: he really has to believe that 'a word has the weight of an actual stone in his hand. The tone of a vowel has the color of a wing', in Robert Duncan's words (Duncan, 1971, vi). Only then may poetic statements assume the status of actual manifestations of material fact. In this sense, it is inadequate to insist on the poet's dedication to language, for what he achieves through words is a movement that goes beyond what *is written* to attain what *is*. Perse will make the claim that the poet is intent on apprehending 'not the *written text*, but the *thing* itself, grasped in its immediacy and totality' (Perse, 1972, 229).

I conceded earlier that such claims for the power of poetic speech can appear exaggerated, and that nobody has ever written anything which has literally affected the three-dimensional environment outside us, except in the indirect sense that a reader may be persuaded to adjust his personal focus on outer reality. It is fairly widespread practice for poets to make extravagant claims for their art, and this has contributed in large part to the credibility gap from which poetry suffers in the eyes of a majority of people. The more poets insist that poetry is literally capable of grasping reality, the more what they say ends up being taken in a metaphorical sense. That is: it is implicitly watered down, as if poets were only makers of symbolic gestures rather than people who truly deliver the goods they promise. Yet, as Suzanne Lilar observes, what more challenging concern could there be than 'the possibility that poetry might consist in constantly relaying to us the vibrant and fresh *perception* of this reality rather than its symbolic representation or its message' (Lilar, 1954, 155)?

Everything depends finally on the reader's attitude. If he has been given to believe that poetry is merely a playing with insubstantial figures, then he will take the claims he reads as so many empty metaphors and will only achieve indirect and minimal contact with the things the poet is trying to convey to him. If on the other hand he adopts the contrary posture – not necessarily one of naive gullibility, but one of thoughtful readiness to adjust his sensibility to the potential fertilisations of allusion or image – then he may find himself in the happy position of being both intellectually stimulated and moved in deeper parts of his being, engaged in such a way that he does not automatically censor the claims of metaphoric discourse and instead allows such extravagance to take shape within the space of his imagination and to make what I have called 'deep sense'.

Reading is an intentional act, and if we speak of someone 'taking in' the meaning of an author, it is because he has truly disposed his mind to accede to the demands of the text, both intellectually and emotionally. Poetry, more than any other literary mode, is an appeal to the freedom of the reader. Mikel Dufrenne suggests that 'poetry asks the reader to be poetic himself: not to be a poet, but to be the poet's collaborator who will accomplish in himself what the poet has created' (Dufrenne, 1961, 84). Reading a poem in an authentic way is to involve oneself fully in its language and its connotations, and the process of discovering the meanings of a poetic text is equally an exploration of the ramifications it sets up within the connotative scheme that exists in the subliminal mind and even the associated sensory network of the reader. Participation in the experience of words means, in this case, not an activity of squeezing meaning out onto a surface where it can be readily disposed in thin sections of dry formulation: rather it is a delving into fertile depths where meaning thickens and reverberates with life, and from which no single slice of intellectual message may be extracted.

'When we read properly', wrote Novalis, 'there opens up within our inner being a genuine, visible world fashioned according to the words' (Novalis, 1962, 412). This world cannot but be subjective in its colouring, at least in the first instance. But can it be otherwise, if there is to be genuine participation in the poem? Can the reader expect entirely to submit to the author's drift and re-create the poetic perceptions exactly as the author intended them to be re-created? It is possible to see poetic texts as containers of hidden energies which wait only to be released. But without a reader, no text can be actualised. The point is made by a phenomenologist, Edo Pivćević, writing about signs at large: 'A sign or a configuration of signs are brought to life in an act of understanding. Without such an act no sign can mean anything' (Pivćević, 1970, 13). This is to say that the poem remains intransitive until I become its animating subject. Those signs on page 74 of *The Complete Poems of Hart Crane* are strictly inert and invisible until the moment when I take the volume down from the shelf, open it at the poem called 'Garden Abstract' and read these lines:

And so she comes to dream herself the tree,
The wind possessing her, weaving her young veins,
Holding her to the sky and its quick blue,
Drowning the fever of her hands in sunlight.

(Crane, 1958, 74)

It is only in the encounter with my imagination, with all the peculiari-
ties specific to my personal sensibility, that the poem can 'take off'
from the page with any chance of achieving a sort of life within the
mind. It is to be expected that my reading will be subjective, for I scan
it through my private reading-glass, shaped by the cultural and existential experiences which are peculiarly mine. In this instance, I come to
the poem with some knowledge of literary history and am thereby pre-
disposed to situate what I read by reference to the Romantic notion
(which I have described above) whereby a human being can feel itself
in communication with natural forms. On the other hand, I shall inevitably bring to the poem my own memories, half-inarticulate, of wind,
trees and the way a woman might move her body, silhouetted on blue.
I may look up during my reading of these lines and look through the
window by my desk, seeing actual trees swaying against the sky. There
will be aspects of the poem which my mind will neglect, since they do
not immediately invite its contact: and what I do not notice, I cannot
account for. And there will be other aspects which my mind magnifies,
savouring a pleasure that will take as long to analyse as it is immediate
and intense – as with the exciting correlation which I infer between the
vein-like patterns of twigs on a tree and the 'young veins' of the
woman's body, both 'woven by the wind' in a rapture of erotic 'possession'. Above all, the reading of the poem at this moment in time will
constitute an event in my own life, and if I communicate my experience to others, I should be disloyal to myself if I censor this dimension
of private import. Each poem is written at a certain date, but each fresh
reading of a poem is an event in the calendar also.

In saying this, I am not arguing for a reading of poetry which should
be subjective to the point of solipsism, excluding all external information, all knowledge of matters such as literary conventions, the explicit
allusions intrinsic to a given historical and social moment, the overall
gist of an author's message as agreed by a consensus of reputable critics
– in short, those matters which have a certain 'objective' relevance to
the situation. What I am arguing is that 'objective interpretation' in isolation is a misguided ideal, and one which can divert the reader from
the genuine pleasure of discovering poems for himself – often also a
process in which he discovers his own most vulnerable and authentic
self. What I want to reject is a view of poetry which might block from
consciousness that dimension of the reading experience which is the
only final justification of poetry, namely its capacity to offer us confirmation that we belong in this world, that we are not trapped behind the
glass.

Beauty, Proust tells us, is always something unique and unrepeatable, not just an arbitrary sample of something pre-existing and ideal. And so it is with the poetic. The sudden fragrance of contact with an enhanced reality, the realisation that we are giving value to some phrase, object or quality because of a response active within some unaccustomed zone of our psychophysical being, the discernment of an aura of deeper significance around those banal acts of perception through which we organise our day-to-day relationship with our environment or with our books — these are experiences which poetry is peculiarly qualified to offer. It is perhaps in the nature of poetic epiphanies that they should be intermittent and ephemeral, even to a point where they seem implausible to the reasoning faculty. Yet those who have known the genuine thrill of crossing that distance which consciousness contemplates, those who, through reading words on a page, have been able to participate in experiences of opening and touching which affect them in ways more profound than any act of intellect, will accept that a poem can be more than a vehicle of mediation, but itself a contact, a presence. The poem is one of the many figures of our reality; when it is fully activated, it can be as meaningfully present to us as any man, any stone, any tree.

NOTES

1. Many surrealist writers have been fascinated by the notion of a dream woman who appears to be physically real. In 'Journal d'une apparition', Robert Desnos records the visitations of a woman who materialised in his bedroom each night over a period of several weeks. 'I have seen her, I have heard her, I have smelled her perfume and sometimes she even touched me. And since sight, hearing, smell and touch are in agreement about recognizing her presence, why should I doubt her reality, — unless I suspect of being illusions those other realities which are commonly recognized and which indeed are only ratified by the same senses?' (Desnos, 1953, 347). In 'Présence à Ravenne', Jean Palou tells what he insists is the true story of the nocturnal apparition of a woman in his hotel bedroom in Ravenna. He concludes that she is none other than Francesca da Rimini, who had died in that building centuries before (Palou, 1957). Michel Leiris writes of his youthful fascination for a beautiful woman in a picture, an allegorical portrayal of Falsehood. So impressed was he that he was later moved to praise a woman's looks with the exclamation 'She is as beautiful as Falsehood', thereby paying implicit tribute to the seductive power of the unreal (Leiris, 1966, 58).

2. The case of August Neter is of interest in this connection. This man was admitted to a psychiatric clinic in Germany in 1907 after having experienced a momentous, epiphany-like hallucination lasting half an hour, during which he saw ten thousand images projected upon a white screen which appeared in the clouds. When Neter later recovered a measure of psychological stability, he devoted himself to painstaking reconstructions of those images in the form of pencil drawings. Evidently the hallucinatory experience had impressed him as a kind of revelation and a powerful exception to his normal experience, notwithstanding the fact that Neter's 'normal' experience was bound up within a psychotic delusional system (see Prinzhorn, 1968, 204ff. and Cardinal, 1972, 94-7).

3. Baudelaire is here conducting a characteristically perverse experiment in purely mental travelling, a voyage without benefit of steam or sail ('sans vapeur et sans voile', Baudelaire, 1961, 124). This impatient

cruise to foreign parts, facilitated by the dreamer's couch rather than a real steamer, is typical of the poet, who only once experienced the actuality of exotic climes, on a voyage to the Indian Ocean at the age of twenty, after which he scarcely set foot outside Paris. It may be noted that the most Francophile of American poets, Wallace Stevens, never once crossed the Atlantic. The topos of the journey-without-leaving-home has a considerable literary lineage in France, from Xavier de Maistre's charming *Voyage autour de ma chambre* (1794) to Joris-Karl Huysmans's *A Rebours* (1884), where the hero stages an artificial visit to England by spending an evening at a phoney tourists' pub in Paris rather than risk the discomfort and undoubted disenchantment of a real Channel crossing. As the hero of Villiers de l'Isle Adam's play *Axël* more or less puts it, 'Travel? Our servants will do that for us!'

4. André Pieyre de Mandiargues has made the claim that Éluard's line about the earth looking as blue as an orange closely prefigured the perceptions of the first cosmonauts when they witnessed the appearance of this planet from a vantage point in outer space (Mandiargues, 1966, 8). An argument which I develop later in this book is that although metaphoric statements cannot literally alter physical facts, they can function as a medium of enhanced perception such that we construe the facts in altered, more poetic, ways. In other words, reality is always relative to our perspective on it.

5. Cf. the title of Dubuffet's assemblage *Le Cabinet logologique*. It may be noted that my argument at the present stage diverges from the position of the Romantic poet Novalis, who coined the term *Logologie* to designate a mode of linguistic activity in which there is both expression and reflection upon the expression – a kind of self-awareness of the Logos in which poetic utterance is raised to a higher power and becomes supremely capable of illuminating the real world. I return to the resonances of Novalis's ideas on language in Chapter 5.

6. A breathless, telegrammatic style of speech is used by Alfred Jingle in Charles Dickens's *The Pickwick Papers*, though the reduction in syntax creates an effect of comedy rather than abstruseness. The writings of Émile Hodinos contain examples of telegrammatic narratives which are elliptical in the extreme. (See his story 'Passion slave' in Thévoz, 1979, 116-18.)

7. A systematic account of the phenomenon of authorial reluctance

to communicate would need to deal with those writers who occult their work completely by destroying it or refusing to have it published at all. Theoretically also, one might conceive of an 'autistic' creator who would not even record his poems on paper, but would keep them safely hidden away in his head! However, I don't think we can get far by speculating on material which is not available for examination, and so my discussion of occultation concerns itself with poetry which exists in the form of printed texts that we can borrow or buy. At least such poetry is accessible to our sight, if not to our intelligence.

8. The story of Trakl's life is one of such riveting gloom that few commentators can forbear to allow its sorry details to feature significantly in their account of the poetry. I would not wish to deny that the facts of Trakl's drug addiction, his relationship with his sister, his suicide and so forth, are integral constituents of the shaping context within which his art flourished. In avoiding explicit biographical discussion here, as elsewhere in this book, I am simply trying to focus attention on the principal area of my concern, the reader's experience of approaching a text in its own right, prior to any enquiry into the psychological or social background.

9. In his book *Language, Truth and Poetry*, Graham D. Martin examines a wide range of evidence drawn from linguistics, semiotics, literary criticism and philosophy and argues that *all* language takes place in a situation of ambiguity and flux: each utterance and each reception of an utterance are subject to vagaries, and for us to construe a given verbal meaning is for us to draw upon resources which make every act of understanding something creative rather than mechanical (see Martin, 1975).

10. Not only sensory but also literary memories can illuminate our reading : a large part of the resources we bring to literature consists, after all, of the literature we have previously assimilated. In my interpretation of Nerval's image, there is an echo of a passage where Wordsworth speaks of the way poetry can give us fresh perceptions of known phenomena, quoting as his example Burns's comparison of sensual pleasure

> To snow that falls upon a river
> A moment white — then gone for ever!
> (quoted in Coleridge, 1957, 182)

It is worth pointing out that in thus isolating a fragment of a poem and seeing it as a kind of independent haiku, an epiphany in its own right, one is implicitly recognising the virtue of the ephemeral poetic moment, a notion which I discuss in Chapter 8.

11. I lack the space to develop a point made most memorably by R.D. Laing in *The Divided Self*, where he demonstrates the meaningful gist of a series of catatonic statements which classical psychiatry had dismissed as sheer nonsense (Laing, 1965, 29ff). Suffice it to say that my own experience of reading schizophrenic texts, such as those edited by Leo Navratil (1971) and Michel Thévoz (1979), is that the sensation of frozen exclusion is far less dominant than the sense of an idiom pressing towards communication. It can be argued that the theme of schizophrenic texts is often the fact of alienation itself, that the 'strangeness' is actually a substantial (thematic) rather than a superficial (stylistic) feature of the writing. A preoccupation with alienation may reflect the writer's desperate desire to transform autism into contact with others. It is notable that many psychotics spontaneously adopt the epistolary form when they write; others emerge as sensitive handlers of poetic language who certainly merit the serious attention of the outside reader. Cf. my article 'Image and Word in Schizophrenic Creation' (in Higgins, 1973, 103-20) and my essay on the schizophrenic poet Alexander (Ernst Herbeck) (in Navratil, 1977, 167-77).

12. A parallel observation is made by Richard Wollheim, who suggests that the Impressionist painters felt justified in putting forward their paintings as being windows onto nature because their own perceptions of nature had been shaped by the practice of looking at paintings (Wollheim, 1970, 119).

13. The many terminological variants should not obscure the gist of what is meant here. Reverdy differentiates between *la réalité*, meaning material existence in its unprocessed state, and *le réel*, meaning that which the poet crystallises in his work. (Elsewhere he somewhat confusingly offers as a synonym for *le réel* the formulation 'la réalité profonde', and also speaks of 'une réalité essentielle'. Reverdy, 1968, 18 and 50.) Breton draws a distinction between the 'réalité relative' witnessed by our senses and the 'réalité absolue' to which abstract thought lends access, and postulates their reciprocal illumination through the faculty of analogical perception (Breton, 1965, 401). Wallace Stevens seeks 'the poem of pure reality, untouched / By trope or deviation'

(Stevens, 1955, 471). In her moving analysis of poetic experience, *Journal de l'analogiste*, Suzanne Lilar speaks of 'the absolute Real made accessible by poetic experience' (Lilar, 1954, 156). Lastly, Novalis defines poetry as 'the authentic absolute Real' (Novalis, 1962, 410).

14. I have elsewhere developed a similar argument concerning the maintenance of a posture of critical openness to both the abstract and the representational dimension in the drawings of the artist Wols. I see that artist's images as operating simultaneously as self-engrossed pure forms (abstractions) *and* as signifying configurations (figures of reality). See my article 'The Later Works of Wols: Abstraction, Transparency, Tao' (in Inch, 1978, 33-43).

15. The poetic character of isolated copses is explored in certain pictures of Paul Nash, especially those depicting Castle Hill and Wittenham Clumps, small hills in Oxfordshire topped by beechwoods (see illustration p. 134). Nash's work at large is a fusion of Surrealist vision and English landscape realism, being devoted to the pictorial representation of a range of natural sites and objects which secrete mystery, fascination, intensity. The poetic is here rendered through an odd dryness of style, which the artist felt to be appropriate to what he saw as the 'magical precision' of his subject. Writing about a garden he loved, Nash touches on the notion of 'the reality of unreality' which was investigated earlier in this book: 'It seemed to respond in a dramatic way to the influence of light. There were moments when, through this agency, the place took on a startling beauty, a beauty to my eyes wholly unreal. It was this "unreality", or rather this reality of another aspect of the accepted world, this mystery of clarity that was at once so elusive and positive, that I now began to pursue' (Nash, 1949, 106-7).

16. Synesthesia — the fusing of disparate sensory perceptions — was known to the German Romantics as well as Baudelaire, and can still be traced as a device of intensification in the work of modern poets, as witness Karl Krolow's 'Azur: blaues Geräusch / des unerklärlichen / Horizonts' (Azure: blue sound / of the inexplicable / horizon) (Krolow, 1966, 34) and Octavio Paz's 'la voz blanca / Del agua enamorada' (the white voice / of the water in love) (Paz, 1971a, 60). The appeal of such images lies in the demand they place on the reader's response: he is *obliged* to attend to his subliminal faculties in order to fashion meaning out of the correlation, as here, of a colour and a sound.

17. Commenting on an even more improbable example of therapeutic practice favoured by the Iakoute people of Siberia, Claude Lévi-Strauss writes: 'The real question is not whether the touch of a woodpecker's beak does in fact cure toothache. It is rather whether there is a point of view from which a woodpecker's beak and a man's tooth can be seen as "going together" ' (Lévi-Strauss, 1966, 9). There is a sense in which mental security based on the perception of structures of analogy is as important to the primitive as physical security. And to see the world as a space of metaphors is to be alive to its poetic dimension. I argue later in this chapter that irrational associations (such as this correlation of a woodpecker's beak and a man's tooth) tend to activate subliminal resources so as to achieve the justification of the metaphoric aberration. The approach of the primitive mentality is, in this sense, to read nature as though it were a Surrealist poem.

18. These remarks are not intended to be more than a passing caricature of Romantic positions, a schema useful to my general argument (in which Symbolist and Surrealist attitudes are also implicated). A closer examination of the Romantic poets would reveal a wide variety of attitudes with regard to the imagination and its effect on the real world. Some Romantics equate poetic vision with the mystical premonition of a superior reality: these are the horizon-gazers, the transcendentalists for whom the present world is but a faulty mirror of a glorious Beyond. Others see poetic vision as a practical faculty, something which can be applied to present actualities, in a perspective of transfiguration here and now. These two basic options lead on to other considerations (religious belief, political positions, and so forth) too numerous to detail here. Broadly speaking, the dilemma for the Romantic is whether the object of his yearning necessarily lies beyond the horizon of this life, or whether he can magically draw that horizon within reach, instituting utopia as something potentially accessible. In such contrasted texts as *Hymnen an die Nacht* and the prose speculations gathered under the heading *Fragmente*, Novalis manages to exemplify both attitudes. Where some will see this as proof of weak-minded vacillation, I see it as evidence of Novalis's existential involvement in a deeply felt dilemma concerning the applicability of poetry to life. That same dilemma is, I feel, still an urgent concern, and my discussion here is an attempt to situate it within a more general poetic perspective.

19. When asked to describe the Zen experience of *satori* (illumination), D.T. Suzuki answered, 'Just like ordinary everyday experience,

except about two inches off the ground!' (quoted in Watts, 1962, 42.)

20. The analogy between the thought processes of the schizophrenic and those of 'seer' poets in the Rimbaldian mould, as well as those of primitives and children, is a seductive one. Of course it is important in any comparison to identify difference as well as similarity. On the one hand, one should be wary of making too facile an equation. For example, the processes of infant thought are simply underdeveloped, the effect of immaturity, while the regressive thinking of the adult schizophrenic may be more accurately envisaged as arising from the dis-integration of mature structures. Again, the mystical thinking of a member of a tribal community may be a socially valued activity, taking place in a context of social esteem markedly different from the context in which the Western psychotic finds himself. On the other hand, it is illuminating to reflect on the shared features of such modes of thought. In essence, these are characterised by the lowering of the barrier between perception and mental representation, between reality as sensed and reality as conceived, and a consequent preference for mythic as opposed to scientific explanations of the world. In such texts as *The Politics of Experience* (Laing, 1967), R.D. Laing has offered some enticing, if hyperbolic, commentaries on the schizoid experience in terms of the visionary potential it offers. In *Awakenings* (Sacks, 1976), Oliver Sacks injects poetic metaphor into cool medical description to evoke the flamboyant unrealities which are the day-to-day experience of patients suffering from post-encephalitic Parkinsonism. While orthodox medical authorities tend to deprecate the excesses of such writings, there is no doubt that they offer important models for the poetic imagination. It is in this regard that I would justify my present toying with the notion that schizophrenic non-differentiation offers a paradigm for a progres-sive mode of reading – a mode which, at the end of Chapter 6, I call 'transparent' and which is concerned to exploit the meanings which arise if the reader can reconcile the literal and the figurative dimensions of a poetic proposition.

21. It may be of interest to quote some other instances where ecsta-tic feeling gives rise to the image of birds flying through the human body:

(a) 'Je vois l'ibis aux belles manières / Qui revient de l'étang lacé dans mon cœur' (Breton, 1966a, 109) (I see the well-mannered ibis / Returning from the pool laced in my heart).

(b) 'Des vols de perroquets traversent ma tête quand je te vois de profil' (Benjamin Péret in Bédouin, 1961, 107) (Flights of parrots cross my head when I see you in profile).

(c) '. . . Les passagères / Hirondelles volant de climat en emoi. / (. . .) Je les vois même errantes sous la lune, / Oiseaux de jour perdus dans mes ombres sans fond' (Supervielle, 1951, 27) (The migrant / Swallows flying from climate to feeling / I even see them wandering beneath the moon, / Birds of daylight lost in my bottomless shadows).

(d) 'Inside me there is a confusion of swallows, / Birds flying through the smoke' (Bly, 1962, 31).

I would hazard the guess that if such imagery is at all widespread, it is because it expresses a collective sense of the poetic experience as being both *fleeting* and *engulfing*. The image of birds flying through the body may also be taken to illustrate the point made at the end of Chapter 11, that the poetic perception of the real implies a simultaneous sense of flight (transcendence) and contact (presence).

BIBLIOGRAPHY

The following is a list of the sources to which reference is made in the text, together with other material consulted in the preparation of this book.

Where the place of publication is unmentioned, this may be assumed to be London in the case of works in English, or Paris in the case of works in French.

Abrams, M.H. (1958), *The Mirror and the Lamp: Romantic Theory and the Critical Tradition*, Norton, New York
Aiken, Conrad (1966), *Preludes*, Oxford University Press, New York
Apollinaire, Guillaume (1956), *Œuvres poétiques*, Gallimard
Aragon, Louis (1924), *Une Vague de rêves*, Hors 'Commerce', Paris
——, (1926), *Le Paysan de Paris*, Gallimard
Arp, Jean (1966), *Jours effeuillés*, Gallimard
Artaud, Antonin (1968), *L'Ombilic des limbes*, Gallimard
——, (1971), *Le Théâtre et son double*, Gallimard
Ashbery, John (1976), *The Double Dream of Spring*, Ecco Press, New York
——, (1977), *Rivers and Mountains*, Ecco Press, New York
Audoin, Philippe (1970), *Breton*, Gallimard
Bachelard, Gaston (1949), *La Psychanalyse du feu*, Gallimard
——, (1960), *La Poétique de la rêverie*, Presses universitaires de France
——, (1961), *La Flamme d'une chandelle*, Presses universitaires de France
Bachmann, Ingeborg (1956), *Anrufung des Grossen Bären*, R. Piper, Munich
Bailly, Jean-Christophe (1971), *Au-delà du Langage: une étude sur Benjamin Péret*, Losfeld
Baker, J.A. (1969), *The Hill of Summer*, Collins
——, (1970), *The Peregrine*, Penguin, Harmondsworth
Balakian, Anna (1965), 'Metaphor and Metamorphosis in André Breton's Poetics', *French Studies*, vol. XIX, no. 1, 34-41
Barker, George (1957), *Collected Poems 1930-1955*, Faber & Faber
Bashō (1966), *The Narrow Road to the Deep North and Other Travel Sketches*, tr. Nobuyuki Yuasa, Penguin, Harmondsworth
Baudelaire, Charles (1961), *Œuvres complètes*, Gallimard

Bazaine, Jean (1953), *Notes sur la peinture*, Seuil
Bédouin, Jean-Louis (1961), *Benjamin Péret*, Seghers
Béguin, Albert (1946), *L'Ame romantique et le rêve*, Corti
Bellmer, Hans (1957), *Petite Anatomie de l'inconscient physique ou l'Anatomie de l'image*, Le Terrain vague
Bergerson, Howard W. (1973), *Palindromes and Anagrams*, Dover, New York
Bernis, Jeanne (1969), *L'Imagination*, Presses universitaires de France
Blake, William (1927), *Poems and Prophecies*, Dent
Blanchot, Maurice (1955), *L'Espace littéraire*, Gallimard
Bly, Robert (1962), *Silence in the Snowy Fields*, Wesleyan University Press, Middletown
Bonnefoy, Yves (1959), *L'Improbable*, Mercure de France
——, (1961), *Rimbaud par lui-même*, Seuil
——, (1967), *Un Rêve fait à Mantoue*, Mercure de France
——, (1970), *Du Mouvement et de l'immobilité de Douve*, Gallimard
——, (1972), *L'Arrière-Pays*, Skira, Geneva
Borges, Jorge Luis (1972), *A Personal Anthology*, Picador
——, (1975), *A Universal History of Infamy*, Penguin, Harmondsworth
Bousquet, Joë (1934), *Une Passante bleue et blonde*, R. Debresse
——, (1946), *Le Meneur de lune*, J.-B. Janin
——, (1973), *Mystique*, Gallimard
Bowie, Malcolm (1978), *Mallarmé and the Art of Being Difficult*, Cambridge University Press
Breton, André (1928), *Nadja*, Gallimard
——, (1952), *Entretiens 1913-1952*, Gallimard
——, (1953), *La Clé des champs*, Sagittaire
——, (1954), with L. Deharme, J. Gracq and J. Tardieu, *Farouche à quatre feuilles*, Grasset
——, (1955), *Les Vases communicants*, Gallimard
——, (1961), with P. Éluard, *L'Immaculée Conception*, Seghers
——, (1963), *Manifestes du surréalisme*, Gallimard
——, (1965), *Le Surréalisme et la peinture*, Gallimard
——, (1966a), *Clair de terre*, Gallimard
——, (1966b), *L'Amour fou*, Gallimard
——, (1968), *Signe ascendant*, Gallimard
——, (1970a), 'En Marge des *Champs magnétiques*', *Change*, no. 7, 9-29
——, (1970b), *Point du jour*, Gallimard
——, (1970c), *Perspective cavalière*, Gallimard
——, (1971), with P. Soupault, *Les Champs magnétiques*, Gallimard
Brett, R.L. (1969), *Fancy and Imagination*, Methuen

Brinkmann, Richard (1965), 'Abstract Lyrics of Expressionism' in *Literary Symbolism*, ed. H. Rehder, University of Texas Press, Austin and London, 109-36

Brophy, Brigid (1966), Foreword to *By Central Station I Sat Down and Wept* by Elizabeth Smart, Panther, 7-15

Burgart, Jean-Pierre (1969), *Failles*, Mercure de France

Burnshaw, Stanley (1970), *The Seamless Web*, Allen Lane The Penguin Press

Caillois, Roger (1965), *Au Cœur du fantastique*, Gallimard

——, (1970), *L'Ecriture des pierres*, Skira, Geneva

——, (1974), *Approches de l'imaginaire*, Gallimard

Cain, Lucienne Julien (1958), 'Valéry et l'utilisation du monde sensible' in *Trois Essais sur Paul Valéry*, Gallimard

Cardinal, Roger (1968), 'André Breton: the Surrealist Sensibility', *Mosaic*, vol. I, no. 2, 112-26

——, (1972), *Outsider Art*, Studio Vista

——, (1973a), 'Pierre Reverdy and the Reality of Signs' in *Order and Adventure in Post-Romantic French Poetry*, ed. E.M. Beaumont et al., Blackwell, Oxford, 206-17

——, (1973b), 'Werner, Novalis and the Signature of Stones' in *Deutung und Bedeutung*, ed. B. Schludermann et al., Mouton, The Hague and Paris, 118-33

——, (1974), 'Enigma', *Twentieth Century Studies*, no. 12, 42-62

——, (1975), *German Romantics*, Studio Vista

——, (1977), ed., *Sensibility and Creation. Studies in Twentieth-Century French Poetry*, Croom Helm

Carroll, Lewis (1939), *The Complete Works of Lewis Carroll*, Nonesuch Press

Caws, Mary Ann (1966), *Surrealism and the Literary Imagination: A Study of Breton and Bachelard*, Mouton, The Hague and Paris

Celan, Paul (1955), *Von Schwelle zu Schwelle*, Deutsche Verlags-Anstalt, Stuttgart

Char, René (1967), *Fureur et mystère*, Gallimard

Charbonnier, G. (1969), *Conversations with Claude Lévi-Strauss*, Cape

Chenu, Roselyne (1971), ed., *L'Imagination créatrice*, A la Baconnière, Lausanne

Christofides, C.G. (1963), 'Gaston Bachelard and the Imagination of Matter', *Revue internationale de philosophie*, vol. LXVI, no. 4, 477-91

Clark, Kenneth (1967), ed., *Ruskin Today*, Penguin, Harmondsworth

Claudel, Paul (1973), *Connaissance de l'est*, Mercure de France

Coleridge, Samuel Taylor (1957), *Poems and Prose*, Penguin, Harmondsworth

Crane, Hart (1958), *The Complete Poems of Hart Crane*, Doubleday, New York

Deguy, Michel (1966), *Actes*, Gallimard

Deleuze, Gilles (1971), *Proust et les signes*, Presses universitaires de France

Desnos, Robert (1953), *Domaine public*, Gallimard

Dubuffet, Jean (1973), *L'Homme du commun à l'ouvrage*, Gallimard

Dufrenne, Mikel (1961), *Le Poétique*, Presses universitaires de France

Duncan, Robert (1968), *Derivations. Selected Poems 1950-1956*, Fulcrum Press

——, (1971), *Bending of the Bow*, Cape

Dupin, Jacques (1971), *L'Embrasure, précédé de Gravir*, Gallimard

Ehrenpreis, Irvin (1972), ed., *Wallace Stevens*, Penguin, Harmondsworth

Ehrenzweig, Anton (1970), *The Hidden Order of Art*, Paladin

Éluard, Paul (1968), *Œuvres complètes*, 2 vols, Gallimard

Follain, Jean (1957), *Tout Instant*, Gallimard

——, (1971), *Espaces d'instants*, Gallimard

Forster, Leonard (1962), *Poetry of Significant Nonsense*, Cambridge University Press

Foucault, Michel (1963), *Raymond Roussel*, Gallimard

Friedrich, Hugo (1956), *Die Struktur der modernen Lyrik*, Rowohlt, Hamburg

Galinsky, G. Karl (1975), *Ovid's Metamorphoses*, Blackwell, Oxford

Garnett, David (1922), *Lady into Fox*, Chatto & Windus

Genette, Gérard (1966), *Figures*, Seuil

George, Stefan (1949), *Der siebente Ring*, H. Küpper, Godesberg

Gibson, Robert (1961), ed., *Modern French Poets on Poetry*, Cambridge University Press

Gracq, Julien (1948), *André Breton*, Corti

——, (1958), *Liberté grande*, Corti

Graham, A.C. (1965), tr., *Poems of the Late T'ang*, Penguin, Harmondsworth

Hamburger, Michael (1969), *The Truth of Poetry*, Weidenfeld & Nicolson

Han-shan (1970), *Cold Mountain. 100 Poems by the T'ang poet Han-shan*, tr. Burton Watson, Columbia University Press, New York and London

Harding, Denys Wyatt (1963), *Experience into Words*, Chatto & Windus

Hawkes, Terence (1972), *Metaphor*, Methuen

Hayner, Paul Collins (1971), *Reason and Existence: Schelling's Philosophy of History*, E.J. Brill, Leiden

Hayter, Alethea (1968), *Opium and the Romantic Imagination*, Faber & Faber

Heftrich, Eckhard (1969), *Novalis: Vom Logos der Poesie*, Klostermann, Frankfurt

Hepburn, R.W. (1972), 'Poetry and "Concrete Imagination": Problems of Truth and Illusion', *British Journal of Aesthetics*, vol. XII, no. 1, 3-18

Higgins, I. (1973), ed., *Literature and the Plastic Arts 1880-1930*, Scottish Academic Press, Edinburgh and London

Hölderlin, Friedrich (1953), *Sämtliche Werke*, vol. II, Kohlhammer, Stuttgart

Hopkins, Gerard Manley (1953), *Poems and Prose of Gerard Manley Hopkins*, Penguin, Harmondsworth

Hugo, Victor (1971), *Les Contemplations* in *Œuvres complètes* vol. IX/1, Club français du livre

Hytier, Jean (1923), *Le Plaisir poétique. Étude de psychologie*, Presses universitaires de France

Inch, Peter (1978), ed., *Circus Wols*, Arc Publications, Todmorden

Jaccottet, Philippe (1970), *Paysages avec figures absentes*, Gallimard

Jackson, Holbrook (1946), *The Reading of Books*, Faber & Faber

Janouch, Gustav (1968), *Gespräche mit Kafka*, S. Fischer, Frankfurt

Jean, Raymond (1965), *La Littérature et le réel*, A. Michel

Jouffroy, Alain (1970), *La Fin des alternances*, Gallimard

Jünger, Ernst (1941), *Das abenteuerliche Herz*, Hanseatische Verlagsanstalt, Hamburg

Kemp, Friedhelm, (1965), *Dichtung als Sprache. Wandlungen der modernen Poesie*, Kösel-Verlag, Munich

Krolow, Karl (1966), *Landschaften für mich*, Suhrkamp, Frankfurt

Kugel, James L. (1971), *The Techniques of Strangeness in Symbolist Poetry*, Yale University Press, New Haven and London

Kurrik, Maire Jaanus (1974), *Georg Trakl*, Columbia University Press, New York and London

Lacroze, René (1938), *La Fonction de l'imagination*, Boivin

Laing, R.D. (1965), *The Divided Self*, Penguin, Harmondsworth

——, (1967), *The Politics of Experience & The Bird of Paradise*, Penguin, Harmondsworth

Lautréamont, Comte de (1953), *Œuvres complètes*, Corti

Lebel, Robert (1955), *Chantage de la beauté*, Éditions de la Beaune

Lecomte, Marcel (1964), *Le Carnet et les instants*, Mercure de France

Lefebve, Maurice-Jean (1965), *L'Image fascinante et le surréel*, Plon
Leiris, Michel (1966), *L'Age d'homme*, Gallimard / Livre de poche
Le Sage, Laurence (1952), *Jean Giraudoux, Surrealism and the German Romantic Ideal*, University of Illinois Press, Urbana
Lévi-Strauss, Claude (1966), *The Savage Mind*, Weidenfeld & Nicolson
Liede, Alfred (1963), *Dichtung als Spiel. Studien zur Unsinnspoesie an den Grenzen der Sprache*, 2 vols, De Gruyter, Berlin
Lilar, Suzanne (1954), *Journal de l'analogiste*, Julliard
Loubère, Joyce A.E. (1972), 'Other Tigers: a Theme in Valéry and Borges', *Comparative Literature*, vol. XXIV, no. 4, 309-18
Luria, A.R. (1969), *The Mind of a Mnemonist*, Cape
Lüschen, Hans (1968), *Die Namen der Steine*, Otto, Thun and Munich
Mabille, Pierre (1949), 'Matta and the New Reality', *Horizon*, vol. XX, no. 117, 184-90
MacNeice, Louis (1949), *Collected Poems 1925-1948*, Faber & Faber
Magliola, Robert (1972), 'The Phenomenological Approach to Literature: its Theory and Methodology', *Language and Style*, vol. V, no. 2, 79-99
Mallarmé, Stéphane (1961), *Œuvres complètes*, Gallimard
Mandelstam, Osip (1977), *Selected Poems*, tr. C. Brown and W.S. Merwin, Penguin, Harmondsworth
Mandiargues, André Pieyre de (1966), 'Préface' in *Capitale de la douleur* by Paul Éluard, Gallimard
Marc, Olivier (1972), *Psychanalyse de la maison*, Seuil
Martin, Graham Dunstan (1975), *Language, Truth and Poetry*, Edinburgh University Press
Mauron, Charles (1968), *Mallarmé l'obscur*, Corti
Mead, Gerald (1978), *The Surrealist Image. A Stylistic Study*, P. Lang, Berne
Michaux, Henri (1946), *Au Pays de la magie*, Horizon, London
——, (1964), *L'Infini turbulent*, Mercure de France
Millet, Louis (1972), *Perception, imagination, mémoire*, Masson
Monnerot, Jules (1945), *La Poésie moderne et le sacré*, Gallimard
Mounin, Georges (1969), *La Communication poétique*, Gallimard
Nash, Paul (1949), *Outline. An Autobiography & Other Writings*, Faber & Faber
Navratil, Leo (1971), ed., *a + b leuchten im Klee. Psychopathologische Texte*, C. Hanser, Munich
——, (1977), ed., *Alexanders poetische Texte*, Deutscher Taschenbuch Verlag, Munich
Nerval, Gérard de (1960 and 1961), *Œuvres*, 2 vols, Gallimard

Novalis (1962), *Werke und Briefe*, Winkler, Munich

Nowottny, Winifred (1962), *The Language Poets Use*, Athlone Press

Onimus, Jean (1966), *La Connaissance poétique*, D. de Brouwer

Oulipo (Ouvroir de littérature potentielle) (1973), *La Littérature potentielle (Créations Re-créations Récréations)*, Gallimard

Ovid (1955), *The Metamorphoses of Ovid*, tr. M.M. Innes, Penguin, Harmondsworth

Palou, Jean (1957), 'Présence à Ravenne', *Le Surréalisme, même*, no. 3, 49-52

Paz, Octavio (1971a), *Configurations*, tr. Muriel Rukeyser *et al.*, New Directions, New York

——, (1971b), with J. Roubaud, E. Sanguinetti and C. Tomlinson, *Renga*, Gallimard

——, (1974), *Children of the Mire*, tr. Rachel Phillips, Harvard University Press, Cambridge and London

Perec, Georges (1969), *La Disparition*, Les Lettres nouvelles

Perse, Saint-John (1972), *Œuvres complètes*, Gallimard

Phillips, Rachel (1972), *The Poetic Modes of Octavio Paz*, Oxford University Press

Pivčević, Edo (1970), *Husserl and Phenomenology*, Hutchinson

Ponge, Francis (1947), *Le Carnet du bois de pins*, Mermod, Lausanne

——, (1961), *Le Grand Recueil: Méthodes*, Gallimard

——, (1967), *Le Savon*, Gallimard

——, (1970), *Entretiens de Francis Ponge avec Philippe Sollers*, Gallimard / Seuil

Poole, Roger (1972), *Towards Deep Subjectivity*, Harper & Row, New York

Poulet, Georges (1964), *Le Point de départ*, Plon

——, (1971), *La Conscience critique*, Corti

Prinzhorn, Hans (1968), *Bildnerei der Geisteskranken*, Springer, Berlin

Proust, Marcel (1954), *A la Recherche du Temps perdu*, 3 vols, Gallimard

Raillard, Georges (1974), *Jacques Dupin*, Seghers

Raymond, Marcel (1963), *De Baudelaire au surréalisme*, Corti

Renaud, Philippe (1969), *Lecture d'Apollinaire*, L'Age d'homme, Lausanne

Reverdy, Pierre (1948), *Le Livre de mon bord*, Mercure de France

——, (1968), *Le Gant de crin*, Flammarion

——, (1969), *Plupart du temps*, 2 vols, Gallimard

——, (1974), *Cette Émotion appelée poésie*, Flammarion

Rexroth, Kenneth (1956), *One Hundred Poems from the Chinese*, New

Directions, New York

——, (1966), *The Collected Shorter Poems*, New Directions, New York

Richard, Jean-Pierre (1954), *Littérature et sensation*, Seuil

——, (1955), *Poésie et profondeur*, Seuil

——, (1961), *L'Univers imaginaire de Mallarmé*, Seuil

Rilke, Rainer Maria (1955 and 1957), *Sämtliche Werke*, vols I and II, Insel, Frankfurt

Rimbaud, Arthur (1960), *Œuvres*, Garnier

Robbe-Grillet, Alain (1953), 'Joë Bousquet le rêveur', *Critique*, no. 77, 819-29

Rousseau, G.S. (1972), ed., *Organic Form. The Life of an Idea*, Routledge & Kegan Paul

Rousseau, Jean-Jacques (1960), *Les Rêveries du promeneur solitaire*, Garnier

Roussel, Raymond (1932), *Nouvelles Impressions d'Afrique*, Lemerre

——, (1963), *Comment j'ai écrit certains de mes livres*, Pauvert

Rovini, Robert (1971), *La Fonction poétique de l'image dans l'œuvre de Georg Trakl*, Faculté des Lettres & des Sciences humaines, Nice

Sacks, Oliver W. (1976), *Awakenings*, Penguin, Harmondsworth

Scheerer, Thomas M. (1974), *Textanalytische Studien zur 'Ecriture Automatique'*, Romanisches Seminar der Universität, Bonn

Schifferli, Peter (1963), ed., *Das war Dada. Dichtungen und Dokumente*, Deutscher Taschenbuch Verlag, Munich

Schlegel, Friedrich (1956), *Schriften und Fragmente*, A. Kröner, Stuttgart

Schwenk, Theodor (1965), *Sensitive Chaos*, Rudolf Steiner Press

Searles, Harold F. (1962), 'The Differentiation between Concrete and Metaphorical Thinking in the Recovering Schizophrenic Patient' in *Collected Papers on Schizophrenia & Related Subjects*, Hogarth Press / Institute of Psychoanalysis

Sewell, Elizabeth (1952), *The Field of Nonsense*, Chatto & Windus

——, (1961), *The Orphic Voice. Poetry and Natural History*, Routledge & Kegan Paul

Sheringham, Michael (1977), 'From the Labyrinth of Language to the Language of the Senses: the Poetry of André Breton' in Cardinal (1977), 72-102

Shroder, Maurice Z. (1961), *Icarus. The Image of the Artist in French Romanticism*, Harvard University Press, Cambridge, Mass.

Sitwell, Sacheverell (1942), *The Homing of the Winds*, Faber & Faber

Söhngen, Gottlieb (1962), *Analogie und Metapher: kleine Philosophie und Theologie der Sprache*, K. Alber, Freiburg and Munich

Starobinski, Jean (1970), *La Relation critique*, Gallimard

Stevens, Wallace (1955), *The Collected Poems of Wallace Stevens*, Faber & Faber

Stewart, Kilton (1975), *Pygmies and Dream-Giants*, Harper & Row, New York

Supervielle, Jules (1951), *Naissances*, Gallimard

Tardieu, Jean (1969), *Les Portes de toile*, Gallimard

Tertz, Abram (1977), *A Voice from the Chorus*, Fontana / Collins

Thévoz, Michel (1978), *Le Langage de la rupture*, Presses universitaires de France

——, (1979), ed., *Écrits bruts*, Presses universitaires de France

Thurley, Geoffrey (1977), *The American Moment. American Poetry in Mid-Century*, Arnold

Todorov, Tzvetan (1970), *Introduction à la littérature fantastique*, Seuil

Trakl, Georg (1972), *Das dichterische Werk*, Deutscher Taschenbuch Verlag, Munich

Tuzet, Hélène (1965), *Le Cosmos et l'imagination*, Corti

Tzara, Tristan (1975), *Œuvres complètes*, vol. I, Flammarion

Valéry, Paul (1962), *Œuvres*, vol. I, Gallimard

Valesio, Paolo (1974), 'On Reality and Unreality in Language', *Semiotica*, vol. X, no. 1, 75-91

Watkins, Alfred (1925), *The Old Straight Track*, Methuen

Watts, Alan W. (1962), *The Way of Zen*, Penguin, Harmondsworth

Wheelwright, Philip (1954), *The Burning Fountain*, Indiana University Press, Bloomington

——, (1960), 'Semantics and Ontology' in *Metaphor and Symbol*, ed. L.C. Knights and B. Cottle, Butterworths Scientific Publications

——, (1962), *Metaphor and Reality*, Indiana University Press, Bloomington

Williams, William Carlos (1963), *Paterson*, New Directions, New York

——, (1970), *Imaginations*, MacGibbon & Kee

Wollheim, Richard (1970), *Art and its Objects*, Penguin, Harmondsworth

INDEX

absence:
    as poetic form 43-4, 200
    veering into presence 105-7, 109,
      178
abstraction 42, 200-1
Aiken, Conrad 146, 147
allusion 69-71, 98-9
    inconsistency of 78-81, 102-3
ambiguity 67, 75, 77, 181
analogical thought 13, 162-3, 173-7,
    185-7, 206, 207, 230n17
'analogistics' *see* analogical thought
analogy, universal *see* correspondences, system of
Apollinaire, Guillaume 146, 181-2
    'Arbre' 52-4, 98-9
Aragon, Louis 27, 112-113
Arp, Hans (Arp, Jean) 110
Artaud, Antonin 182, 220
Ashbery, John 54-6, 151
associations, poetic *see* response to
    poetry, associative
automatic writing *see* Surrealism

Bachelard, Gaston 99, 133, 135
Bachmann, Ingeborg 113
Baker, J.A. 114-16, 133
Ball, Hugo 61-2, 99-100
Barker, George 135-6
Bashō 166-7, 179
Baudelaire, Charles 27, 34, 129, 143,
    161, 196, 225-6n3
Bazaine, Jean 42
Béguin, Albert 163
Bellmer, Hans 141
Blake, William 166
Blanchot, Maurice 48, 63
Bly, Robert 129-30, 165, 232n21
Bonnefoy, Yves 71, 108-9, 132, 146,
    150, 152, 154
Borges, Jorge Luis 30-1, 42, 97, 116
Bousquet, Joë 11, 118-19, 141, 147,
    153, 166
    imaginary woman 26-7, 30, 91
Breton, André 32, 71, 151, 220,
    228n13, 231n21
    analogical thought 176, 207

Champs magnétiques, Les 48-50,
    51, 113
    elective attractions 132, 141-2, 143
    imagination as reality 14, 25-6,
      29, 114
    metaphor, justification of 180-1
    transfiguration of perceptions
      203
Brinkmann, Richard 89
Brophy, Brigid 189
Burgart, Jean-Pierre 46

Carroll, Lewis, *pseud.* (Charles
    Dodgson) 31, 40-1
Celan, Paul 63, 164-5
Char, René 63, 82, 107, 111-2, 144,
    151
Claudel, Paul 133
Cocteau, Jean 27
Coleridge, Samuel Taylor 22-3, 68,
    135, 178
consciousness as alienation 213-15,
    217-19
contact:
    attunement to material reality
      123, 145, 149, 177, 208, 220-1
    immediacy of poetic language
      110-11, 113, 147-9, 178-9, 221
convertibility of signs 185, 191
correspondences, system of 13, 159,
    161-3, 164, 167-70, 189
Crane, Hart 222-3
creative observation *see* poetic
    perception
criticism of poetry:
    analytical 11
    phenomenological 15, 106
Cubism 46

Dadaism 100
    and language 61
Degas, Edgar 213-15, 219
Deguy, Michel 176
derealisation 39-42, 50, 63, 98, 120
Desnos, Robert 57-8, 225
dreams in waking life 174
Dubuffet, Jean 57

242